Advanced Research Methods in Hospitality and Tourism

The Advanced Research Methods in Hospitality and Tourism book makes a great contribution to literature by providing a cutting-edge overview on research methods used in hospitality and tourism. A range of useful chapters written by experts in our field focus on different topics including mixed-method research methods, scale development, application of neuromarketing, and text mining approaches. This is a comprehensive methodology overview from world-class experts, and the readers can get extensive knowledge and experiences on different research methods. The book will support researchers and students undertaking research, and it is therefore highly recommended.

Professor Dimitrios Buhalis
Bournemouth University Business School,
UK and The Hong Kong Polytechnic University, SAR China
Editor-in-Chief of *Tourism Review*

... a must have research methods book for hospitality and tourism researchers and practitioners. It provides clear guidelines for the use of various research methodologies. It's full of important information for those of us who conduct research in hospitality and tourism field. Make sure you read this book to learn from the best researchers in the field.

Dogan Gursoy Taco Bell Distinguished Professor
Hospitality Business Management
Washington State University
Editor-in-Chief of *Journal of Hospitality Marketing and Management*

This is the source to explore and learn about the latest research methods in the hospitality and tourism field. A must-read for all graduate students and faculty who are serious about performing scholarly work in our field.

Professor Sheryl F. Kline
Aramark Chaired Professor and Deputy Dean
Alfred Lerner College of Business & Economics,
University of Delaware

Advanced Research Methods in Hospitality and Tourism

EDITED BY

FEVZI OKUMUS

University of Central Florida, USA

S. MOSTAFA RASOOLIMANESH

Taylor's University, Malaysia

And

SHIVA JAHANI

University of Central Florida, USA

United Kingdom – North America – Japan – India – Malaysia – China

Emerald Publishing Limited
Howard House, Wagon Lane, Bingley BD16 1WA, UK

First edition 2022

Reprints and permissions service
Contact: permissions@emeraldinsight.com

British Library Cataloguing in Publication Data
A catalogue record for this book is available from the British Library

ISBN: 978-1-80117-551-7 (Print)
ISBN: 978-1-80117-550-0 (Online)
ISBN: 978-1-80117-552-4 (Epub)

INVESTOR IN PEOPLE

Table of Contents

List of Figures

Chapter 10

List of Tables

About the Contributors

Elizabeth Agyeiwaah is an Assistant Professor at the Faculty of Hospitality and Tourism Management, Macau University of Science and Technology, Avenida Wai Long, Taipa, Macau. She received her PhD at the Hong Kong Polytechnic University. Her research interests include sustainable tourism development, small and medium tourism enterprises, and tourist studies.

John Ap (**PhD**, Texas A&M) is a Professor in Tourism Management at the Macao Institute for Tourism Studies. He is Director of the Global Centre for Tourism Education & Training and Visiting Professor in the School of Tourism Management. His areas of expertise include: impacts of tourism; tourist behavior; theme parks, tourism planning; and research methods. Prior to becoming an academic, he was a town planner who specialized in recreation and tourism planning with over 11 years' professional experience.

Jaylan Azer is Assistant Professor of Marketing at Adam Smith Business School, University of Glasgow, Scotland, UK. Her research interest focuses within the services domain on the complementary concepts of actor/customer engagement, value co-creation, and Service-dominant Logic (SDL). Within this domain, she has a focus on consumer behavior and its impact in digital contexts, especially social online networks. Her research has been published in marketing and service journals including the *Journal of Business Research*, *Journal of Service Management*, *Journal of Marketing Management*, and *Journal of Services Marketing and the Proceedings of International Conferences.* Dr Azer has led research and business projects sponsored by Visit Scotland and Scottish Tourism Alliance, and has been a recipient of external research and impact grants from the Economic and Social Research Council (ESRC).

Ali Bavik is an Assistant Professor at the Macau Institute for Tourism Studies (IFTM). Dr Bavik completed his PhD at the University of Otago. His research expertise is hospitality marketing and hospitality management, organizational culture, tourist behavior, and corporate social responsibility. He has several published journal articles and conference papers on topics related to tourism and hospitality management and marketing. He was recognized as the Outstanding Author Contribution Award Winner by Emerald under the Literati Network Awards for Excellence 2017. Currently, he is serving on the editorial board of the *Journal of Hospitality and Tourism Insights* and *The Service Industries Journal.*

Giovanna Bertella is Associate Professor at the School of Business and Economics, UiT – The Arctic University of Norway, Tromsø. She received her PhD from the Department of Sociology, Political Science and Community Planning at UiT. Her research interests include management, entrepreneurship/innovation, marketing, tourism and leisure studies (nature- and animal-based tourism, rural tourism, food tourism), food studies (plant-based food), and futures studies (scenarios). She has published articles in various peer-reviewed journals and contributed to several books.

Hakan Boz is Associate Professor at Usak University's School of Applied Sciences, Turkey. Prior to joining the academia, he held various positions in the tourism and hospitality sector. His research focuses on gaining a deeper understanding of consumer and employee behaviors by using psychophysiological and neuromarketing tools.

Neil Carr is a Professor in the Department of Tourism, University of Otago. His research focuses on understanding behavior within tourism and leisure experiences, with a particular emphasis on children and families, sex, and animals (especially dogs).

Martin Gannon is Lecturer in Entrepreneurship at the University of Edinburgh Business School. His work has a diverse focus, incorporating entrepreneurial philanthropy, family business management, sustainability management, destination management, consumer behavior, and tourism and hospitality management. His published works can be found across a range of internationally leading outlets. Dr Gannon currently serves on the editorial board of *Tourism Management Perspectives* and the *International Journal of Contemporary Hospitality Management*.

Andrea Insch is an Associate Professor at the University of Otago, Dunedin, New Zealand. Before undertaking her doctorate at Griffith University in Brisbane, Andrea worked at Queensland's Department of State Development. In 2005 Andrea moved to New Zealand to join the Marketing Department at the Otago Business School. Andrea's research expertise is interdisciplinary, connecting marketing, urban studies, and tourism. Andrea is the Book Review Editor and Regional Editor (Australia and New Zealand) for *Place Branding and Public Diplomacy*.

Shiva Jahani is a Data Scientist and Tourism and Hospitality Scholar. She leverages her data science expertise as a statistician and graduate faculty in the College of Community Innovation and Education at the University of Central Florida as well as a Research Fellow at Orblytics LLC – an international data science and scholarly writing firm. She applies her tourism and hospitality expertise as the Associate Editor of the *Journal of Hospitality and Tourism Insights* (JHTI). Dr Jahani has served as an invited board member and researcher of the World Academy for the Future of Women (WAFW). She has published over 20 articles in refereed journals as well as several methodological white papers on a variety of topics. Dr Jahani's research includes invited collaborations on funded projects from funders such as: (1) FEMA, (2) NSF, and (3) FDA.

Balvinder Kaur Kler, Senior Lecturer in Tourism, is also Director of the Borneo Tourism Research Centre at the Faculty of Business, Economics and Accountancy, Universiti Malaysia Sabah. Her research explores people–place relationships, specifically the meanings and attachments to place from both a resident and tourist perspective. Her publications combine the application of sense of place to niche tourism markets. She continues to wander in the world of interpretative inquiry expanding her understanding of qualitative methods. She received her PhD in Tourism from the University of Surrey.

Erdoğan Koc is a Professor of Marketing at Faculty of Economics and Administrative Sciences, Bandırma Onyedi Eylül University, Turkey. He is the chair and head of the Department of Business Administration. He serves on the editorial boards of a number of journals. His research primarily focuses on the human behavior element (both as consumer and employee) in tourism and hospitality particularly by using psychophysiological and neuromarketing tools.

Chen Feng Kuo (Andy) is an Assistant Professor at the Macau Institute for Tourism Studies (IFT). Dr Kuo received his PhD from Purdue University in Hospitality and Tourism Management after receiving an MS from Cheng Kung University in Taiwan in Transportation and Communication Management Science. Dr Kuo was chairman of the hospitality management department at Tunghai University in Taiwan and also served on the faculty. Dr Kuo has held several consulting positions in the hospitality area including being foodservice operations consultant for the 2009 Kaohsiung World Games and for the 2017 Taipei Summer Universiade. Also, he acted as management consultant for the 85 Sky Tower Hotel.

Paulin Wong Poh Lin is Senior Lecturer and Head of Programme at the Faculty of Business and Management, Quest International University, Malaysia. She obtained her PhD from Universiti Malaysia Sabah (UMS). Her academic pursuit includes understanding place meanings, especially among host community in tourism destinations. She is currently a reviewer for the *Malaysian Journal of Qualitative Research* and an Associate Editor for the *Journal of Social Sciences and Business*.

Eva Martin-Fuentes is a Senior Lecturer for the Department of Business Management at the University of Lleida (Spain) where she has been recognized with the Teaching Excellence Award for the areas of tourism management and social media. She has been coordinator of Social Media Marketing (MSc) at the University of Lleida, academic secretary of the Business Management Department, and currently, she is Vice-Dean of Institutional Relations and Employability of the Faculty of Law, Economics and Tourism. She holds an international PhD in Engineering and Information Technologies. She is postdoctoral researcher in the Research Group on Tourism and Social Knowledge Economy, and she has been Visiting Academic for the University of South Australia. Her research interests focus on e-tourism, especially in the hospitality industry, and she has published articles in several journals, such as *Annals of Tourism Research*, the *International Journal of Hospitality Management, Sustainability, Tourism Management, Journal of Hospitality and Tourism Management*, among others.

Juan Pedro Mellinas is Assistant Professor of Marketing at University of Murcia (Spain). His research interests are focused on tourism satisfaction and User Generated Content (UGC) using online reviews in websites like Booking.com or TripAdvisor as main data source. The most prominent of his research is focused on describing, questioning, and criticizing the current online review collection systems in the tourism field. He has described the controversies that the use of different scales and methodologies can create in capturing and presenting information and also the subjectivity of these reviews and, to a certain extent, their questionable reliability in the measurement of some items. His articles have appeared in *Tourism Management, Annals of Tourism Research, International Journal of Hospitality Management*, and *Tourism Review*, among other journals.

Parisa Saadat Abadi Nasab has recently completed her PhD studies at the University of Otago. Her research interests include the areas of sociology of leisure, family leisure, family photography, qualitative inquiries, and visual data analysis. Working with migrant women to understand how leisure can help with their community integration, resettlement, and home-making in New Zealand, she is also highly interested to expand her research knowledge in understanding leisure experiences of underserved communities (women, migrants, refugees).

Fevzi Okumus is the CFHLA Preeminent Chair Professor within the Hospitality Services Department at the University of Central Florida's Rosen College of Hospitality Management. He has over 160 refereed journal articles, three books, 12 book chapters, and 90 conferenced presentations and reports. As of August 1, 2021, his publications have received over 13,300 citations and he has an h-index of 55. He has chaired/cochaired and served on numerous PhD dissertation and master thesis committees. He is the Editor-in-Chief of the *International Journal of Contemporary Hospitality Management* (IJCHM) (IF: 6.514) and the *Journal of Hospitality and Tourism Insights* (JHTI). He has received numerous prestigious research awards and recognitions.

Gozde Ozturk is currently an Information Technology Teacher in the Education of Ministry, Turkey. She graduated the PhD program in 2020 from the Department of Tourism Management, Faculty of Tourism, Aydın Adnan Menderes University, Turkey. Her research interest areas are data mining, text mining, graph mining, and association rule mining.

S. Mostafa Rasoolimanesh is an Associate Professor and Director of the Centre for Research and Innovation in Tourism (CRiT), in Taylor's University, Malaysia. His research interest areas include sustainable tourism, heritage tourism, community participation, residents' perceptions, and urban sustainability. Moreover, he has used advanced quantitative analysis such as partial least squares structural equation modeling in most of his papers. He has published widely in high-impact journals. Mostafa is an editorial team and board member of several reputed tourism and hospitality journals.

Ismail Shaheer is a Postdoctoral Fellow in the Department of Tourism, University of Otago. His research focuses on tourist behavior, ethics, social media, and media-induced tourism. Before undertaking his doctorate, he worked at the Maldives Tourism Promotion Board (now Maldives Marketing & Public Relations Corporation) for more than 10 years marketing the Maldives as a tourist destination.

Babak Taheri is Professor of Marketing at Nottingham Trent University and has held a number academic and research leadership positions in the past. He is also Honorary Professor of Marketing at the Business School at University of Aberdeen. He has an established reputation in the marketing field with a specific expertise in services marketing management, consumer behavior and tourism, leisure and cultural consumption. The innovative nature of his research traces its roots to multidisciplinary work and to the methodologically robust measurement and assessment of key concepts. He has published consistently in internationally rated top-tier journals with high impact factors (over 100 academic publications) and held funds from bodies in the EU and UK such as Horizon 2020 and Innovate UK Research Grant. Professor Taheri currently serves as Senior Editor for *Tourism Management Perspectives* and Associate Editor for *The Service Industries Journal* and the *International Journal of Contemporary Hospitality Management*. He is also on the editorial review board of several social science journals, including the *Journal of Business Research* and *Journal of Travel Research*.

Abdullah Tanrısevdi is currently a Professor in Tourism Marketing, Research Methods, and Special Interest Tourism at the Department of Tourism Guiding, Faculty of Tourism, Aydın Adnan Menderes University, Turkey. He visited Oklahoma State University (OSU) – Center for Hospitality and Tourism Research (CHTR) as a visiting scholar in 2011, and received a postdoc from the University of South Florida in 2015. He is the Editor-in-Chief of the Adnan Menderes University *Journal of Travel and Tourism Research*.

Trudie Walters is an Independent Researcher from Ōtepoti/Dunedin, Aotearoa New Zealand. Her research platform is centered on events and leisure as interdisciplinary lenses through which to understand the inner workings and values of society.

Chapter 1

Introduction

S. Mostafa Rasoolimanesh, Shiva Jahani and Fevzi Okumus

Over the last 20 years, the number of hospitality and tourism peer-reviewed journals has grown from 10 to 300 (and counting) – an average of 145% increase per year and a total 2,900% increase over 20 years (Nunkoo, 2018). Over this period, research in the hospitality and tourism industry has grown in breadth and depth, and the questions needing answers have grown in complexity. As such, scholars need to apply advanced research methodologies (Ali, Rasoolimanesh, Sarstedt, Ringle, & Ryu, 2018; Hadinejad, Moyle, Scott, & Kralj, 2019; Okumus, Koseoglu, & Ma, 2018; Rasoolimanesh, Ringle, Sarstedt, & Olya, 2021; Rasoolimanesh, Wang, Mikulić, & Kunasekaran, 2021; Rasoolimanesh, Wang, Roldán, & Kunasekaran, 2021; Tavakoli & Wijesinghe, 2019). To this end, the editors have produced this book that introduces advanced research methodologies relevant to current research in hospitality and tourism.

This first chapter provides a preview of the chapter content in this book. A paragraph is dedicated to each chapter. Methodologies covered in this chapter include mixed-method approaches to tourism and hospitality research, scale development, psychophysiological tools, importance of archival materials, the importance and challenges of ratings and review in online databases, text mining, scientific inquiry, qualitative analysis of social media historical data, Q-methodology incorporating photo-elicitation, and research ethics.

In Chapter 2, Jaylan Azer, Babak Taheri, and Martin Gannon have provided a critical view on mixed-method approaches to tourism and hospitality research. They highlighted the growth and popularity of mixed-methods research (MMR) over recent decades compared to mono-qualitative and mono-quantitative approaches. The authors discussed (1) research paradigm, (2) reasons to apply mixed-methods designs, (3) rigorousness of MMR, (4) advantages and challenges of MMR, and (5) guidelines for application of MMR in tourism and hospitality research.

In Chapter 3, Elizabeth Agyeiwaah has highlighted the exploratory sequential mixed-methods design with an example of small tourism enterprises in Ghana. She examined the application of exploratory sequential mixed-methods design, which involves the first phase of qualitative data collection and analysis that informs the second phase of quantitative data collection for a thorough

Advanced Research Methods in Hospitality and Tourism, 1–4

Copyright © 2023 S. Mostafa Rasoolimanesh, Shiva Jahani and Fevzi Okumus
Published under exclusive licence by Emerald Publishing Limited
doi:10.1108/978-1-80117-550-020221001

explanation of the results. This design is applied in the context of small accommodation enterprises (e.g., homestay) to highlight its advantages.

Ali Bavik, Kuo Chen-Feng, and John Ap have illustrated the scale development process in Chapter 4. The authors of this chapter state that numerous scales have been developed and utilized in the tourism and hospitality field, yet their psychometric properties have not been systematically reviewed. This gap compromises researchers' ability to develop better measures and make better measurement decisions. The authors reviewed 56 scales and related development procedures as well as summarized the psychometric properties of the scales. Ali et al. provided recommendations for future tourism and hospitality scale development.

Hakan Boz and Erdogan Koc have discussed the role and potential of psychophysiological tools of research in tourism and hospitality in Chapter 5. Encounters between customers and service providers often include frequent (and sometimes intense) contact and social interactions, which may determine customers' satisfaction and dissatisfaction. As such, examining customers' emotional reactions and the correlation with their satisfaction outcomes aids researchers and practitioners in understanding how customers' emotions may influence planning, marketing, implementation, and satisfaction. Psychophysiological tools, often referred to as neuromarketing tools, allow researchers to collect realistic data regarding customers' emotions related to service encounters. The authors explained and discussed the use of tools such as the electroencephalography (EEG), eye tracker, the Galvanic skin response, and facial expression recognition.

Parisa Saadat Abadi Nasab, Neil Carr, and Trudie Walters in Chapter 6 have highlighted the importance of archival material and how, despite its secondary nature, it can provide first-hand information for researchers. By providing a variety of examples from tourism, hospitality and leisure, the authors demonstrated how this underused data can be a valuable resource for these areas of study. To illustrate how to use archival material as data, the authors provided a step-by-step process to analyzing archival photographs. The authors also discussed the challenges and ethical considerations associated with using archival material while also providing suggestions for the use of this data source in future studies.

In Chapter 7, Juan Pedro Mellinas and Eva Martin-Fuentes have highlighted the importance and challenges of ratings and reviews in online databases as a new source of data for tourism research. Data from websites like TripAdvisor are replacing or complementing traditional questionnaires and interviews. However, TripAdvisor does not provide information on sample design and the possible biases that this could entail. The authors proposed a methodology to estimate the percentage that the sample of self-interviewed individuals accounts for over the total population under study in order to calculate the reliability of the results obtained.

In Chapter 8, Gozde Ozturk and Abdullah Tanrisevdi have illustrated text mining approach with an example from cruise tourism. Text mining studies extract information and meaning from texts as viable data. This process does not lend itself well to manual analysis of individuals' thoughts and feelings. Therefore, studies that automatically reveal meaningful information have become a necessity. In response to this need, sentiment analysis studies have developed. Sentiment analysis applies natural language processing techniques to automatically identify and analyze subjective information in natural language settings. This chapter sheds light on researchers and practitioners about sentiment analysis in hospitality and tourism. The technical details described throughout the chapter with a case study to provide clear insights and guidelines for researchers to apply this method.

Ismail Shaheer, Neil Carr, and Andrea Insch have discussed qualitative analysis of social media historical data in Chapter 9. Social media is noted for its usefulness and contribution to destination marketing and management. Social media data is particularly valued as a source to understand issues such as tourist behavior and destination marketing strategies. Among the social media platforms, Twitter is one of the most utilized in research. The use of Twitter in research poses two significant considerations which are the challenge of obtaining historical data and the importance of qualitative data analysis. To address these two points, the authors presented a hands-on approach to collecting historical data from the Twitter platform. As such, they argued that retrieving tweets using hashtags and keywords on the Twitter website provides a corpus of tweets that is valuable and sufficient for research, especially for qualitative inquiries. In addition, the value of qualitative analysis of Twitter data is presented, demonstrating how such an approach captures more in-depth information, enables appreciation and inclusion of the non-conventional language used on social media, enhances understanding of the relationship between individual elements in a message, distinguishes between *noise* and useful information, and recognizes information as the sum of all parts in the data.

In Chapter 10, Paulin P.L. Wong and Balvinder Kaur Kler have highlighted an innovative qualitative method to collect data to understand host community place meanings by combining focus group interviews and visitor employed photography with an adapted Q-methodology. This chapter elaborates on original qualitative methods used to collect data consisting of verbal and pictorial techniques, and an adapted Q-methodology incorporating photo-elicitation. The research design for data collection is provided as a guideline to illustrate how the study progressed through two essential parts. This study contributes to a gap in method on how to extract pictorial measures on a collective basis to systematically produce group place meanings.

In Chapter 11, Giovanna Bertella has discussed the research ethics of examining animals' roles in tourism and hospitality. In recent decades, an increasing number of scholars have been interested in exploring animals and their roles in the context of tourism, hospitality, and leisure. Recent studies have covered both the practical and theoretical aspects of this topic, sometimes including considerations of animal ethics. The author argued that it is time to reflect on the research ethics and the methodological implications of such emerging perspectives. This chapter presented a literature review addressing the recent shift in tourism, hospitality, and leisure studies from human/animal dualism and anthropocentrism toward a recognition and inclusion of the animals' perspectives. He developed a set of guidelines for a methodology to underpin research about and with animals, inspired by the ecofeminist care tradition and elaborated according to the reviewed literature and the author's personal experience. The guidelines involve reflexivity, philosophical and practical clarifications of the research perspective and content, the researchers' knowledge of animals, and the possible impact of such research on the animals. Three main approaches are identified: a fictional approach, multispecies ethnography, and a multispecies technology-based approach.

Finally, Chapter 12 written by the editors has summarized and synthesized the recommendations provided by the authors of each chapter for applications on the illustrated methods in hospitality and tourism research.

References

Ali, F., Rasoolimanesh, S. M., Sarstedt, M., Ringle, C. M., & Ryu, K. (2018). An assessment of the use of partial least squares structural equation modelling (PLS-SEM) in hospitality research. *International Journal of Contemporary Hospitality Management, 30*(1), 514–538. doi:10.1108/IJCHM-10-2016-0568

Hadinejad, A., Moyle, B. D., Scott, N., & Kralj, A. (2019). Emotional responses to tourism advertisements: The application of FaceReader™. *Tourism Recreation Research, 44*(1), 131–135.

Nunkoo, R. (Ed.). (2018). *Handbook of research methods for tourism and hospitality management.* Cheltenham; MA: Edward Elgar Publishing.

Okumus, B., Koseoglu, M. A., & Ma, F. (2018). Food and gastronomy research in tourism and hospitality: A bibliometric analysis. *International Journal of Hospitality Management, 73*, 64–74.

Rasoolimanesh, S. M., Ringle, C. M., Sarstedt, M., & Olya, H. (2021). The combined use of symmetric and asymmetric approaches: Partial least squares-structural equation modelling and fuzzy-set qualitative comparative analysis. *International Journal of Contemporary Hospitality Management, 33*(5), 1571–1592. doi:10.1108/IJCHM-10-2020-1164

Rasoolimanesh, S. M., Wang, M., Mikulić, J., & Kunasekaran, P. (2021). A critical review of moderation analysis in tourism and hospitality research toward robust guidelines. *International Journal of Contemporary Hospitality Management, 33*(12), 4311–4333. doi:10.1108/IJCHM-02-2021-0272

Rasoolimanesh, S. M., Wang, M., Roldán, J. L., & Kunasekaran, P. (2021). Are we in right path for mediation analysis? Reviewing the literature and proposing robust guidelines. *Journal of Hospitality and Tourism Management, 48*, 395–405.

Tavakoli, R., & Wijesinghe, S. N. (2019). The evolution of the web and netnography in tourism: A systematic review. *Tourism Management Perspectives, 29*, 48–55.

Chapter 2

A Critical View on Mixed-Method Approaches to Tourism and Hospitality Research

Jaylan Azer, Babak Taheri and Martin Gannon

Abstract

Mixed methods research (MMR) represents an alternative methodological approach, combining qualitative and quantitative research styles, and enabling researchers to explore complex phenomena in detail. This chapter provides a critical view of mixed methods research and its application in social science research, with examples from tourism and hospitality used to guide those aiming to undertake mixed-methods research projects. The chapter provides insight into the characteristics of MMR, distinguishing it from a multi-method approach. It also provides a detailed explanation of different MMR designs and highlights the advantages and challenges of adopting a mixed-methods approach. Moreover, the chapter discusses approaches to analysis which are pivotal to MMR design. Finally, the chapter concludes with recommendations for researchers hoping to adopt a mixed-methods approach.

Keywords: Mixed-methods; research design; hospitality research design; tourism research design; social sciences research design; alternative research design

Introduction

The popularity of mixed methods research (MMR) has grown over recent decades, with its position alongside singular qualitative and quantitative approaches to research now firmly established (Gibson, 2017; Teddlie & Tashakkori, 2009). Serving as a "third way," a mixed-method approach is not concerned with replacing traditional qualitative or quantitative techniques but it instead combines the strengths of each in order to minimize and/or negate any

Advanced Research Methods in Hospitality and Tourism, 5–24
Copyright © 2023 Jaylan Azer, Babak Taheri and Martin Gannon
Published under exclusive licence by Emerald Publishing Limited
doi:10.1108/978-1-80117-550-020221002

weaknesses therein (Johnson, Onwuegbuzie, & Turner, 2007; Khoo-Lattimore, Mura, & Yung, 2019). Accordingly, a mixed-method approach to research can be broadly characterized as:

> The type of research in which a researcher or team of researchers combines elements of qualitative and quantitative research approaches (e.g., use of qualitative and quantitative viewpoints, data collection, analysis, inference techniques) for the broad purpose of breadth and depth of understanding and corroboration.
>
> (Johnson et al., 2007, p. 123)

Nevertheless, while the *combined* deployment of qualitative and quantitative techniques is core to MMR, some ambiguity remains regarding the differences between multi-method and mixed-method approaches to research. In contrast with MMR, multi-method approaches combine multiple qualitative methods (e.g., case studies and ethnography) *or* multiple quantitative methods (e.g., surveys and experiments) (Harrison & Reilly, 2011). Therefore, multi-method research reflects the notion of multiple operationalism favored by early social science researchers, with this originally introduced to improve the validity of research findings (Campbell & Fiske, 1959). In the 1970s, multi-method approaches evolved, moti- vated by a desire to convey the potential for triangulation born from the deploy- ment of quantitative and qualitative data sources as a means of cross-validation (Denzin, 1978; Jick, 1979). However, despite the shared concession that using a range of methods can help to strengthen research processes, an emphasis on mul- tiple operationalism, convergent validation, and methodological triangulation is more closely related to a multi-method, as opposed to mixed-method, approach to research (Harrison & Reilly, 2011; Johnson et al., 2007).

Accordingly, MMR extends beyond simple triangulation in pursuit of validation (Creswell, 2014; Johnson & Onwuegbuzie, 2004), serving instead to legitimize studies underpinned by pragmatic philosophical assumptions by integrating both qualitative and quantitative methods to answer research questions that cannot be addressed using a single method (Creswell & Clark, 2011; Doyle, Brady, & Byrne, 2009). As such, there is a range of circumstances where a mixed-methods approach proves most appropriate. For example, under conditions where one source of data is considered insufficient or incomplete; initial results require further explanation; or where a research project has multiple phases. To this end, the decision to adopt MMR in pursuit of research aims is often pragmatic, paradigmatically underpinned by a combination of assumptions from potentially incongruous viewpoints. This chapter, therefore, begins by discussing the paradigmatic foundations of MMR prior to discussing the approach itself in greater depth.

Research Paradigm

MMR is characterized by heated discourse concerning the incongruity between the multiple perspectives required to appropriately deploy a mixed-method design and established understanding of research philosophy (Khoo-Lattimore et al., 2019). Moreover, the complexity of MMR's paradigmatic foundations is exemplified by how this approach is operationalized in practice; those conducting MMR must embrace ontological, epistemological, and axiological viewpoints from a range of (often competing) methodological traditions (Table 1). Accordingly, debate has centered on *whether, how*, and *the extent to which* research paradigms should be 'mixed,' irrespective of the functional benefits of adopting a mixed-method approach.

Table 1. Competing Characteristics of MMR.

Criteria	Explanation
Uses of positivism:	Positivists claim that reality is "out there," capable of being accessed and understood with the right tools, whereas post-positivists believe that reality can never truly be comprehended. As a result, Post-positivists typically use multiple methods to capture "reality" as much as possible.
Acceptance of postmodern sensibilities:	Postmodern researchers argue that the positivist method is one way of telling a story, and that this might be no better or no worse than any other method. Therefore, these researchers seek alternative methods for assessing their study. However, positivists and post-positivists contend that what they do is good science, free of individual bias and subjectivity, and they see postmodernism as an attack on reason and truth.
Capturing the individual's point of view:	Qualitative researchers argue that quantitative researchers may not capture the subject's view because they prioritize empirical materials. In response, some quantitative researchers consider qualitative studies as less objective.
Examining the constraints of everyday life:	Quantitative scholars rely on probabilities derived from the study via randomization, whereas qualitative researchers seek a case-based position that directs their attention to the particular cases.

Source: developed by authors based on Creswell (2014), Guba and Lincoln (2005), and Harrison and Reilly (2011).

Given the core differences in research philosophy outlined in Table 1, some scholars go so far as to advocate against mixing research paradigms and subsequent methodological strategies entirely, with this perspective on MMR captured by the moniker "incompatibility thesis" (Guba & Lincoln, 2005). Accordingly, this perspective contends that the two prevailing research paradigms (positivism and constructivism) are fundamentally incompatible, with irrevocable ontological, epistemological, and axiological differences. Furthermore, those adopting this perspective suggest that the diversity in views characteristic of positivism and constructivism are fundamentally incompatible to reasoning (e.g., deductive vs. inductive), legitimizing knowledge, generalizing findings (e.g., nomothetic versus ideographic statements) and accepting causal relations (Bryman, 2006b), further stressing the incompatibility of MMR design more generally.

Nevertheless, two main research paradigms are typically adopted to justify an MMR approach to social science research, with this also evidenced across hospitality and tourism studies. First, *pragmatism* (problem-based or objective-based) is proposed as a paradigm capable of prompting mutual dialogue between the (apparent) empirical and theoretical/philosophical incongruences core to MMR (Khoo-Lattimore et al., 2019). A pragmatic underpinning challenges the notion that "predetermined frameworks" form truth and knowledge (Easterby-Smith, Thorpe, & Jackson, 2012, p. 32) and, therefore, researchers can use any methodological approach to tackle research questions and problems (Maarouf, 2019).

Methodologically, pragmatism contends that a research project can sit within an inductive or deductive research phase at different intervals (Baggio & Mariani, 2019; Teddlie & Tashakkori, 2009). Accordingly, an "abductive" approach to reasoning is proposed as a practical alternative, with this used to support a process of inquiry that assesses previous inductive results (Morgan, 2007). At this abductive stage, the goal is to explore the data, identify patterns, and suggest plausible hypotheses via discreet categories. Subsequently, the deductive approach enables forming logical and testable propositions based upon plausible premises, with inductive reasoning serving to approximate the truth in parallel to pragmatically guiding the general inquiry (Teddlie & Tashakkori, 2009). This abductive approach is employed when sequentially integrating qualitative and quantitative methods, serving as the philosophical bedrock of much MMR design (Baggio & Mariani, 2019; Morgan, 2007).

Second, *post-positivist* perspectives can serve as a response to the shortcomings of positivism. Generally, a positivist philosophy encourages researchers to perceive reality objectively, leaving little room for the subjective interpretation of results (Hudson & Ozanne, 1988). Accordingly, Ackroyd and Fleetwood (2000) identify the functional drawbacks of reducing research philosophy to two opposed perspectives:

> We arrive at the commonly held position that there are two basic perspectives on offer: either the world is objectively and unproblematically available and capable of being known by the systematic application of the empirical techniques common to

positivism, or not knowable objectively at all; and in the place of claims to objectivity, we find that what is known is merely the product of discourses.

Ackroyd and Fleetwood (2000, pp. 3–4)

As such, while positivism assumes that causal relationships among variables can be verified, an alternative post-positivist approach suggests that reality can only be known probabilistically, making the falsification of null hypotheses, not the verification of hypotheses, the order of the day (Harris, 2008).

Post-positivism theory concedes that it is impossible for scholars to be value-free while retaining the goal of observable reality central to positivism. Thus, Post-positivists openly reflect on the assumptions, methods, and results shaping their research (Schurr, 2007). From an ontological viewpoint, one of the most common post-positivist perspectives is that of critical realism, which Schurr (2007, pp. 165–166) defines as "[a perspective in which] reality exists in time and space independent of the human mind, maybe observed, and is more enduring than our perception of it." Critical realism contends that researcher observation is vulnerable to mistakes and that theoretical foundations are not set in stone but instead open to revision as studies progress (Trochim, 2006). Accordingly, critical realism suggests that objectivity can be gained through the collective critique of extant work (Johnson & Duberley, 2003) while also demonstrating no favor toward different data collection methods beyond those considered most appropriate to the research aim (Ackroyd & Fleetwood, 2000).

As such, post-positivist perspectives contend that the adoption of intensive qualitative methods can help to reveal individual motives, while extensive quantitative methods can prove crucial in illuminating the more general characteristics of any phenomena under investigation. Therefore, this perspective is consistent with the functional aspects of MMR design, with this approach allowing the researcher to adequately examine both observable and non-observable conditions (Ackroyd & Fleetwood, 2000). While scholars have often traditionally felt obliged to use single quantitative or single qualitative methods, recent moves toward pragmatism and post-positivism argue against the polarization of research along philosophical lines (Ercikan & Roth, 2006). Nevertheless, as steadfast adherence to a sole research paradigm can encourage inherent bias (Deshpande, 1983), some researchers continue to challenge methodological norms, as evidenced by a concerted shift toward adopting MMR design. To this end, acknowledging the ever-evolving and multi-layered nature of research contexts, the increased adoption of MMR has led to significant epistemological and ontological advancement in hospitality and tourism scholarship in recent decades (Khoo-Lattimore et al., 2019).

Reasons to Adopt an MMR

Generally, research problems likely to benefit from the adoption of a mixed-method approach are those in which one data source is likely to prove insufficient. However, MMR is appropriate when results are likely to require further explanation; experimental findings require generalization; the core experimental design must be extended upon or improved; multiple cases must be compared; and participant involvement is required. Over recent years, authors adopting MMR have raised a range of reasons for doing so (also referred to as 'rationales') (Bryman, 2006a). This section discusses the three core rationales underpinning MMR design.

Corroboration

Quantitative and qualitative data differ in how they respectively provide richness of understanding or a general understanding of phenomena. Qualitative and quantitative methods capture different perspectives, yet each has its limitations. For example, results emerging from qualitative research are typically ungeneralizable. Conversely, while quantitative studies typically draw upon large sample sizes, detailed understanding of phenomena at an individual level is often limited. Therefore, the drawbacks of one method are balanced with the strengths of the other, with a combined qualitative and quantitative approach capable of providing a more holistic understanding of the phenomena under investigation than either approach in isolation. Further, under some circumstances, using one data source alone may prove insufficient; one view may not tell the full story. Under such circumstances, using a solely qualitative or quantitative approach to address a research problem may be inadequate, and thus an MMR design can serve to strengthen results through corroboration.

Explaining Initial Results

In some instances, the results of a study may not provide a complete understanding of a research problem, with further explanation required to adequately identify core findings. Under such circumstances, mixed methods can be used, with a second study employed to better-explain primary inquiry results (Creswell & Clark, 2018). A typical situation in which this challenge emerges is when quantitative findings require further clarification with regards to how they apply in practice (Khoo-Lattimore et al., 2019). For example, while experimental studies provide quantitative results regarding the prevalence of specific outcomes, a subsequent qualitative study can be used to provide greater insight into the process leading to these outcomes, alongside their likely impact at an individual level (Cash, Stankovic, & Storga, 2016). On the other hand, qualitative data can be used for studies investigating emerging phenomena as the initial means of in-depth exploration, with subsequent quantitative data deployed to better-understand its impacts, mechanisms, and effects at a larger scale (Gannon, Taheri, & Olya, 2019). Accordingly, qualitative and quantitative methods can work together to provide a more robust, detailed explanation of initial research results irrespective of the order of deployment.

To Administer Measurement Instruments

At times, researchers may not be able to fully identify or articulate the core questions under investigation, measurement variables, and/or any theories underpinning the study (Creswell & Clark, 2018). MMR is ideal under such circumstances, where it is recommended to start by exploring via qualitative data to better-understand the variables, theories, or questions which require further research. Afterward, a quantitative study can test and generalize nascent findings captured in the exploration phase. This mixed-method research design encourages the administration of more accurate quantitative instruments, with the initial qualitative stage capable of filling a researcher's knowledge gaps.

Types of Mixed Methods Designs

While the rationale for adopting a mixed-method approach is clear and consistent, there remains debate about how this is enacted in practice. Accordingly, there are four core mixed-method designs: convergent parallel design, explanatory sequential design, exploratory sequential design, and an embedded design (Creswell & Clark, 2011) (Table 2). Each is classified under two main categories: sequential or concurrent (Harrison & Reilly, 2011). When employing a sequential design, researchers start with one data collection method and then, following initial analysis, continue with another before reaching a final analysis stage. In contrast, researchers conduct research activities simultaneously when conducting MMR framed by concurrent design (Creswell & Clark, 2011; Teddlie & Tashakkori, 2009).

Table 2. MMR Designs.

Design	Timing	Merging
Convergent Parallel	Concurrent: quantitative and qualitative at the same time	Merging data during interpretation or analysis
Embedded	Concurrent or sequential	Embed one type of data within a larger design using the other type of data
Explanatory	Sequential: quantitative followed by qualitative	Connect data between the two phases
Exploratory	Sequential: Qualitative followed by quantitative	Connect data between the two phases

Source: developed by authors based on Creswell and Clark (2011) and Teddlie and Tashakkori (2009).

Choice of Mixed Methods Design

When adopting a mixed-methods design there are some aspects to consider:

The Timing

Researchers must consider timing regarding the collection of qualitative and quantitative data: will this be conducted in phases (sequentially) or gathered at the same time (concurrently)? If data are collected sequentially, the qualitative OR quantitative stage can be enacted first. However, this is contingent upon the researcher's original intent and the core aim of their study (Creswell & Clark, 2011; Teddlie & Tashakkori, 2009). For example, if a research project comprises two studies, with the second study informed by the results of the first, then a sequential research design is most appropriate because there is no possibility of running both strands simultaneously. To illustrate, when qualitative data are collected first, the intent is to explore the topic with participants, with this then expanded through a second phase in which data are collected from a larger number of people (Creswell, 2009). However, when data are collected concurrently, both quantitative and qualitative data are gathered simultaneously, and the implementation of each is simultaneous (Teddlie & Tashakkori, 2009).

The Priority of the Respective Strands

It is also crucial to consider the weight or priority of qualitative or quantitative methods enacted within a focal study. This is categorized as follows: equal priority, quantitative priority, or qualitative priority (Teddlie & Tashakkori, 2009). Researchers may perceive both the qualitative and quantitative studies underpinning their MMR as holding equal priority as both play an equally important role in addressing the research problem (Creswell & Clark, 2011). Conversely, the prioritization of one type of study (qualitative or quantitative) depends on (1) the interests of the researcher, (2) the audience for the study, and (3) what the investigator seeks to emphasize in the study (Teddlie & Tashakkori, 2009). To illustrate, prioritization in MMR is dependent on whether quantitative or qualitative information is emphasized first, the extent of the treatment of one type of data or the other in the project, or the preference toward a primarily inductive (i.e., generating themes via qualitative means) or deductive approach (i.e., testing a theory) (Creswell, 2014; Creswell & Clark, 2011).

The Level of Interaction

This refers to whether the qualitative and quantitative data are connected, kept separate, or merged (Creswell & Clark, 2018). In other words, the level of interaction between different datasets can be either independent or interactive (Creswell & Clark, 2011). When the design of a study (either qualitative or quantitative) depends on the results of another study (again qualitative or quantitative), then this is a connected level of interaction (Creswell & Clark, 2011; Teddlie & Tashakkori, 2009). In MMR, connected interaction is often demonstrated between the results of data analysis pertaining to the first phase of the research, with this used to help design data collection enacted during the second phase of research (Creswell, 2009). For example, Azer and Alexander (2018) conceptualized forms of negative online reviews in a qualitative study before using these newly-conceptualized categories in a quantitative study to investigate their impacts on other actors' attitudes and behavioral intentions (Azer & Alexander, 2020a, 2020b).

However, in other instances, any interaction between data emerging from different study phases can be avoided, with this separation used strategically to shape MMR design (Teddlie & Tashakkori, 2009). For example, in a two-phase project that begins with a quantitative phase, the data analysis and study results can be used to identify participants for qualitative data collection in a follow-up phase. Further, researchers may wish to merge qualitative and quantitative data (Creswell, 2009). For example, a researcher might collect both quantitative and qualitative data concurrently and merge the two databases by transforming qualitative themes into counts and comparing these counts with descriptive quantitative data. Finally, the researcher may avoid merged, connected, and separated interaction between strands. Instead, researchers can embed a secondary form of data within a larger study (Creswell & Clark, 2018). For example, some studies may have a primary aim to collect one form of data yet draw upon another to provide supporting information.

Application of MMR Design: The Example of Scale Development

Scale development is one of the core approaches for associating abstract concept(s) (i.e., scale or measurement constructs) to empirical indicants. It is concerned with the accuracy of a measurement instrument and the concepts it measures rather than the truthfulness of the measurement. Researchers must first define the concept (i.e., scale or measurement construct) and its possible sub-components (i.e., sub-dimensions of the measurement construct). Proper measurement of constructs is of utmost significance in behavioral and social sciences and represents an important field of inquiry (Churchill, 1979; Netemeyer, Bearden, & Sharma, 2003). Researchers apply combinations of several different qualitative and quantitative methods in order to develop practical scales, with this extending to tourism and hospitality research (e.g., Dedeoglu, Taheri, Okumus, & Gannon, 2020; Hosany & Gilbert, 2010; Taheri, Jafari, & O'Gorman, 2014; Taheri, Jafari, & Okumus, 2017; Taheri, Gannon, Cordina, & Lochrie, 2018). Typically, five sequential steps are required when conducting scale development, with each step drawing upon several different methods (Churchill, 1979; Netemeyer et al., 2003). The scale development process is, therefore, a pertinent example of MMR in practice, capturing multiple strands of research while also demonstrating the importance of interaction therein:

(1) The domain definition step: "the literature should indicate how the variable has been defined previously and how many dimensions or components it has" (Churchill, 1979, p. 67).

(2) Item generation step: deductive (i.e., develop items based on existing theory), inductive (i.e., develop items based on experience), or hybrid (i.e., a combination of both inductive and deductive). In-depth interviews, focus groups, Delphi and/or panel rating methods are common.

(3) Initial item reduction step: uses initial quantitative questionnaire (and exploratory factor analysis) to identify potential sub-scales.

(4) Initial validation step: uses the main quantitative questionnaire (and confirmatory factor analysis) to validate the findings from Step 4. This step confirms factor structure by examining the statistical significance of the model and relationships between subscales and items (i.e., dimensionality).

(5) Final validation or replication step: uses a quantitative follow-up questionnaire with different samples and normally from different context/culture (but also test-retest reliability assessment) to validate findings from Step 5.

MMR Rigor

When evaluating the rigor of MMR, it is typically apposite to assess how rigorous each phase (e.g., qualitative and quantitative) is. However, such an assessment does not necessarily demonstrate the rigor of the method adopted and enacted via MMR as a whole, as it overlooks the integration of multiple methods and whether each works congruently in pursuit of the research aim. As such, to help authors understand rigor within MMR, Reilly and Jones (2017) developed guidelines for assessing rigor regarding the qualitative and quantitative stages of MMR (Table 3).

Advantages of Mixed-Methods

MMR allows researchers to harness the strengths and offset the weaknesses of both quantitative and qualitative research (Creswell & Clark, 2018). For example, quantitative research is typically argued to be weak regarding encouraging researchers to understand the context under investigation, particularly under circumstances where participant voices are typically overlooked. Fortunately, when adopting an MMR approach, the qualitative research phase can make up for these weaknesses. However, it has its deficiencies, such as the bias born from the researchers' interpretations and the limited generalizability of findings. Accordingly, the advantages of one approach can offset the flaws of the other (Doyle et al., 2009; Morgan, 2007). This is true of the researcher, too; conducting mixed methods research enhances the skills of researchers and increases their expertise in a wider range of research methods.

Using mixed methods, researchers can employ different data collection tools without feeling constrained by those typically concomitant with qualitative or quantitative research (Teddlie & Tashakkori, 2009). MMR thus bridges the

Table 3. Guidelines for Evaluating Rigor Within MMR.

Criteria	High	Medium	Low
Data collection	Formal: Uses MMR strategies to design and conduct data collection	Informal: collects quantitative and qualitative data but overlooks the importance of MMR design more generally.	Single-method primacy. No discussion of multiple methods.
Data analysis	Multiple sources of data are analyzed together. The advantages of each method are recognized, with this used to offset methodological flaws therein.	All collected data, across both types, is analyzed. However, support for each phase of data collection is poor.	Relies upon one method of analysis. Analysis of different types of data is not linked.
Data integration	Types of data are mixed following the research design adopted. Data and findings are displayed jointly.	There is a degree of integration, but how each type of data interacts is overlooked regarding the depth of discussion.	Data is not integrated. Some collected data is not presented.
Mixed methods design type	Acknowledges its position as MMR and identifies the type of design adopted (e.g., concurrent embedded). Incorporates a figure or model to demonstrate the MMR design visually.	Offers insight into how each type of data was collected and methodology adopted more generally.	Descriptively addresses the interaction between dominant and secondary research phases (e.g., 'interviews helped develop our questionnaire')
Elements of writing	Demonstrates understanding of contemporary MMR literature. Core work is cited	Acknowledges that it is MMR in nature but does not cite relevant studies. Similar articles	Discussion of the MMR approach is not provided.

Table 3. *(Continued)*

Criteria	High	Medium	Low
	comprehensively – both methodological literature and examples of MMR within the study field. In addition, it is clear regarding signposting the MMR nature of the study (e.g., title, keywords, abstract, method, etc.).	across the discipline are cited, though not necessarily with clarity regarding the methodological approach. Failing to cite the mixed methods literature. MMR nature is unclear at first glance (e.g., reference to MMR is missing in the title, keywords, abstract, etc.)	
The rationale for employing mixed methods	The overall rationale for undertaking MMR is provided. This is extended to show relevance to the study's research question. Finally, the value of adopting an MMR approach specific to the research context is provided.	It is clear with regards to why multiple types of data are used. However, does not provide the rationale for using MMR design within the context of the study.	The rationale is missing or unclear.

Source: adapted from Reilly and Jones (2017).

often-combative rift between quantitative and qualitative scholars (Creswell & Clark, 2018), with this proving useful for social, behavioral, and human science researchers. Accordingly, MMR encourages researchers to draw upon multiple philosophical paradigms rather than limit themselves to associating certain paradigms with distinct approaches to research (Johnson et al., 2007). Importantly, MMR enables researchers to combine inductive and deductive logic by adopting an abductive perspective (Morgan, 2007); encouraging paradigmatic thought that embraces and bridges quantitative and qualitative research, such as pragmatism (Morgan, 2007). Finally, and most practically, MMR provides scholars with a greater opportunity to produce a range of outputs (e.g., a quantitative article, a qualitative article, and a methodological article) from a single study (Creswell & Clark, 2018).

Challenges of Conducting Mixed-Method Approaches

There are also several difficulties in undertaking MMR. This includes challenges associated with developing conceptual models from multi-source data, concerns regarding resource intensity (both time and financial), and the possibility of researcher bias. According to Creswell and Clark (2018), the core challenges of conducting MMR are highlighted in Table 4.

Approaches to Analysis

Mixed-method data analysis and interpretation approaches can take a non-integrative approach or a separate analysis with some integration during the analysis and interpretation phase (Greene, Caracelli, & Graham, 1989). Typically, quantitative and qualitative data are analyzed separately within MMR before combining data and results (Creswell & Clark, 2011). Although mixed method researchers do not always combine their findings (Bryman, 2006a, 2007), a lack of integration can limit the importance of subsequent findings. Furthermore, integrating quantitative and qualitative findings can potentially offer valuable insights that researchers could not otherwise discover (Bryman, 2007). Nevertheless, when analyzing MMR data, there remains a potential barrier to integration related to the "incompatibility thesis" debate discussed earlier. In order to preclude any potential problems regarding this point, no opportunities to "quantitize" qualitative data or the opposite are considered in this thesis (Bryman, 2007; Khoo-Lattimore et al., 2019).

Integration is pivotal within MMR design as different methodological approaches contribute to understanding a complex phenomenon interdependently (Caracelli & Greene, 1993). For example, when applying SED, the analysis from the second study should be dependent on that of the first, otherwise it would not be an instance of sequential mixed data analysis (Teddlie & Tashakkori, 2009). In addition, the quantitative phase validates any generated themes from the qualitative phase (Creswell, 2014; Teddlie & Tashakkori, 2009).

MMR in Hospitality and Tourism

Innovative mixed-method data collection and analysis has been employed to investigate phenomena across social science research, with hospitality and tourism research proving no different. Therein, several authors have adopted a mixed-method approach to, for example, study traveler behaviors in online reviews (Azer & Alexander, 2018; Wei, Miao, & Huang, 2013), destination image perception (Hunter & Suh, 2007), develop place brand models (Hanna & Rowley, 2015), investigate culture in tourism research (Ryan & Gu, 2010; Weiler & Yu, 2007), and empirically examine pragmatism in tourism research (Pansiri, 2006). Table 5 illustrates some recent examples of MMR across the field.

Table 4. Challenges of Conducting Mixed-Methods.

Challenge	How to Overcome?
Ethical considerations	Researchers must acknowledge, understand, and address ethical concerns regarding undertaking research with human subjects.
Researchers' skills	It is recommended that researchers develop skills concerning both quantitative and qualitative research. Solid foundations in this regard allow researchers to undertake MMR. At worst, those undertaking MMR must understand data collection and analysis techniques associated with quantitative and qualitative research.
Time and resources	Reflect on whether MMR is appropriate given time constraints and resources. MMR involves collecting multiple sources and forms of data with associated resource constraints. Further, analysis of multiple types of data can be time-consuming and costly. Therefore, researchers must be aware of the time required to gain approval, reach participants, collect and analyze data, analyze, and integrate results from multiple study phases. The complexity of this approach and the associated resource intensity is contingent upon whether MMR adopts a single-phase, two-phase, or multi-phase design.
Educating others about the value of Mixed-Methods	MMR is considered a contemporary methodology by some, with others holding misconceptions about mixed methods more generally. Thus, it may prove crucial to educate others on the nature of MMR. This can be achieved by identifying the exemplary deployment of MMR across extant literature and signposting peers accordingly.

Source: developed by authors based on Creswell and Clark (2018).

Table 5. Recent Tourism and Hospitality Studies Adopting Mixed/Multi Methods

Authors	Methods	Research Purpose
Jahandideh, Golmohammadi, Meng, O'Gorman, and Taheri (2014)	Survey and interviews and Delphi method	This study combines Hofstede's (1980, 2001) and Schwartz's (2006) cultural dimensions to form a new theoretical model examining cross-cultural consumer complaint behavior. The results address the implicit assumption in previous cross-cultural studies that Asian consumers are homogeneous in their behavior, revealing a significant difference in Arab and Chinese consumer complaint behavior.
Wells, Manika, Gregory-Smith, Taheri, and McCowlen (2015)	Survey and interviews	This study sheds light on the antecedents of employee environmental behavior and the effects of a social marketing intervention in a tourism organization using a mixed-methods longitudinal approach.
Azer (2018)	Netnography followed by experimental studies	Conceptualize forms and triggers of negatively valenced influencing behavior on TripAdvisor's online reviews and their impacts on travelers attitudinal and behavioral outcomes
Gannon et al. (2019)	Survey and interviews	Investigate how experiential purchase quality influences experience self-connection and braggart word-of-mouth for both first-time and repeat visitors,

Table 5. *(Continued)*

Authors	Methods	Research Purpose
Taheri and Thompson (2020)	Survey and interviews	This study examines how ski resorts can manage sustainable events while also balancing the needs of consumers and local workers
Taheri, Chalmers, Wilson, and Arshed (2021)	Survey and interviews	This paper incorporates two complementary studies, one focusing on value creation, the other on perceived value in medical tourism.
Taheri, Pourfakhimi, Prayag, Gannon, and Finsterwalder (2021)	Survey and interviews	This study investigates whether the antecedents of co-creation influence braggart word-of-mouth (WoM) in a participative leisure context, theorizing the concept of co-created food wellbeing and highlighting implications for interactive experience co-design.

Source: developed by authors.

Concluding Remarks

This chapter provides a critical view of MMR adoption within social science research more generally, with some specific examples pertaining to the tourism and hospitality disciplines. The chapter provides insight into the characteristics of MMR, demonstrating how it differs from a multi-method approach. By briefly discussing the underpinning characteristics of two core philosophical paradigms that support an MMR approach, this chapter encourages researchers to consider a range of aspects before deciding to adopt mixed methods in pursuit of research objectives. The rationale for adopting MMR is likely to shape research design. Accordingly, researchers are recommended to consider whether the central purpose of adopting a mixed-method approach is based on a desire to corroborate results, explain initial results, or for the robust administration of quantitative research instruments.

This chapter also explains different MMR designs, demonstrating key differences therein. Beyond the nature of the research problem, other factors influence MMR design. First, the timing of each study phase; it is recommended that the researchers consider the timing factor very specifically and decide whether different methods can be enacted simultaneously, or whether it is crucial for the study to be phased and sequential? Moreover, it is recommended that researchers determine whether their research problem is best addressed using concurrent, embedded, explanatory, or exploratory designs. Second, the priority of each phase is important; researchers are therefore recommended to decide whether greater importance is placed upon the qualitative or the quantitative phase as this will determine which design they should follow. Third, it is recommended that researchers determine the interaction level between each strand of research; should data be connected, kept separate, or merged at the analysis stage?

It is also recommended that researchers consider both the advantages and the challenges associated with MMR. This chapter discusses the advantages of adopting a mixed-method approach (e.g., one method's strengths counterbalance the weak points of another; corroboration of evidence; being well-suited for interdisciplinary research and adopting multiple philosophical perspectives to guide the inquiry). However, it also recognizes that MMR can be challenging and resource-intensive and that researchers must possess an appropriate range of skills, time, and resources to conduct MMR effectively. Finally, the chapter discusses approaches to analysis, emphasizing that researchers should consider that integration is pivotal in MMR design as different methodological approaches contribute to understanding a complex phenomenon interdependently, and that a lack of integration delimits the chances to make the most of collected data.

References

Ackroyd, S., & Fleetwood, S. (2000). *Realist perspectives on management and organisations.* London: Routledge.

Azer, J. (2018). *Negatively-valenced influencing behaviour: Forms, triggers and impacts.* PhD in Marketing. University of Strathclyde. Retrieved from https://ethos.bl.uk/OrderDetails.do?uin=uk.bl.ethos.814006

Azer, J., & Alexander, M. (2018). Conceptualizing negatively valenced influencing behavior: Forms and triggers. *Journal of Service Management, 29*(3), 468–490.

Azer, J., & Alexander, M. (2020a). Negative customer engagement behaviour: The interplay of intensity and valence in online networks. *Journal of Marketing Management, 36*(3–4), 361–383.

Azer, J., & Alexander, M. (2020b). Direct and indirect negatively valenced engagement behavior. *Journal of Services Marketing, 34*(7), 967–981.

Baggio, R., & Mariani, M. (2019). The relevance of mixed methods for network analysis in tourism and hospitality research. *International Journal of Contemporary Hospitality Management.* doi:10.1108/IJCHM-04-2019-0378

Bryman, A. (2006a). Integrating quantitative and qualitative research: How is it done? *Qualitative Research, 6*(1), 97–113. doi:10.1177/1468794106058877

Bryman, A. (2006b). Paradigm peace and the implications for quality. *International Journal of Social Research Methodology*, *9*(2), 111–126. doi:10.1080/13645570600595280

Bryman, A. (2007). Barriers to integrating quantitative and qualitative research. *Journal of Mixed Methods Research*, *1*(1), 8–22. doi:10.1177/2345678906290531

Campbell, D., & Fiske, D. (1959). Convergent and discriminate validation by the multi-trait-multi-method matrix. *Psychological Bulletin*, *56*(2), 81–105.

Caracelli, V., & Greene, J. (1993). Data analysis strategies for mixed-method evaluation designs. *Educational Evaluation and Policy Analysis*, *15*(2), 195–207.

Cash, P., Stankovic, T., & Storga, M. (2016). *Experimental design research: Approaches, perspectives, applications*. Cham: Springer.

Churchill, G. A. (1979). A paradigm for developing better measures of marketing constructs. *Journal of Marketing Research*, *16*(February), 63–73.

Creswell, J. (2009). *Research design: Qualitative, quantitative, and mixed methods approaches* (3rd ed.). London: Sage Publications.

Creswell, J. (2014). *A concise introduction to mixed methods research*. Thousand Oaks, CA: Sage publications.

Creswell, J., & Clark, P. (2011). *Designing and conducting mixed methods research*. London: Sage Publications.

Creswell, J., & Clark, P. (2018). *Designing and conducting mixed methods research* (3rd ed.). Thousand Oaks, CA: Sage publications.

Dedeoglu, B. B., Taheri, B., Okumus, F., & Gannon, M. (2020). Understanding the importance that consumers attach to social media sharing (ISMS): Scale development and validation. *Tourism Management*, *76*(Feb), 1–16.

Denzin, N. (1978). *The research act: A theoretical introduction to sociological methods*. New York, NY: McGraw-Hill.

Deshpande, R. (1983). Paradigms lost: On theory and method in research in marketing. *Journal of Marketing*, *47*(4), 101–110.

Doyle, L., Brady, A., & Byrne, G. (2009). An overview of mixed methods research. *Journal of Research in Nursing*, *14*(2), 175–185. doi:10.1177/1744987108093962

Easterby-Smith, M., Thorpe, R., & Jackson, P. (2012). *Management research*. Los Angeles, CA: Sage.

Ercikan, K., & Roth, W. (2006). What good is polarizing research into qualitative and quantitative? *Educational Researcher*, *35*(5), 14–23. doi:10.3102/0013189x035005014

Gannon, M., Taheri, B., & Olya, H. (2019). Festival quality, self-connection, and bragging. *Annals of Tourism Research*, *76*, 239–252.

Gibson, C. B. (2017). Elaboration, generalization, triangulation, and interpretation: On enhancing the value of mixed method research. *Organizational Research Methods*, *20*(2), 193–223.

Greene, J., Caracelli, V., & Graham, W. (1989). Toward a conceptual framework for mixed-method evaluation designs. *Educational Evaluation and Policy Analysis*, *11*(3), 255–274. doi:10.3102/01623737011003255

Guba, E., & Lincoln, Y. (2005). Competing paradigms in qualitative research. In N. L. Denzin & Y. S. Lincoln (Eds.), *Handbook of qualitative research* (pp. 105–117). Thousand Oaks, CA: Sage.

Hanna, S., & Rowley, J. (2015). Towards a model of the place brand web. *Tourism Management*, *48*(1), 110–112.

Harris, M. M. (2008). *Handbook of research in international human resources.* New York: Lawrence Erlbaum Associates.

Harrison, R., & Reilly, T. (2011). Mixed methods designs in marketing research. *Qualitative Market Research: An International Journal, 14*(1), 7–26. doi:10.1108/13522751111099300

Hofstede, G. (1980). Culture and organizations. *International Studies of Management & Organization, 10*(4), 15–41.

Hofstede, G. (2001). *Culture's consequences: Comparing values, behaviors, institutions and organizations across nations.* Thousand Oaks: Sage publications.

Hosany, S., & Gilbert, D. (2010). Measuring tourists' emotional experiences toward hedonic holiday destinations. *Journal of Travel Research, 49*(4), 513–526.

Hudson, L. A., & Ozanne, J. L. (1988). Alternative ways of seeking knowledge in consumer research. *Journal of Consumer Research, 14*(4), 508–521.

Hunter, W., & Suh, Y. (2007). Multi-method research on destination image perception: Jeju standing stones. *Tourism Management, 28*(1), 130–139.

Jahandideh, B., Golmohammadi, A., Meng, F., O'Gorman, K. D., & Taheri, B. (2014). Cross-cultural comparison of Chinese and Arab consumer complaint behavior in the hotel context. *International Journal of Hospitality Management, 41*, 67–76.

Jick, T. (1979). Mixing qualitative and quantitative methods: Triangulation in action. *Administrative Science Quarterly, 24*(4), 602–611.

Johnson, P., & Duberley, J. (2003). Reflexivity in management research. *Journal of Management Studies, 40*(5), 1279–1303.

Johnson, B., & Onwuegbuzie, J. (2004). Mixed methods research: A research paradigm whose time has come. *Educational Researcher, 33*(7), 14–26.

Johnson, B., Onwuegbuzie, A., & Turner, L. (2007). Toward a definition of mixed methods research. *Journal of Mixed Methods Research, 1*(2), 112–133. doi:10.1177/1558689806298224

Khoo-Lattimore, C., Mura, P., & Yung, R. (2019). The time has come: A systematic literature review of mixed methods research in tourism. *Current Issues in Tourism, 22*(13), 1531–1550.

Maarouf, H. (2019). Pragmatism as a supportive paradigm for the mixed research approach: Conceptualizing the ontological, epistemological, and axiological stances of pragmatism. *International Business Research, 12*(9), 1–12.

Morgan, D. (2007). Paradigms lost and pragmatism regained. *Journal of Mixed Methods Research, 1*(1), 48–76. doi:10.1177/2345678906292462

Netemeyer, R. G., Bearden, W. O., & Sharma, S. (2003). *Scaling procedures: Issues and applications.* Thousand Oaks, CA: Sage.

Pansiri, J. (2006). Doing tourism research using the pragmatism paradigm: An empirical example. *Tourism and Hospitality Planning & Development, 3*(3), 223–240.

Reilly, T. M., & Jones, R. (2017). Mixed methodology in family business research: Past accomplishments and perspectives for the future. *Journal of Family Business Strategy, 8*(3), 185–195.

Ryan, C., & Gu, H. (2010). Constructionism and culture in research: Understandings of the fourth Buddhist Festival, Wutaishan, China. *Tourism Management, 31*(2), 167–178.

Schurr, P. H. (2007). Buyer-seller relationship development episodes: Theories and methods. *Journal of Business & Industrial Marketing, 22*(3), 161–170.

Schwartz, S. (2006). A theory of cultural value orientations: Explication and applications. *Comparative Sociology, 5*(2–3), 137–182.

Taheri, B., Chalmers, D., Wilson, J., & Arshed, N. (2021a). Would you really recommend it? Antecedents of word-of-mouth in medical tourism. *Tourism Management, 83.* in press.

Taheri, B., Gannon, M. J., Cordina, R., & Lochrie, S. (2018). Measuring host sincerity: Scale development and validation. *International Journal of Contemporary Hospitality Management, 30*(8), 2752–2772.

Taheri, B., Jafari, A., & O'Gorman, K. (2014). Keeping your audience: Presenting a visitor engagement scale. *Tourism Management, 42,* 321–329.

Taheri, B., Jafari, A., & Okumus, B. (2017). Ceremonious politeness in consuming food in VFR tourism: Scale development. *Service Industries Journal, 37*(15–16), 948–967.

Taheri, B., Pourfakhimi, S., Prayag, G., Gannon, M., & Finsterwalder, J. (2021b). Towards co-created food wellbeing: Culinary consumption, braggart word-of-mouth, and the role of participative co-design, service provider support, and C2C interactions. *European Journal of Marketing, 55*(9), 2464–2490.

Taheri, B., & Thompson, J. (2020). Generating socially responsible events at ski resorts. *International Journal of Hospitality Management, 91,* 102695.

Teddlie, C., & Tashakkori, A. (2009). *Foundations of mixed methods research.* London: Sage.

Trochim, W. M. K. (2006). *Research methods knowledge base.* Retrieved from http://www.socialresearchmethods.net/kb/contents.php

Weiler, B., & Yu, X. (2007). Dimensions of cultural mediation in guiding Chinese tour groups: Implications for interpretation. *Tourism Recreation Research, 32*(3), 13–22.

Wei, W., Miao, L., & Huang, Z. (2013). Customer engagement behaviors and hotel responses. *International Journal of Hospitality Management, 33*(1), 316–330. doi: 10.1016/j.ijhm.2012.10.002

Wells, V. K., Manika, D., Gregory-Smith, D., Taheri, B., & McCowlen, C. (2015). Heritage tourism, CSR and the role of employee environmental behaviour. *Tourism Management, 48,* 399–413.

Chapter 3

An Exploratory Sequential Mixed Methods Design: A Research Design for Small Tourism Enterprises in Ghana

Elizabeth Agyeiwaah

Abstract

This chapter examines the application of exploratory sequential mixed methods design in the context of small accommodation enterprises (i.e., home-stay). This study, therefore, discusses the exploratory sequential mixed methods of data collection and analysis and provides practical illustrations based on a study of small tourism enterprise sustainability practices in Ghana. The findings demonstrate that mixed methods overcome the weaknesses of a mono-method and offer an in-depth understanding of tourism and hospitality phenomena. In addition to providing a practical guide to emerging tourism scholars, the current study highlights the ability of mixed methods to develop emerging practitioners' skills in both qualitative and quantitative data. In conclusion, the exploratory sequential mixed methods design offers pragmatic data collection techniques that are non-existent in mono-methods. Accordingly, it is recommended for exploring research questions when there is limited information and high flexibility is needed.

Keywords: Mixed methods; exploratory sequential; small tourism enterprises; sustainability; research design; Ghana

Introduction

As a multi-dimensional, multi-faceted, and multi-scalar concept (Hopwood, Mellor, & O'Brien, 2005), sustainability has attracted scholarly interest within the context of small tourism enterprises (Roberts & Tribe, 2008). The studies that have been conducted have employed various techniques, including case studies (Bergin-Seers & Jago, 2007; Scheyvens & Russell, 2012), grounded theory method

---
Advanced Research Methods in Hospitality and Tourism, 25–45

Copyright © 2023 Elizabeth Agyeiwaah

Published under exclusive licence by Emerald Publishing Limited

doi:10.1108/978-1-80117-550-020221003

(Kornilaki, Thomas, & Font, 2019), scenarios and interviews (Biggs, Hall, & Stoeckl, 2012; Hassanli & Ashwell, 2020), and quantitative survey (Font, Garay, & Jones, 2016). Nonetheless, when conducting sustainability studies among small tourism enterprises such as home-stay, assessing their sustainable practices within diverse contexts is a methodological challenge. Addressing such a challenge requires a mixed method design that addresses multiple epistemological foci (Klassen, Creswell, Clark, Smith, & Meissner, 2012).

As the "third" methodological movement with a strong association with pragmatism, mixed methods research emerged from the paradigm battles of the 1980s among the purists who argue that research approaches should not be mixed (Cameron, 2009; Creswell, 2014). However, many proponents have provided several arguments to support the need for mixed methods. According to Johnson and Onwuegbuzie (2004), the mixed methods design is an outcome-based approach that is action-oriented and eliminates doubts. According to Brady and Collier (2010), it has the potential for mutual learning while Neuman (2006) suggests that it helps to develop a better understanding and explanation of a complex social phenomenon.

Such perceived pluralistic strengths of combining qualitative and quantitative approaches have stimulated the growing application of mixed methods designs in educational research (Johnson & Onwuegbuzie, 2004), organizational research (Cameron, 2009), management research (Jogulu & Pansiri, 2011), quality of life research (Klassen et al., 2012), and tourism studies (Khoo-Lattimore, Mura, & Yung, 2019). For many tourism scholars, the "epistemological eclecticism" of mixed methods that address complex and multi-faceted research questions stimulates its methodological relevance and adoption (Singh, Milne, & Hull, 2012). Others are intrigued by the possibility of drawing meta-inferences from integrating quantitative and qualitative methodologies. However, surprisingly current sustainable tourism studies have given limited attention to how mixed research approaches can be used to unpack the complexities of sustainability in tourism (Iaquinto, 2016).

Despite the growing importance of small tourism enterprises' contribution to sustainable development (Roberts & Tribe, 2008), there is a lack of attention on their research methods with a few exceptions that elaborate how fore-sighting methods can be employed to examine the sustainability of small firms (e.g., Tilley & Fuller, 2000). Although calls for advanced methodologies for examining the tourism phenomenon have increased (Ateljevic & Doorne, 2000; Noy, 2008), such calls are more crucial within sustainable tourism research where diverse stakeholders are involved and, thus, pluralistic mixed approaches that practically address underlying research questions are required. More importantly, while evidence exists on the popularity of sequential mixed methods over concurrent designs in sustainable tourism research (Molina-Azorín & Font, 2016), there is little information on how the approach has been implemented in the various studies.

Indeed, tourism researchers have shown immense interest in the application of mixed methods designs (Khoo-Lattimore et al., 2019), but studies on how these methods can be applied among small tourism enterprises are limited. While this study acknowledges the significant contribution of previous studies that applied either quantitative surveys or qualitative interviews, it is the position of this book chapter that a combination of both approaches will inject an intellectual vitality through the associated divergences of both quantitative and qualitative methods. This brings into focus the question of how this integration can be achieved, a question that all researchers and methodologists must ask before deciding to combine qualitative and quantitative approaches (Johnson & Onwuegbuzie, 2004). In addressing this question through reflexivity as suggested by Bourdieu (2004), the objective of this chapter is to examine how an exploratory sequential mixed method is applied to unpack sustainability practices among small tourism enterprises. Providing a guideline on the application of such a method can assist other researchers working in similar areas as well as early career researchers seeking to employ sequential mixed method designs. This chapter is organized as follows. The next section briefly elaborates on mixed methods designs in tourism and zeroes in on the specific design (i.e., exploratory sequential method). This is followed by a guideline on how this approach can be implemented using a case study. Finally, a concluding section is provided, highlighting some important recommendations for future researchers.

Literature Review

Mixed Methods Research and Its Application in Tourism Studies

Mixed methods research combines qualitative and quantitative techniques, approaches, and concepts into one study to gather or analyze data. Such an approach aligns with the pragmatic philosophy which builds on the fundamental principle that mixing research methods should be implemented in a manner that allows the researcher to respond to significant questions that facilitate practical results (Johnson & Onwuegbuzie, 2004). It is this core tenet that many researchers and methodologists find convincing (e.g., Johnson & Onwuegbuzie, 2004; Morse, 1991; Tashakkori & Teddlie, 1998), including tourism scholars (e.g., Font et al., 2016; Iaquinto, 2016; Koteyko, Jaspal, & Nerlich, 2013; Molina-Azorín, Tarí, Pereira-Moliner, López-Gamero, & Pertusa-Ortega, 2015).

The evolution of mixed methods designs has led to the invention of a gamut of typologies for its implementation (Cameron, 2009). Some methodologists differentiate between multi-method designs and mixed methods designs (Morse, 2003) whereas others distinguish between mixed-model designs and mixed methods designs (Johnson & Onwuegbuzie, 2004; Mertens, 2014). Multi-method designs imply the use of two or more methods in the same study where the methods are kept separate and not mixed. mixed methods design, which the current book chapter aligns with, is a type of design where researchers combine two or more approaches of qualitative and quantitative within the same project (Morse, 1991). This differs from mixed-model designs that include quantitative as well as qualitative methods in the same study or across different aspects of the study (Johnson & Onwuegbuzie, 2004). Despite the plethora of designs, nine parsimonious designs have been proposed based on a combination of four themes, namely

Degree of importance	Concurrent	Sequential
Equal importance	QUAL + QUAN	QUAL → QUAN QUAN → QUAL
Dominant status	QUAL + quan	QUAL → quan qual → QUAN
	QUAN + qual	QUAN → qual quan → QUAL

Fig. 1.   Mixed Methods Design Matrix Showing Nine Different Designs. *Note*: "qual" denotes qualitative, "quan" denotes quantitative, "+" symbolizes concurrent, "→" stands for sequential, capital letters imply high importance, and lower-case letters imply low importance. *Source*: Developed based on Johnson and Onwuegbuzie (2004, p. 22).

concurrent, sequential, equal status, and dominance (Fig. 1). Thus, researchers as part of mixing qualitative and quantitative approaches should decide whether to give equal status to each approach or allow one approach to dominate. In addition, there is also the decision as to whether to conduct each phase sequentially or concurrently. Such a decision is related to the research intention. Examples of such intentions include *triangulation* which seeks convergence and corroboration of results from varied methods; complementarity which clarifies findings of one method with a different method; *initiation* which seeks to discover inconsistencies leading to reframing research questions; *a developmental purpose* that uses the findings of one approach to guide the other approach; and *expansion* which uses different methods to extend the scope of a study (Johnson & Onwuegbuzie, 2004; Molina-Azorín & Font, 2016). Mixed methods are usually employed for expansion and developmental purposes other than complementarity and triangulation in most tourism research (Molina-Azorín & Font, 2016).

Based on the purpose of expansion, Kasim (2009), for example, employed simultaneous mixed methods designs with a dominance of quantitative method (QUAN + qual) to examine environmental management awareness and attitudes among small and medium hotels in Kuala Lumpur. The author developed a Likert scale questionnaire from the literature, complemented with open-ended questions to achieve this objective. Kim and Han (2010), for developmental purposes, employed a sequential equivalence mixed methods design (QUAL → QUAN) to understand the intentions toward the payment of standard hotel prices in South Korean green hotels. Following Fishbein and Ajzen (1980)'s elicitation suggestions, Kim and Han (2010) interviewed four hotel managers, five hotel customers, and five hospitality academics using a focus group in addition to an open-ended survey with 30 hotel customers. Following this process, final questionnaires were developed through the elicitation process. Lynch, Duinker, Sheehan, and Chute (2010) for extension purposes employed concurrent equivalent mixed methods designs (QUAN + QUAL) to examine motivations and satisfaction of cultural tourists' participation in authentic Mi'kmaw in Nova Scotia in addition to the perspectives from the Mi'kmaw host. Consequently, quantitative surveys were used to examine tourists' perspectives whereas key informant interviews were conducted to ascertain the Mi'kmaw host perspectives concurrently. Specifically, within small tourism research, Sampaio, Thomas, and Font (2012) examined the engagement and disengagement in environmental management among small enterprises based on a chronological equivalence mixed methods technique for expansion purposes. In their study, the quantitative stage of the research comprised a self-completion questionnaire for owner-managers. The qualitative stage, on the other hand, focused on owner-managers who were part of the quantitative study.

Several other examples of the use of mixed methods designs for other purposes such as complementarity and triangulation have also been documented in tourism studies (see Bonilla Priego, Najera, & Font, 2011; Dawson, Stewart, Lemelin, & Scott, 2010; Ryan, Chaozhi, & Zeng, 2011). Generally, these studies favor sequential mixed methods designs over concurrent mixed methods designs (Molina-Azorín & Font, 2016); however, research on how to implement these designs remains scarce.

Exploratory Sequential Mixed Methods Design in Tourism

Exploratory sequential mixed methods are characterized by the first phase of a qualitative approach which informs the second stage of quantitative data to clarify the study findings. This design is usually adopted to develop better measurements among a few groups of respondents under study (qualitative) and to see how such results can be extended onto a bigger group (quantitative) (Creswell, 2014). The use of the expression "exploratory" signifies the design, implying that the qualitative method precedes the quantitative approach; whereas the word "sequential" is used to denote the order of implementation approach applied to the data collection process where data is collected in different phases against other concurrent designs (Morse, 1991; Tashakkori & Teddlie, 1998). Like many mixed methods designs, it is at the discretion of researchers' conducting exploratory sequential studies to decide the priority of quantitative and qualitative aspects leading to either equal status or dominant status (Johnson & Onwuegbuzie, 2004). Hence, the complexity of designing exploratory sequential methods can take three different forms (Fig. 2). The first exploratory sequential typology of mixed methods design accords equal importance to both qualitative and quantitative methods. An example is a study conducted by Canavan (2014) that examined the relevance of sustainable tourism in the UK. In this study, 32 in-depth interviews with local residents and tourists were conducted over 24 months. This qualitative approach aided the process of developing an emergent theory that aided the

Exploratory sequential design

Equal status	QUAL → QUAN
Dominant status	QUAL → quan
	qual → QUAN

Fig. 2.   Exploratory Sequential mixed method Design Matrix. *Note*: "qual" stands for qualitative, "quan" stands for quantitative, "→" denotes for sequential, capital letters connote high importance, and lowercase letters connote low importance. *Source*: Developed based on Johnson and Onwuegbuzie (2004).

development of the quantitative questionnaire in the second stage of the study for a better result interpretation.

The second type of exploratory sequential mixed methods design is where the qualitative method is dominant over the quantitative approach. An example is a study by Walker and Moscardo (2014) that examined the experience of passengers of cruise expeditions, including their perceptions of the benefits of such experiences, the nature of interpretation provided, and sustainability values. Their mixed methods design involved a sequential approach with a qualitative dominance using ethnographic techniques. By employing a laddering interviewing technique, the authors asked respondents to specify relevant elements of the product attributes and their perceived benefits. They further questioned why those benefits were important and this help in the identification of personal important values represented in attribute-benefit-value chains. The techniques employed in this study are a combination of mixed approaches with a predominance of qualitative in the first phase with additional quantitative measures in the analysis stage.

The third type of exploratory sequential mixed methods design is where the qualitative approach precedes a quantitative approach but in a less dominant manner. An example is a study by Reichel, Uriely, and Shani (2008) that examined tourist attitudes regarding a conceptual planning approach in ecotourism. In this study, the authors employed an earlier qualitative approach to assist the development of dominant quantitative research. A three-stage questionnaire development process involving literature review, focus group panel of researchers, and in-depth interviews were used to identify useful measures of tourist attitudes. After obtaining the measures for attitudes, new questions were added to survey 453 tourists in various languages.

The preceding studies illustrate the over-reliance of exploratory sequential designs for developmental and expansions purposes. When conducted appropriately, exploratory sequential mixed methods design facilitates the development of theory and research instrument with a complete understanding of the research problem. However, there are some challenges to be aware of. One major challenge relates to the decision point of interface – i.e. what aspects of the findings in the qualitative stage should be the focus of the quantitative stage? Other challenges surround the point of convergence – i.e. at what point should the results be merged? Additionally, deciding reasonable sample sizes for both stages can be challenging as well as the interpretation of results from both phases (Creswell, 2014; Klassen et al., 2012). How these questions can be addressed is illustrated through a guideline and a practical case study.

Guidelines to Implement the Method

Following the practical tourism examples on the three distinct kinds of exploratory sequential mixed methods designs, this book chapter develops a guideline (Fig. 3) to implement the exploratory sequential mixed methods design. The

Phase 1

Step 1: Developing the qualitative instrument
Step 2: Deciding the sample size and data site
Step 3: Selecting target participants
Step 4: Deciding the interview procedures & data collection
Step 5: Analyzing the qualitative results

Phase 2

Step 6: Framing the quantitative phase and instrumentation
Step 7: Deciding the quantitative sample and data collection
Step 8: Analyzing the quantitative data

Interpretation stage

Steps 9: **Interpretation and presentation of results**

Fig. 3.   Guidelines for Implementation (Author's Construct).

section is divided into the two major phases or sequences that characterize this design.

Phase 1

Step 1: Developing the Qualitative Instrument

The first stage of exploratory sequential is to develop the qualitative tool for data collection. The qualitative instrument stage usually begins with a detailed analysis of literature (based on one's research questions) to decide the instrument design. The first question at this stage is to determine the kind of interviews to be conducted that is, whether structured interviews or unstructured interviews. In terms of a structured interview, it is imperative to establish the degree of structuredness – semi-structured or complete structure. Thus, researchers must decide whether to use in-depth interviews, structured interviews, or focus group discussions. This choice is dependent on the study's research question and objectives. In-depth interviews adopt an intensive and unstructured style that allows the interviewer and target respondents to openly speak about the issue under discussion. Semi-structured interviews, however, provide a framework for examining experiences in instances of inadequate subjective knowledge (McIntosh & Morse, 2015). Focus group discussions help to gather information from a group via an interactive session led by a moderator (Stewart, Shamdasani, & Rook, 2009). From the existing literature, an interview protocol could be developed that asks respondents to express their views on specific questions relating to the broader question of the study.

Step 2: Deciding the Sample Size and Data Site

Once interview questions have been established to deal with specific research questions, a decision on the sample size and data collection location is pertinent. While at this qualitative phase the sample size should be smaller than the quantitative phase (Creswell, 2014), researchers must still determine the right data size. There are several rules for deciding sample sizes depending on whether this qualitative stage is predominant, less dominant, or equivalent to the quantitative aspects. If the researcher chooses an equivalent sequential design, the qualitative stage must cover a substantial number of respondents to provide useful information for the second stage. While sample sizes in qualitative research have been debated (Boddy Clive, 2016), Sandelowski (1995) argues that qualitative sample sizes should be adequate to allow detailed analysis. Some methodologists suggest that 10 to 15 sample sizes may be acceptable for a homogenous population (Bertaux, 1981; Sandelowski, 1995). Cresswell (1998), however, suggests that a range between 20 and 30 samples is typical. Others contend that a sample size of 20 may be too small while a sample size of 40 may be too large for grounded theory studies. Thus, sample size ranges between 20–30 and 15–30 are recommended for grounded theory and case study research respectively (Marshall, Cardon, Poddar, & Fontenot, 2013). From these suggested sample sizes, it is recommended that a qualitative sample size above 20 is adequate for useful insights into a phenomenon. The sample size decision should be followed by a choice of a data collection site for both pre-testing and actual data collection.

Step 3: Selecting Target Participants
Selecting whom to interview is an important part of the design. The researcher must decide on an appropriate sampling technique that is suitable for the intended sample size. There are several qualitative non-probability sampling techniques for mixed methods research, including purposive sampling, convenience sampling, accidental sampling, and snowball sampling (Creswell, 2014; Teddlie & Yu, 2007). At this stage, the sampling techniques can be used individually or combined to obtain the required target respondents for the initial phase of the mixed methods designs. However, researchers should note that given the non-probability nature of these sampling techniques, some characteristic groups (e.g., more males or more females) may be dominant but may be typical of the target group.

Step 4: Deciding the Interview Procedures and Data Collection
After selecting the target respondents, researchers need to plan the interview procedures. The next question relates to how the interviewer intends to conduct the interview. For example, the interview can be performed face-to-face, via Skype, or by telephone. In most instances, the approach that is convenient, less costly, and yields maximum results is considered. Since observational information constitutes an important aspect of qualitative studies, conducting interviews via telephone may deny the researcher the opportunity for close observation. In such an instance, a face-to-face interview is recommended. Thus, the research question and the purpose of the study must inform the kinds of procedures to be adopted to ensure that the right results are derived from the study.

In addition, when to conduct the interview is an important consideration for researchers. In-depth interviews, for example, are intensive interactions that may last more than 30 minutes. Consequently, both the interviewer and the interviewee must have ample time for such an uninterrupted conversation. The choice of time must be convenient for the interviewee. Once such considerations have been resolved, data collection can commence.

Step 5: Analyzing the Qualitative Results
Following the qualitative data collection, data analysis must be performed to identify which aspects of this phase should be incorporated into the next phase. Several data analytical approaches, including grounded theory (open, axial, and selective coding approaches) and the development of a theoretical model (Strauss & Corbin, 1997) that can be tested at the quantitative phase are available. Other content analytical coding such as thematic analysis (Attride-Stirling, 2001) are also useful for developing themes that can be used for developing scale items at the quantitative stage. Here, researchers can employ data management software such as NVIVO or QDA Miner (Lewis & Maas, 2007).

Phase 2

Step 6: Framing the Quantitative Phase and Instrumentation
The first task at this stage is to identify themes from the qualitative study that require further explanation. This involves determining which items must be included and excluded at this second phase of the quantitative data collection (Creswell, 2014). At this point, it is needful to have some criteria for inclusion. The research questions are the core guiding principles. Researchers must develop key aspects from the qualitative results that require further explanation. This can be done through the development of a questionnaire to be surveyed among a larger group for deeper analysis. Consequently, the questionnaire, for example, can begin with quotes from the qualitative data while quantitative variables can be developed from the qualitative themes identified during the analysis.

Step 7: Deciding the Quantitative Sample and Data Collection
Once instrument design has been completed, sample sizes must be determined for both pre-testing and actual data collection. It is common for the sample size at this stage to have a different and larger group than the qualitative stage since the exploratory sequential moves from smaller qualitative groups to a larger quantitative group for generalization (Creswell, 2014). For generalization purposes, sample sizes should be substantial enough to reflect the population being studied.

Following sample size determination, the designed instrument must be pilot tested to ensure that the chosen items are valid and measure what they are supposed to measure. Reliability tests are also important at this stage, and this could be done using Cronbach's alpha statistic (Pallant, 2013). Actual data collection follows the refinement of the instrument. Here, the researcher decides whether to conduct an online survey, mail the questionnaire or personally administer questionnaires. The approach as discussed previously depends on time, money, other resources (e.g., research assistants), and considerations of the effectiveness of the approach to yield the best outcomes.

Step 8: Analyzing the Quantitative Data
After data collection, data cleaning must be done to ensure that only completed instruments are analyzed. Several analytical procedures can be followed at this stage based on the research questions. For example, factor analysis is a good tool to identify dimensions whereas cluster analysis (e.g., Two-step or K-means) is a good tool to identify groups that are similar within and different from other groups for comparisons. Cluster membership can be created with further analysis of variance (ANOVA) computation. Quantitative analysis such as Chi-square can be computed if the researcher seeks to test for differences and relationships among categorical items. Importantly, each analysis should be purposefully conducted to address a specific problem rather than merely flaunting statistical skills.

Step 9: Interpretation and Presentation of Results
The final stage is the interpretation and presentation of the results. This section requires the researcher to make meaning from both stages of the research.

Typically, the qualitative results are first interpreted, followed by the quantitative results. Since both data sets are usually drawn from different samples but the same population, a comparison may not be appropriate. Comparing the two datasets may also not be necessary because the small qualitative sample is often generalized to a larger population (Creswell, 2014).

A Case Study of Exploratory Sequential Mixed Methods in Tourism Through Reflexivity

Bourdieu (2004) argues that reflexivity in mixed methods research is necessary for methodological reflection and refinement. In this vein, this book chapter presents a case study of how the nine steps proposed above were applied through a reflection of my PhD thesis that examined sustainability issues among small tourism enterprises using the exploratory sequential mixed methods designs. Since the illustration is based on my personal experience, "I" is used as a first-person singular pronoun in some instances to explain my involvement and application of the guidelines suggested.

The purpose of the above-named project was to assess how small tourism enterprise performance can be improved within the framework of sustainable development. Specifically, the study answered the following research questions: What do home-stay owners know about sustainable development? Do home-stay owners care about sustainable development and are willing to be sustainable? Do owners apply sustainable practices as part of their business operations? What is the role of business reasons on the sustainable performance of the home-stay sector? What are the performance issues/constraints, capabilities, and obstacles of the home-stay sector of Ghana? These questions were so multifaceted that a mono-method was inadequate to yield insightful outcomes. Hence, this study followed Johnson and Turner (2003)'s argument that in mixed methods research, multiple strategies and approaches are conducted in such a way that it leads to a superior outcome of complementary strength and non-overlapping weaknesses. Specifically, the exploratory sequential mixed methods design, which is relevant for exploring a new phenomenon, was employed to develop a suitable sustainability instrument for the home-stay business. This is because home-stay business characteristics are unique and there are no existing measures for this small tourism enterprise. I chose an equal priority sequential mixed methods design and how the design was conducted is illustrated below. Moreover, even though the pilot test preceded the actual data, I discuss both simultaneously under the guidelines owing to space constraints.

Step 1: Developing the Qualitative Instrument

I started the sequential mixed methods designs by developing an interview protocol based on an extensive meta-analysis of the literature on sustainability, in general, and small tourism enterprises, in particular (see Agyeiwaah, McKercher, & Suntikul, 2017). Based on the findings, I developed an initial in-depth interview that was made up of a broad list of questions on the dimensions of sustainability for an initial pilot study with owner-managers of home-stay accommodation. Some of the specific questions included: "What do you know about sustainability?" "What do you know about economic sustainability?" Other open-ended questions were also asked on owner-managers care, willingness and practices of sustainability as well as performance issues and capabilities. For example, "What are your major business performance constraints?" However, a semi-structured interview tool was adopted for the actual qualitative data collection following the pilot study – this has been explained under "Step 4".

The semi-structured interview schedule was divided into eight sections. First, the owners' location needed to be captured to understand the role context plays in sustainability. Besides, the number of rooms, years of operation, employee number, and the nature of the job were also captured for proper profiling of the respondents. These questions were important to unpack the dynamics of the business in various homes and settings (Agyeiwaah, 2020a, 2020b). Following this section, questions related to owner business goals, business reasons, and attributes were asked to unpack the intentions for operating home-stay in Ghana and what owners hoped to achieve. However, it was later found that most owners gave the same/similar responses to both personal goals and business reasons – this may be attributed to the similarity in the local translation used.

Step 2: Deciding the Sample Size and Data Site

This stage involved the decision of how many target respondents would be suitable for pilot -testing as well as the actual data collection for the qualitative data. The pre-test took place in Kumasi, the second-largest city in the Ashanti Region of Ghana. For the pre-testing of instruments, I decided a sample size of about five to 10 owner-managers was appropriate while 30 respondents were considered acceptable for the actual study. The most challenging issue here was where to locate these small tourism businesses. The starting point was non-governmental organizations in Ghana that are mediators for this accommodation. Hence, I contacted these organizations within that city (Kumasi for pre-test) while those in Cape Coast were contacted for the actual data. Both organizations gave a list of owner-managers for data collection. However, to expand the list, some sampling techniques were used for selection.

Step 3: Selecting Target Participants

Practically, Steps 2 and 3 sometimes occur simultaneously. During this stage, it was important to use purposive and snowball sampling techniques because owner-managers have relevant information about other owner-managers and could, therefore, make recommendations for the pilot sample. Following lessons from the pilot study, the same sampling procedures were used to recruit 30 owner-managers in a different metropolis, namely the Cape Coast Metropolis, Ghana. This metropolis is one of the important tourism hubs in Ghana with its enormous castles and forts and other cultural attractions. As indicated in the previous section above, the actual data collection employed semi-structured interviews.

While deciding the sample sizes, I also thought about ways to select the owner-managers of the small accommodation enterprises. As mentioned earlier, given the specific nature of the business, only those involved in the day-to-day running of the business were selected. In cases where couples were involved, the one who was predominantly involved in the business was purposely selected to respond to questions related to the sustainability practices of the business.

Step 4: Deciding the Interview Procedures and Data Collection

To observe the various accommodation and take photos as well, face-to-face meetings at various homes were mostly preferred to telephone/Skype interviews. Consequently, I visited various homes for the pre-testing based on the schedules proposed by owner-managers since the interview required that they interact with me for at least one hour. Only five respondents participated in the pre-test interview and the interactions were audio-recorded for transcription. The feedback from this pre-test informed the choice of a semi-structured interview. For example, during the pre-test interview data collection, when owner-manager were asked openly about their daily practices and willingness toward sustainability, they were not willing to provide specific information relevant to the study. Many owner-managers, for instance, were keen to report what they do only at the expense of what they do not practice. Moreover, broader terms such as economic sustainability were not clear to respondents. Hence, it became necessary to revise the instrument by adding more specific issues (e.g., income, expenditure, employment). This structured design was also needed to ensure consistency among research assistants.

The actual data collection procedure started after all relevant NGOs had been contacted to provide home-stays within the Cape Coast Metropolis. I first visited all the owner-managers, explained the purpose of the study to them, and sought their consent. I also inquired of their convenient time for the interviews to take place. Many preferred to participate in the interview at home while a few preferred to be interviewed at the workplace. After scheduling the interviews, I visited each home with the help of a research assistant to conduct the interview. With the help of the semi-structured interview, the process lasted between 45minutes to two hours. All interviews were audio-recorded, and photos were also taken.

Step 5: Analyzing the Qualitative Results

Before analyzing the qualitative transcripts, I coded all audio records and corresponding interview schedules for easy tracking. All files were saved in relevant folders in Dropbox. All the recorded interviews were transcribed for individual respondents using the back-to-back translation method. During the data analysis, the transcription involved typing out the actual information given by each respondent and saving the information in the respondent's name in Word and portable document format (PDF), which was then uploaded into the QDA Miner for analysis. These two formats were required for successful upload into the data analysis software. Hence, transcription and upload were done for 26 respondents out of the 30 who participated in the study. The use of QDA was preferred to other qualitative software as it facilitates the development of a dendrogram as well as saves all transcripts in an Excel format for future use. The data analysis procedure helped to identify key issues that were relevant to answering the research questions. By employing the QDA Miner software, I was able to create inductive codes with specific colors and to organize them into basic, organizing, and global themes following qualitative thematic analysis procedures (Attride-Stirling, 2001). For example, information related to owner-managers knowledge of sustainability were coded as either "Don't know" (e.g., "I have not heard it and I have no idea what it is"), "Have heard" (e.g., "I don't know what it is, but I have heard about it on the radio) or "Superficial" (e.g., "sustainability means maintenance or improvement of something"). These responses were organized under the organization theme – Knowledge of sustainability, which falls under the research question: what do home-stay owners know about sustainable development?

Step 6: Framing the Quantitative Phase and Instrumentation

After the qualitative data analysis, the quantitative phase had to be framed based on the outcome of the qualitative study. Here, I had to decide which aspects of the qualitative requires further explanation at the quantitative stage. The questionnaire used for this purpose had eight sections, but I will highlight four sections to show how this design allows researchers to be pragmatic in their inclusion and exclusion of relevant themes. First, some aspects of demographics (e.g., age, sex, marital status) were repeated while new aspects (years of business experiences) were added based on the qualitative insights. Second, from the qualitative interviews, I learned that each owner had different reasons for starting their business and this informed their practices and what they considered important. Hence, at the quantitative phase, based on the fourth research question of the study ("What is the role of business reasons on the sustainable performance of the home-stay sector?"), my first section examined business reasons following the qualitative themes and additional themes extracted from Getz and Carlsen (2000, p. 551). I used open-ended questions because the sample at this point was still larger, and it was possible to identify new themes that capture broader business reasons. My aim for this categorical question was to group their business reason's themes using cluster analysis and compare them statistically with different practices. This analytical procedure will be elaborated under the analysis section.

Third, in line with explaining some key aspects, certain background issues were not part of the objectives but shed light on some daily practices that emerged from the qualitative stage. For instance, owner-managers exhibited certain environmental attitudes that were important to be explored to understand their views on sustainability. Hence, a section of the questionnaire examined respondents' worldview using the New Ecological Paradigm Scale (see Dunlap, Van Liere, Mertig, & Jones, 2000) and a six-point Likert scale of *Strongly disagree (1); Disagree (2); Neither agree nor disagree (3); Agree (4); Strongly Agree (5), and Don't know (6).*

Fourth, another section of the questionnaire examined sustainability awareness, concern, willingness, and practices using a categorical sustainability application scale employed by Freestone and McGoldrick (2008). This scale was adapted in this study. The specific statements about sustainable practices by owner-managers identified from the qualitative phase were used as the assessment. For example, on economic sustainability, specific items included home-stay revenue and expenditure and they were accompanied by a statement that asked respondents whether they sell local items to make revenue. In sum, through the qualitative phase, specific statements relevant to the small tourism enterprise and which were understandable to the owners were identified using a bottom-up approach.

Step 7: Deciding the Quantitative Sample and Data Collection

The decision on the sample size was based on the availability of respondents at the three chosen sites (Tamale, Cape Coast, and Akropong-Mamfe) and not any statistical analysis since there was no sampling frame. These sites were chosen out of the many cities in Ghana because of the proliferation of home-stay accommodation with identifiable organizations to facilitate the data collection. The three cities were visited and overall, 150 enterprises were identified. The next step was to visit the various home-stay enterprises to confirm their current operation and seek the owner's consent. It was discovered during the visit that 120 owners were in operation and could participate in the survey in the chosen three sites. The questionnaire was personally administered to the owners in their various local languages even though the original design was in English. The data collection started with training research assistants after which data collection commenced concurrently in different cities with the help of the assistants.

Step 8: Analyzing the Quantitative Data

Following the data collection, analysis followed with an initial inspection and cleaning using box plots and basic descriptive statistics to identify outliers and incomplete questionnaires. Two questionnaires were excluded, resulting in 118 instruments for analysis. Cluster analysis was the initial technique used to identify groups and compare sustainability practices. This was guided by one of the research questions that sought to examine sustainable performance. It was important to cluster owner-managers and compare differences with other dependent variables of interest such as sustainability application, environmental attitude, business goals, sustainable tourism attitudes, performance constraints, and obstacles. Other analytical techniques employed included one-way analysis of variance, chi-square, and factor analysis.

Steps 9: Interpretation and Presentation of Results

The results interpretation and presentation occurred simultaneously. The interpretation of the results was presented such that the qualitative chapter came first, followed by the quantitative chapter. Since both data sets were collected differently and separately to generalize the small sample over a larger population, it was relevant to keep each aspect separate and make references where necessary. So, I decided to present a separate qualitative section where I interpreted the different sustainability knowledge I identified and the various level of concern, willingness, and practices of small tourism enterprises. This qualitative section made use of quotes to support the various themes identified. For example, as part of answering the questions what do home-stay owners know about sustainable development? I identified three types of knowledge and interpreted their demographics and business profiles. This grouping was further used to compare owner-managers concerns, willingness, and practices.

In addition to this chapter, a separate chapter was devoted to discussing the quantitative results where all statistical procedures were presented in tables and charts. For example, the open-ended questions on business reasons resulted in six broad categorical themes: income (29.7%), social interaction (28.8%), cultural exchange (22.0%), altruism (11%), personal satisfaction (7.6%), and opportunities (0.8%). These themes were used for clustering respondents into four groups (*income seekers, social interaction seekers, culture exchange seekers, and altruism seekers*) using the two-step cluster analysis. These clusters facilitated the comparison in addition to a prior qualitative chapter that discussed the different knowledge levels and practices of the 26 owner-managers interviewed. The combination of qualitative and quantitative approaches resulted in deeper insights and superior outcomes that could not have been provided by a single approach.

Conclusion and Recommendations

As sustainable tourism research among small tourism and hospitality enterprises continues to develop, pragmatic approaches for exploring the phenomenon are essential. Mixed methods research has been found to offer pluralistic insight that addresses complex research questions. While the application of mixed methods by tourism scholars is skewed toward sequential designs (Khoo-Lattimore et al., 2019), hardly do such studies provide guidelines and practical examples for implementation. To address this issue, the current book chapter examined the application of exploratory sequential mixed methods designs to the investigation of sustainability among small tourism enterprises. The chapter indicates that mixed methods research overcomes the weaknesses of single approaches to yield superior outcomes based on research questions (Johnson & Turner, 2003). For instance, in the current case study, the qualitative instrument detected the depth of understanding of respondents without imposing any form of understanding on them. If an initial quantitative approach was adopted for respondents to tick options, it would have yielded results that may not be a true reflection of their knowledge. Consequently, the strength of the qualitative phase provided credible results that can be replicated in other (similar) contexts. Secondly, beginning with a qualitative study resulted in contextually relevant themes that reflect the context and can be understood by a larger population. Generally, the quantitative phase allowed larger group evaluation through rigorous statistical analysis that was absent in the qualitative phase, resulting in a comprehensive understanding of the phenomenon (Johnson & Onwuegbuzie, 2004). This study, thus, illustrates the value of mixed methods, especially to emerging tourism researchers. The success of this methodology, however, hinges on the ability of researchers to possess competencies in both techniques (Cameron, 2009). This study, thus, holds methodological implications for tourism research. That is, most studies on sustainability in large companies have employed quantitative approaches (e.g., Alzboun, Khawaldah, Backman, & Moore, 2016; Fraj, Matute, & Melero, 2015) that may be at odds with small tourism enterprises whose services are personalized and, therefore, require pluralistic methodologies to understand the dynamics of their business (Kasim, 2009).

Even though many researchers are challenged with the question of when the exploratory sequential mixed methods design is useful for addressing complex questions (Johnson & Onwuegbuzie, 2004), some recommendations have been suggested. First, the exploratory sequential mixed methods designs are recommended for researchers who want to develop quantitative research instruments that can better measure the targeted group contextually. This approach provides a bottom-up approach to survey instrument development as it relies on a smaller group to generalize items on a bigger group. Secondly, this design is recommended for researchers seeking to expand the range of their research by applying different approaches to understand the phenomenon under study. However, researchers seeking to triangulate results may not find the approach helpful as convergence is not central to the exploratory sequential mixed methods design. Finally, as six months were used for data collection for the case study presented in this chapter, it is recommended that human resources, financial resources, and time be considered when planning to use this approach. In this regard, the approach may not be suitable for researchers with limited time and resources. In conclusion, this chapter has discussed the exploratory sequential mixed method design and provided practical illustrations of how it could be implemented using a case study of sustainability practices among small businesses.

It can thus be concluded that, overall, the exploratory sequential mixed method overcomes the weaknesses of a mono-method by providing initial qualitative knowledge of tourism and hospitality phenomena in addition to quantitative information. Based on these strengths, this chapter recommends this design for exploring issues when little is known and to develop the best fit instrument for the tourism and hospitality phenomena.

42 *Elizabeth Agyeiwaah*

References

Agyeiwaah, E. (2020a). A social-cognitive framework of small accommodation enterprise sustainability practices. *International Journal of Tourism Research, 22*(5), 666–676.

Agyeiwaah, E. (2020b). The contribution of small accommodation enterprises to sustainable solid waste management. *Journal of Hospitality and Tourism Management, 44*, 1–9. doi:10.1016/j.jhtm.2020.04.013

Agyeiwaah, E., McKercher, B., & Suntikul, W. (2017). Identifying core indicators of sustainable tourism: A path forward? *Tourism Management Perspectives, 24*, 26–33.

Alzboun, N., Khawaldah, H., Backman, K., & Moore, D. (2016). The effect of sustainability practices on financial leakage in the hotel industry in Jordan. *Journal of Hospitality and Tourism Management, 27*, 18–26. doi:10.1016/j.jhtm.2016.03.001

Ateljevic, I., & Doorne, S. (2000). 'Staying within the fence': Lifestyle entrepreneurship in tourism. *Journal of Sustainable Tourism, 8*(5), 378–392.

Attride-Stirling, J. (2001). Thematic networks: An analytic tool for qualitative research. *Qualitative Research, 1*(3), 385–405.

Bergin-Seers, S., & Jago, L. (2007). Performance measurement in small motels in Australia: (Funded by the sustainable tourism co-operative research centre). *Tourism and Hospitality Research, 7*(2), 144–155. doi:10.1057/palgrave.thr.6050036

Bertaux, D. (1981). From the life-history approach to the transformation of sociological practice. In D. Bertaux (Ed.), *Biography and society: The life history approach in the social sciences* (pp. 29–45). London: Sage.

Biggs, D., Hall, C. M., & Stoeckl, N. (2012). The resilience of formal and informal tourism enterprises to disasters: Reef tourism in Phuket, Thailand. *Journal of Sustainable Tourism, 20*(5), 645–665. doi:10.1080/09669582.2011.630080

Boddy Clive, R. (2016). Sample size for qualitative research. *Qualitative Market Research: An International Journal, 19*(4), 426–432. doi:10.1108/QMR-06-2016-0053

Bonilla Priego, M. J., Najera, J. J., & Font, X. (2011). Environmental management decision-making in certified hotels. *Journal of Sustainable Tourism, 19*(3), 361–381.

Bourdieu, P. (2004). *Science of science and reflexivity*. Cambridge: Polity.

Brady, H. E., & Collier, D. (2010). *Rethinking social inquiry: Diverse tools, shared standards*. Lanham, MD: Rowman & Littlefield Publishers.

Cameron, R. (2009). A sequential mixed model research design: Design, analytical and display issues. *International Journal of Multiple Research Approaches, 3*(2), 140–152.

Canavan, B. (2014). Sustainable tourism: Development, decline and de-growth. Management issues from the Isle of Man. *Journal of Sustainable Tourism, 22*(1), 127–147. doi:10.1080/09669582.2013.819876

Cresswell, J. W. (1998). *Qualitative inquiry and research design: Choosing among five traditions*. Thousand Oaks, CA: Sage.

Creswell, J. W. (2014). *Research design: Qualitative, quantitative and mixed methods approaches* (4th ed.). Thousand Oaks, CA: Sage Publications.

Dawson, J., Stewart, E. J., Lemelin, H., & Scott, D. (2010). The carbon cost of polar bear viewing tourism in Churchill, Canada. *Journal of Sustainable Tourism, 18*(3), 319–336.

Dunlap, R. E., Van Liere, K. D., Mertig, A. G., & Jones, R. E. (2000). New trends in measuring environmental attitudes: Measuring endorsement of the new ecological paradigm: A revised NEP scale. *Journal of Social Issues, 56*(3), 425–442.

Fishbein, M., & Ajzen, I. (1980). *Understanding attitudes and predicting social behavior.* Englewood Cliffs, NJ: Prentice-Hall.

Font, X., Garay, L., & Jones, S. (2016). Sustainability motivations and practices in small tourism enterprises in European protected areas. *Journal of Cleaner Production, 137*, 1439–1448. doi:10.1016/j.jclepro.2014.01.071

Fraj, E., Matute, J., & Melero, I. (2015). Environmental strategies and organizational competitiveness in the hotel industry: The role of learning and innovation as determinants of environmental success. *Tourism Management, 46*, 30–42. doi:10.1016/j.tourman.2014.05.009

Freestone, O. M., & McGoldrick, P. J. (2008). Motivations of the ethical consumer. *Journal of Business Ethics, 79*(4), 445–467.

Getz, D., & Carlsen, J. (2000). Characteristics and goals of family and owner-operated businesses in the rural tourism and hospitality sectors. *Tourism Management, 21*(6), 547–560.

Hassanli, N., & Ashwell, J. (2020). The contribution of small accommodations to a sustainable tourism industry. *Current Issues in Tourism, 23*(3), 261–264.

Hopwood, B., Mellor, M., & O'Brien, G. (2005). Sustainable development: Mapping different approaches. *Sustainable Development, 13*(1), 38–52.

Iaquinto, B. L. (2016). Strengths and weaknesses of using mixed methods to detect the sustainable practices of backpackers: A reflexive account. *Journal of Cleaner Production, 111*, 479–486.

Jogulu, U. D., & Pansiri, J. (2011). Mixed methods: A research design for management doctoral dissertations. *Management Research Review, 34*(6), 687–701. doi:10.1108/01409171111136211

Johnson, R. B., & Onwuegbuzie, A. J. (2004). Mixed methods research: A research paradigm whose time has come. *Educational Researcher, 33*(7), 14–26.

Johnson, B., & Turner, L. A. (2003). Data collection strategies in mixed methods research. In A. M. Tashakkori & C. B. Teddlie (Eds.), *Handbook of mixed methods in social and behavioral research* (pp. 297–319). Thousand Oaks, CA: Sage Publications.

Kasim, A. (2009). Managerial attitudes towards environmental management among small and medium hotels in Kuala Lumpur. *Journal of Sustainable Tourism, 17*(6), 709–725.

Khoo-Lattimore, C., Mura, P., & Yung, R. (2019). The time has come: A systematic literature review of mixed methods research in tourism. *Current Issues in Tourism, 22*(13), 1531–1550.

Kim, Y., & Han, H. (2010). Intention to pay conventional-hotel prices at a green hotel–a modification of the theory of planned behavior. *Journal of Sustainable Tourism, 18*(8), 997–1014.

Klassen, A. C., Creswell, J., Clark, V. L. P., Smith, K. C., & Meissner, H. I. (2012). Best practices in mixed methods for quality of life research. *Quality of Life Research, 21*(3), 377–380.

Kornilaki, M., Thomas, R., & Font, X. (2019). The sustainability behaviour of small firms in tourism: The role of self-efficacy and contextual constraints. *Journal of Sustainable Tourism, 27*(1), 97–117. doi:10.1080/09669582.2018.1561706

Koteyko, N., Jaspal, R., & Nerlich, B. (2013). Climate change and 'climategate' in online reader comments: A mixed methods study. *The Geographical Journal, 179*(1), 74–86. doi:10.1111/j.1475-4959.2012.00479.x

Lewis, R. B., & Maas, S. M. (2007). QDA Miner 2.0: Mixed-model qualitative data analysis software. *Field Methods, 19*(1), 87–108.

Lynch, M.-F., Duinker, P., Sheehan, L., & Chute, J. (2010). Sustainable Mi'kmaw cultural tourism development in Nova Scotia, Canada: Examining cultural tourist and Mi'kmaw perspectives. *Journal of Sustainable Tourism, 18*(4), 539–556.

Marshall, B., Cardon, P., Poddar, A., & Fontenot, R. (2013). Does sample size matter in qualitative research? A review of qualitative interviews in IS research. *Journal of Computer Information Systems, 54*(1), 11–22.

McIntosh, M. J., & Morse, J. M. (2015). Situating and constructing diversity in semi-structured interviews. *Global Qualitative Nursing Research, 2*. doi:10.1177/2333393615597674

Mertens, D. M. (2014). *Research and evaluation in education and psychology: Integrating diversity with quantitative, qualitative, and mixed methods*. Thousand Oaks, CA: Sage Publications.

Molina-Azorín, J. F., & Font, X. (2016). Mixed methods in sustainable tourism research: An analysis of prevalence, designs and application in JOST (2005–2014). *Journal of Sustainable Tourism, 24*(4), 549–573.

Molina-Azorín, J. F., Tarí, J. J., Pereira-Moliner, J., López-Gamero, M. D., & Pertusa-Ortega, E. M. (2015). The effects of quality and environmental management on competitive advantage: A mixed methods study in the hotel industry. *Tourism Management, 50*, 41–54. doi:10.1016/j.tourman.2015.01.008

Morse, J. M. (1991). Approaches to qualitative-quantitative methodological triangulation. *Nursing Research, 40*(2), 120–123.

Morse, J. M. (2003). Principles of mixed methods and multimethod research design. *Handbook of Mixed Methods in Social and Behavioral Research, 1*, 189–208.

Neuman, W. L. (2006). *Science and research. Social research methods: Qualitative and quantitative approaches* (6th ed.). Boston, MA: Pearson.

Noy, C. (2008). Pages as stages: A performance approach to visitor books. *Annals of Tourism Research, 35*(2), 509–528.

Pallant, J. (2013). *SPSS survival manual*. London: McGraw-Hill Education.

Reichel, A., Uriely, N., & Shani, A. (2008). Ecotourism and simulated attractions: Tourists' attitudes towards integrated sites in a desert area. *Journal of Sustainable Tourism, 16*(1), 23–41.

Roberts, S., & Tribe, J. (2008). Sustainability indicators for small tourism enterprises–an exploratory perspective. *Journal of Sustainable Tourism, 16*(5), 575–594.

Ryan, C., Chaozhi, Z., & Zeng, D. (2011). The impacts of tourism at a UNESCO heritage site in China–a need for a meta-narrative? The case of the Kaiping Diaolou. *Journal of Sustainable Tourism, 19*(6), 747–765.

Sampaio, A. R., Thomas, R., & Font, X. (2012). Why are some engaged and not others? Explaining environmental engagement among small firms in tourism. *International Journal of Tourism Research, 14*(3), 235–249. doi:10.1002/jtr.849

Sandelowski, M. (1995). Sample size in qualitative research. *Research in Nursing & Health, 18*(2), 179–183.

Scheyvens, R., & Russell, M. (2012). Tourism and poverty alleviation in Fiji: Comparing the impacts of small-and large-scale tourism enterprises. *Journal of Sustainable Tourism, 20*(3), 417–436. doi:10.1080/09669582.2011.629049

Singh, E., Milne, S., & Hull, J. (2012). Use of mixed-methods case study to research sustainable tourism development in South Pacific SIDS. In K. F. Hyde, C. Ryan, & A. G. Woodside (Eds.), *Field guide to case study research in tourism, hospitality and leisure (advances in culture, tourism and hospitality research volume 6)* (pp. 457–478). Bingley: Emerald Publishing Limited.

Stewart, D. W., Shamdasani, P. N., & Rook, D. W. (2009). Group depth interviews: Focus group research. *The Sage Handbook of Applied Social Research Methods, 2*, 589–616.

Strauss, A., & Corbin, J. M. (1997). *Grounded theory in practice.* Thousand Oaks, CA: Sage.

Tashakkori, A., & Teddlie, C. (1998). *Applied social research methods series.* International Education and Professional Publishers (Vol. 46). Thousand Oaks, CA: SAGE Publications.

Teddlie, C., & Yu, F. (2007). Mixed methods sampling: A typology with examples. *Journal of Mixed Methods Research, 1*(1), 77–100.

Tilley, F., & Fuller, T. (2000). Foresighting methods and their role in researching small firms and sustainability. *Futures, 32*(2), 149–161.

Walker, K., & Moscardo, G. (2014). Encouraging sustainability beyond the tourist experience: Ecotourism, interpretation and values. *Journal of Sustainable Tourism, 22*(8), 1175–1196.

Chapter 4

Systematic Review of Scale Development Practices in the Field of Tourism and Hospitality

Ali Bavik, Chen-Feng Kuo and John Ap

Abstract

Numerous scales have been developed and utilized in the tourism and hospitality field, yet, their psychometric properties have not been systematically reviewed and evaluated. This gap compromises researchers' ability to develop better measures and improve measurement decisions. In this current study, 56 scales were identified and evaluated in terms of their psychometric properties. It was found that most scales were imperfect in measuring tourism and hospitality domains, and most scales did not provide explicit information about the scale development procedures that were adopted. The scale development procedure and psychometric properties of the reviewed scales are summarized, evaluated, and recommendations are made for future tourism and hospitality scale development.

Keywords: Scale development; scale guideline; tourism; hospitality; systematic review; measurement

Introduction

Scale development is the primary resource of building knowledge in the social sciences (Hinkin, 1995) refers to the scale, that is measurement, as the process of building constructs based on items that describe and attempt to measure attributes in a numerical system. Advancing knowledge and theory in any discipline or field of study will be challenging if we do not have proper measures. Tourism and hospitality constitute multi-disciplinary fields of study and the industry also has multiple stakeholders. As a major focus of tourism and hospitality research is social science-based, it focusses on dynamic human relationships and faces problems with the accuracy (i.e., true value/meaning) and precision

Advanced Research Methods in Hospitality and Tourism, 47–85
Copyright © 2023 Ali Bavik, Chen-Feng Kuo and John Ap
Published under exclusive licence by Emerald Publishing Limited
doi:10.1108/978-1-80117-550-020221004

(i.e., consistency of reproducibility) of the questionnaires used (Stening & Zhang, 2007), which may lead to difficulties in understanding the outcomes of research (Netemeyer, Bearden, & Sharma, 2003). As tourism and hospitality research has been increasing, some research areas grow and as a result, existing measurements may become less applicable, and "niche measurements" may be required. Fifty-six studies thus far have developed scales on various areas such as tourism impact ((Ap & Crompton, 1998), ecotourism scales (Boley, Ayscue, Maruyama, & Woosnam, 2017; Lee & Jan, 2018), cultural scales (Bavik, 2016; Dawson, Abbott, & Shoemaker, 2011; Tepeci & Bartlett, 2002), food experience (Choe & Kim, 2019; Ko, 2018), and shopping (Choi, Law, & Heo, 2016).

Our existing knowledge on scale development does not postulate a holistic understanding and application of scale development procedures in the tourism and hospitality fields. Furthermore, existing scales developed in tourism and hospitality have not been comprehensively evaluated, and we do not know whether these scales have adopted appropriate and/or rigorous procedures. Specifically, (1) What are the common problems and pitfalls in developing scales? Moreover, (2) What are the best practices in scale development that may help improve future studies? Therefore, to address these research questions, three objectives are proposed, as follows:

(1)   To provide a systematic review of scale development steps and procedures (i.e., Churchill, 1979; DeVellis, 2016; Gerbing & Anderson, 1988; Hinkin, 1995; Netemeyer et al., 2003) and scale development research published in the tourism and hospitality literature;
(2)   To assess, evaluate and critique the theoretical and methodological approaches adopted for scales developed in tourism and hospitality; and
(3)   To provide suggestions for better practices in future scale development in tourism and hospitality.

Review of Scale Development in the Methodological Research Literature

An overview of the literature addressing the methodological aspects of scale development is provided in the next section, namely in terms of item generation, scale development, and scale assessment. The seminal works by Churchill (1979) and De Vellis (2016) and those of other research methodologists are compiled, reviewed, and synthesized to provide a comprehensive overview of the proper steps and procedures that should be followed when developing a scale. Although these studies provide different steps to develop a scale, they may be summarized into three main steps.

Item Generation (Theoretical Soundness)

In scale development research, the initial item pool generation, relevance, and representativeness in measurement are quintessential. Content validity and precise measurement are mandatory to accurately test research questions (Hair, Anderson, Tatham, & Black, 1998; Hooper, Coughlan, & Mullen, 2008; Tabachnick, Fidell, & Osterlind, 2001). The term *content validity* refers to "the degree to which elements of an assessment instrument are relevant to, and representative of the target construct for a particular assessment purpose" (Haynes, Richard, & Kubany, 1995, p. 238). De Vellis (2011) indicated that it is vital to ensure that all dimensions are well represented in the scale. The first step of the item generation stage begins with an extensive review of scales in the relevant literature "in which a solid theoretical definition of the construct and its domain are delineated and outlined" (Netemeyer et al., 2003, p. 9). This is regarded as the backbone of the scale as the quality of the item pool would help achieve valid and reliable measures (Hair, Money, Samouel, & Page, 2007). There are three approaches to generate the initial items, which are categorized as deductive (i.e., a statement used in a questionnaire), inductive (i.e., an interview question), or in some cases, a combination of the two.

The first approach is "deductive", also known as "logical partitioning" or the "top-down" approach (Cooper, Schindler, & Sun, 1998). Deductive item generation examines the existing literature to define constructs, and in some instances, the items may even represent a construct (DeVellis, 2011). The second approach is "inductive" or "bottom-up" (Hinkin, 1995, 1998), which allows the researcher to obtain wide-ranging explanations about an individual's behavior (Berg, 2001). Hence, the interview results may reveal potential contextual factors regarding the phenomenon (Patton, 2002). Furthermore, Bentz and Shapiro (1998, p. 123) pointed out that the inductive approach "...depicts more complex organizational realities and processes more accurately and fully." In-depth interviews are a common data collection method employed by qualitative researchers (Berg, 2001). Therefore, item generation is based upon qualitative input from the target population through interviews, focus groups, expert panels, and academicians. Both these different approaches have their advantages and disadvantages. Hinkin (1995) emphasized that inductive item generation is more valuable "when there is often little theory involved at the outset as one attempts to identify constructs to generate measures from individual responses" (p. 969).

The third option combines both inductive and deductive approaches. Hinkin (1995) has suggested that researchers utilize the mixed-method approach in order to maintain the advantages of both the quantitative method involving the collection of data from large samples. This is regarded by some as being more objective and through qualitative methods involving in-depth examination of the phenomena, getting the bigger picture of reality, and being more intimate and familiar with the subject area. Onwuegbuzie and Johnson (2006, p. 48) also pointed out that mixed research "involves combining complementary strengths and non-overlapping weaknesses of quantitative and qualitative research." Thus, a mixed methodological approach is suggested for better scale development. Consequently, this approach generates a comprehensive item pool, covering a wide range of ideas that facilitates the scale's generalizability by offering an all-inclusive, realistic, and accurate picture of the construct's characteristics and complexities.

One of the most challenging issues in conducting interviews is asking "the right questions," which according to Churchill (1979) requires the questions to be inclusive and reflect the significant elements of the investigated phenomena. Furthermore, De Witte and Van Muijen (1999, p. 593) highlighted that "asking the right questions is more important than having solutions." The reason is that the questions should cover a broad range of sensations to grasp a high degree of content validity (Sireci, 1998).

Furthermore, King and Horrocks (2010) suggested that content validity can be achieved by including subjects who are directly involved in the investigated phenomenon or "judged" to be experts of the phenomenon. According to Hinkin (1995, p. 969), expert panel members or judges refer to "a sample of respondents who were subject matter experts to provide critical incidents that are subsequently used to develop items." Expert panel members and/or judges should be selected among people who have knowledge, expertise, direct involvement, and extensive work experience with the constructs. De Vellis (2016) highlighted that role of the expert panel/judges include but is not limited to rating items based on relevance, modifying the items, rating items based on their importance (i.e., low, moderate, or high), helping define theoretical meaning, identifying ambiguous items, and/or providing new viewpoints on how to categorize the items. Consequently, the role of the expert panel/judges may differ based upon the characteristics of a construct. Netemeyer et al. (2003) pointed out that the scale developer is also an expert on the scale phenomenon who plays a crucial role in the effective formation of an item pool and its subsequent assessment.

Meanwhile, the related literature has revealed that there is no universal rule concerning the number of experts and/or judges essential for content validation. Further, a comparison of related studies on this subject shows a lack of congruity (Bearden, Netemeyer, & Teel, 1989; Hinkin, 1995; Lee & Crompton, 1992). Netemeyer et al. (2003) have suggested that using as many judges as possible may contribute to greater validity. Based on the remarks received from the panel, the researcher can then modify the questionnaire and improve the overall quality and validity of the scale questionnaire (Hornby & Symon, 1994).

The purification of the scale continues with an assessment of *face validity*, which implies that an instrument in a practical situation should appear practical, pertinent, and related to the purpose of the study. Therefore, the instruments should be valid and appear to be valid to respondents. The research instrument is checked with a small pilot sample to confirm face validity. This procedure helps the researcher evaluate the overall comments about the instrument and that it: is at an appropriate reading level, comprises straightforward and easy-to-read instructions, and has an easy-to-use response format. Consequently, Hinkin (1995, p. 970) stated that this process "serve[s] as a pre-test. It will permit the deletion of items deemed to be conceptually inconsistent."

It is also crucial to consider any bias that may be produced by a survey item(s) (Podsakoff, MacKenzie, & Podsakoff, 2012). Podsakoff, MacKenzie, Jeong-Yeon, and Podsakoff (2003) highlighted, "the problem with ambiguous items is that they often require respondents to develop their own idiosyncratic meanings of them. This issue may either increase random responding or increase the probability that respondents' own systematic response tendencies may come into play" (p. 883). Some of the typical response biases include:

- *leniency biases* – like versus dislike;
- *mood state* – positive or negative affectivity;
- *item demand characteristics* perception of hidden messages in the items;
- *common scale anchors* – frequent use of the same *anchor points* – e.g., extremely, always, and never;
- *item priming effects* – the sense of item may trigger salient meaning;
- *item embeddedness* – positively or negatively worded items influence the evaluation of the items); and
- *acquiescence biases* – to agree or disagree (Brace, 2006; Podsakoff et al., 2012).

Moreover, social desirability (tendency to answer questions consistent with favorable cultural norms (Mick, 1996). Consequently, to avoid the aforementioned critical pitfalls and based on the study purpose, researchers should consider and utilize various common response bias controls in the questionnaire design (see Table 4).

Finally, before the scale development procedure commences, it is also essential to consider the measurement model to ensure construct validity. Two well-known reflective and formative models are commonly employed to assess the constructs (Schhwab, 1980). Traditional scale development generally draws on reflective measures where the changes in latent variables directly "reflect" the assigned item changes. The path of causality goes from the construct to the measures. The construct illustrates a variation in the measures. Hence, reflective items have conceptual unity in that all variables should correspond to the construct's definition. It has been highlighted that reflective indicator are greatly interchangeable and cover similar aspects of the construct. With a reflective measure, it has been suggested that the items that present low item-to-total correlations should be removed from a scale to enhance reliability in terms of internal consistency so that removal of an item does not alter the essence of the underlying construct (Schwab, 1980).

In contrast, formative measures are designed to completely grasp the latent construct and the direction of causality following from the indicators to the construct (Diamantopoulos & Winklhofer, 2001). Formative indicators may share some similarities to define the construct, but formative indicators conceptually and sufficiently, which serve as a function of an indicator defining the latent variable (Coltman, Devinney, Midgley, & Venaik, 2008). These indicators need not co-vary and can be mutually exclusive. Thus, formative measures may not be suitable for theory testing as removing an indicator may change the latent construct (MacKenzie, Podsakoff, & Jarvis, 2005). Consequently, it has been suggested that the measurement model type must be determined by considering both the theoretical and directional relationship between the latent construct and indicator(s) (Bollen & Lennox, 1991).

Scale Development

In the second step, a pilot is recommended to create a parsimonious measurement scale (Netemeyer et al., 2003). Pilot studies are essential to verify and support construct validity as it allows the deletion of items that may be conceptually inconsistent. The pilot study sample is one of the crucial issues that play an essential role in the scale development process (Hinkin, 1998). Thus, the population and the sample should be selected cautiously. *Population* refers to the specific group relevant to the research project (Zikmund & Babin, 2009). The *sample* refers to a portion of aggregate elements representing the whole population (Bearden et al., 1989). While there is no universal number of participants recommended for a pilot study, De Vellis (2003) has indicated at least 50, while Hinkin (1998) has suggested 150 participants.

After data collection, "a researcher has a relatively little theoretical or empirical basis for making strong assumptions about how many common factors exist" (Fabrigar, Wegener, MacCallum, & Strahan, 1999, p. 277). Therefore, the procedures suggested by Churchill's (1979) item reduction technique should be followed in the initial purification of the scale. Some common statistical techniques for item reduction include Principal Component Analysis (PCA), Principal Axis Analysis (PAA), Exploratory Factor Analysis (EFA), and item-to-total correlation (DeVellis, 2003; Fabrigar et al., 1999). According to Thompson (2004, p. 5), *EFA* "summarize relationships in the form of a more parsimonious set of factor scores used in subsequent analyses." Following the factorial composition that emerges from EFA, it should be tested to confirm the generalizability of the taxonomic constructs (Netemeyer et al., 2003).

At this stage, factor extraction is essential to determine the appropriate number of factors to examine. One way of choosing a type of rotation is assessing the theoretical relationships among the studied factors (Kaiser, 1958). For example, the researcher should use oblique rotation if the identified items and factors are conceptually interrelated. If the items and factors are conceptually distant or mutually independent, the researcher should choose orthogonal rotation. Consistent with the theory and the purpose of the investigation, the researcher needs to consider the inter-factor correlations. De Vellis (2016) has suggested that orthogonal rotation is more suitable for factor extraction when the inter-factor correlations are mostly below 0.15, assuming that the factors are independent, that is uncorrelated to each other. Regardless of the rotation, the data should also be assessed and based on correlations between factors to check whether the data combines some factors in conceptually larger factors (i.e., word of mouth + revisit intention = loyalty). Consequently, scale purification may be undertaken through reliability analysis, whereby Cronbach alpha tests are used to assess the internal consistency of the overall scale and items within each factor (Cronbach, 1951, 1972). The scale development procedure may also involve using qualitative and quantitative research project management software tools. With the qualitative approach, the data based upon open-ended questions or comments must be reviewed to identify the factors. Some researchers may prefer conventional means such as manual "pen and post-it." Some researchers have used mind-mapping software such as Mindjet (see Bavik, 2016). There are also commonly used qualitative and mixed-method analysis software such as statistical and qualitative data analysis software (NVIVO) and Atlas.ti, which allows researchers to organize and analyze the unstructured text, image, audio, and video data.

A commonly used software for scale development and validation is Statistical Package for the Social Sciences (SPSS), which allows researchers to conduct various analyses such as factor analysis, group analysis, reliability analysis, regression analysis, and survey and sampling analysis. SPSS can also allow one to test meditation, moderated mediation, and mediated moderation (see Hayes, 2012), but it cannot be used to undertake the more complicated structural equation modeling (SEM). AMOS, LISREL, Mplus, and SmartPLS are the most popular software used to conduct confirmatory factor analysis (CFA). The notable differences between the software pertain to the interface and the availability of different options and fit indices. For example, AMOS and SmartPLS have a functional graphical interface, while AMOS offers several bootstrap capabilities (Ali, Bakhshi, Azarkeivan, & Biglarian, 2016). LISREL and SmartPLS are the most commonly used software for general linear modeling SEM, while Mplus is more popular for testing an integrated modeling framework that allows researchers to handle continuous, categorical, observed, and latent variables. LISREL and Mplus interfaces have a similar list of fit indices except for "fit function value" and Goodness-of-Fit Index (GFI) (see Narayanan, 2012). From the practical point of view, LISREL and Mplus can only be used in specific programming and/or language and command.

Scale Assessment (Structural Validity)

The researcher should confirm whether the new scale has construct validity and reliability. *Construct validity* is defined as "representing the correspondence between a construct conceptual definition of a variable. Furthermore, operational procedures are needed to measure or manipulate that construct" (Schwab, 1980, p. 5). Thus, when the main data is collected in the second stage, purification of this new data set is necessary. The researcher should also determine the adequacy of the sample size and address how many questionnaires should be collected. The choice of appropriate sample size is also dependent on several factors such as the type of sample, time, budget, and what kinds of analyses are needed to achieve the research's aim (Churchill, 1979; Hinkin, 1998). Fowler (1995) noted that the sample size is recognized as a sign of having a robust data set. For any regression-based technique, 200 responses are suggested as being adequate to validate any claims from the data set (Hair et al., 1998; Pallant, 2007). As sample size increases, sources of error, such as bias, usually evident in questionnaire formulation, can often be significantly reduced (Creswell, 2009; Creswell, Plano Clark, Gutmann, & Hanson, 2003). With structural equation modeling (SEM), there is no generally accepted figure for sample size in the absolute sense, but larger samples are always preferable (Hair et al., 2007). Bearden et al. (1989) emphasized that to reduce the risk of drawing erroneous conclusions from the

SEM analysis, researchers should use a sample of more than 200. MacCallum and Austin (2000) and Hair et al. (2007) also advised that a minimum of 200 cases is needed to obtain accurate conclusions in model testing when using LISREL. By keeping both these rule of thumb figures and the calculated minimum number in mind, the minimum sample size required for the adequacy of the sample and robustness of the results in any research is considered to be at least 200.

Similar to the pilot study, the researcher should utilize the same rigorous data testing with the selected population(s). The data distribution with either a highly skewed nature or high Kurtosis indicates non-normality, which has random effects on specification or estimation (Nunnally, 1978). This non-normality may occur due to outlier cases in the data set. Factor analysis and structural equation modeling require variables to be normally distributed (Tashakkori, 2006). Therefore, researchers should employ data screening processes to examine the data set's univariate and multivariate normality (Bollen, 1990; Thompson, 2004). Normality in the data is typically addressed in the estimation process (Hair et al., 1998, 2007). It has been suggested by.

Jöreskog and Sörbom (1993) that absolute skewness values should not go beyond 2.00, while the absolute values of Kurtosis should not exceed 3.0. In addition to assessment for normality, the scale should be evaluated in terms of sampling adequacy. The Kaiser-Meyer-Olkin Measure (KMO) and Bartlett's Test of Sphericity are commonly used for measuring sampling adequacy (Hair et al., 2007). It has been recommended that KMO results higher than 0.60 indicate that the sample size is enough to run the subsequent tests. As mentioned above, construct validity is an integral part of construct validation and several rules of thumb are available to assess the adequacy of such measures (Creswell, 2009). Construct validity involves assessing content validity, face validity, uni-dimensionality, discriminant validity, and convergent validity.

As content validity and face validity should be achieved during the early stages of scale development, assessing uni-dimensionality should be further tested as evidence of construct validity. *Uni-dimensionality* is defined as "an assumption underlying the calculation of reliability and is demonstrated when the indicators of a construct have an acceptable fit on a single-factor or one-dimensional model (DeVellis, 2011). In other words, only one factor accounts for the covariance among the items (Hair et al., 1998, p. 641). *Reliability* is the degree to which items within a given construct vary together and show that given construct's internal consistency (Tabachnick et al., 2001). Different types of reliability issues need to be addressed in the scale development process. First, the scale must have inter-rater reliability, which indicates whether the multiple respondents have consistently scored on the same items. Another reliability issue is internal consistency, which shows whether all the items in the scale measure the same construct (Hair et al., 1998). These two aspects of reliability are principally related to internal reliability, where the results manifest the inter-item consistency and all the items' relationships at a single point in time. However, a single measurement may not always be representative. Therefore, a scale should be collected at different points of time to obtain external reliability where the results present consistency of scale with other measurements over time. Test-retest reliability requires testing the same scale items from the same respondents' overtime to ensure external reliability and construct validity. The last type of reliability is the alternate form of reliability, which refers to theoretical consistency with other measures with similar or the same results on the same construct (Fidell et al., 2001). External validity can be obtained over time. The internal reliability can be confirmed during the scale development process.

Nunnally (1978) suggests that scales should have an alpha level equivalent of 0.70 or higher to be considered reliable. However, (Hair et al. stated (1998, p. 118), "exploratory, early research scales with an α *(alpha)* greater than 0.60 are satisfactory." Low reliability suggests that the factor has low internal consistency. Consequently, according to Hinkin (1995), low-reliability scores indicate scale construction problems.

During purification of the scale, convergent validity is regarded as another component of construct validity. Evidence of convergent validity can be obtained in various ways. The term *convergent validity* refers to how the scale is related to other measures or indicators of the same construct (Chao, O'Leary-Kelly, Wolf, Klein, & Gardner, 1994). If a scale measures the construct it is meant to measure; then the scale is expected to be highly related to other scales or indicators of the same construct (Schwab, 1980). Fornell and Larcker (1981) suggested that convergence can be determined by examining the average variance extracted (AVE), and they indicated that convergent validity could be established if the AVE score for a construct exceeds the 0.50 threshold, which implies that the variance captured by the construct is higher than the variance associated with an error.

Once the researcher confirms uni-dimensionality and convergent validity, the next step is to assess discriminant validity. *Discriminant validity* provides evidence of how a construct differs from other constructs. Discriminant validity can be assessed in multiple ways (Fornell & Larcker, 1981; Schwab, 1980). One way of testing discriminant validity involves analyzing the confidence interval for all the possible construct correlations. Peter (1981, p. 36) stated that "discriminant validity is determined by demonstrating that a measure does not correlate very highly with another measure from which it should differ." If the estimated confidence interval (+/− two standard errors) is not greater than 0.85, this provides additional discriminant validity evidence (Nunnally & Bernstein, 1994). Another way to test discriminant validity is by comparing the Cronbach's alpha of a construct to its correlations with other model variables (Cronbach, 1972). The alpha values should be over 0.70 for each factor and the aggregate overall reliability (Hair et al., 2007).

Finally, discriminant validity can be further obtained through confirmatory factor analysis (CFA) (Gerbing & Anderson, 1988; Saxe & Weitz, 1982). Meredith (1993) proposed four levels of a factorial test to increase equality constraints on four measurement elements: (1) model structure/specifications, (2) loadings, (3) intercepts, and (4) residual variances that constitute sufficient evidence for Measurement Invariance (MI). Wu, Li, and Zumbo (2007) stated the necessity for testing equality in all these four elements to support MI decisions. Besides, the good model fit could be indicated by root mean square error of approximation (RMSEA) $\leq$ 0.05–0.08 and/or the comparative fit index (CFI) $\geq$ 0.9 or 0.95 (Cheung & Rensvold, 2002; Fan & Sivo, 2005; Hu & Bentler, 1998; Marsh, Wen, & Hau, 2004; Vandenberg & Lance, 2000). The chi-squared ($\chi 2$) test of fit is not appropriate for indicating model fit due to its susceptibility to sampling size and model complexity (Cheung & Rensvold, 2002).

This compilation and review of the pertinent scale development literature have provided a fairly comprehensive treatise and detailed explanation of the relevant steps and procedures involved in developing scale measures. This review also provides a benchmark of what is required and expected in developing a rigorous scale.

Methodology for This Evaluation Study

The methods used in this assessment, evaluation, and critique of the scale development papers are discussed in this section, which includes the search strategy, paper selection criteria, data extraction, and quality assessment. The limitations of this evaluation are also addressed.

Search Strategy

The authors carried a systematic review to evaluate the tourism and hospitality scale measurements based on the Preferred Reporting Items for Systematic Reviews and Meta-Analyses (i.e., PRISMA) guidelines. To date, there has been little agreement on the study selection process, and for this study, the identified and selected measures were obtained from the Web of Science covering the period from 1970 to August 2019. The search terms used were "scale development" and "scale measurement" in the title section. The studies retrieved from each database were imported into the Citavi 6.3 (Reference Management and Knowledge organization) software library.

Inclusion and Exclusion Criteria

Fig. 1 presents a flowchart summarizing the procedures chosen for identifying and selecting studies. Three criteria were selected for identifying papers for evaluation: (1) journal studies in the tourism and hospitality domain; (2) tourism and hospitality journal studies in the Social Sciences Citation Index (SSCI) list; and (3) journal studies that endeavor to develop scales in the tourism and hospitality domain. Meanwhile, the following sources were excluded: (a) book chapters, conference papers, and editorial notes; (b) non-English journal studies; and (d) journal studies that were not primarily aimed at the development of a new scale.

Data Extraction and Quality Assessment

Data were extracted based on the PRISMA guidelines for reporting systematic reviews. All studies and references were coded and stored in the Citavi library.

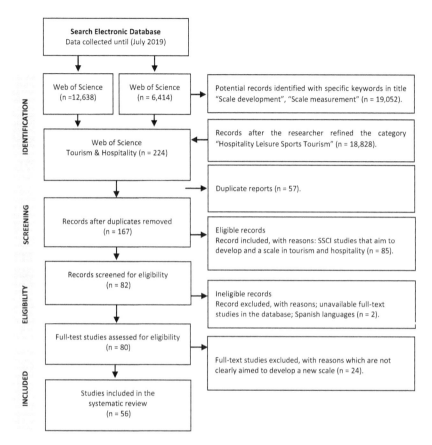

Fig. 1.   Flow Chart of Procedures for Study Selection.

The initial screening of studies was undertaken by reading the titles, keywords, and abstracts. Two of the researchers screened all potentially related studies and reviewed them independently. At the final inclusion phase, it was evaluated by all three authors. The studies selected for evaluation are presented in Table 1 with the recording of the characteristics of the study, including author(s), year of publication, main theme, country, scale name and purpose, scale guideline(s) used, number of factors, initial and final number of items, and the lost a percentage of items in the final scale.

The theoretical and methodological assessment of the scales were based on the three stages of item generation, scale development, and structural validity (see Table 2). The theoretical approaches were evaluated by determining whether the studies used a panel of experts and employed pre-tests to determine face validity and content validity. To check criterion validity, scales were assessed based on the dimensionality of the construct. Notably, the researchers assessed whether the study employed controls for social desirability response bias, the type of item reduction technique employed, and sample size adequacy. In the last stage, to

Table 1. Descriptive Characteristics of the Reviewed Scales in Tourism and Hospitality Studies.

Author(s) Year	Main Theme	Location	Scale Name and Purpose	Scale Guideline	Factors	Initial Item Pool	Final Pool	Lost %
Choe and Kim (2019)	T	Hong Kong	A scale of local food consumption value from a tourist perspective (TLFCV)	(Churchill, 1979; DeVellis, 2003; Chung & Petrick, 2010; Kim & Eves, 2012)	6	71	33	53.5
Choi et al. (2019)	H	Thailand S. Korea	Hotels' environmental management initiative (HEMI)	*	3	77	24	68.8
Jorgenson et al. (2019)	T	US	Tourism autobiographical memory scale (TAMS)	*	2	8	8	0.0
Liu, Wang, Huang, and Tang (2019)	T	Taiwan	Festival gamification scale (FGS)	Churchill (1979)	5	33	16	51.5
Lu et al. (2019)	T	US	Service robot integration willingness (SRIW)	(Churchill, 1979; Lin & Hsieh, 2011)	6	153	36	76.5
Omuris (2019)	H	Turkey	Workplace friendship in hospitality organizations (*)	(Creswell & Clark, 2001; Denscombe, 2008; Johnson, Onwuegbuzie, & Turner 2007)	6	71	65	8.5
Tsaur and Tu (2019)	T	Taiwan	Tour leaders' cultural competence (TLCC)	(Churchill, 1979; Tsaur, Yen, & Chen, 2010	10	45	36	20.0
Ying and Wen (2019)	T	China	Chinese tourists' motivations for commercial sex when traveling overseas (*)	(Churchill's, 1979; DeVellis, 2003; Netemeyer et al., 2003)	8	32	25	21.9

Author (Year)	T/H	Country	Scale	Source				
Bui and Wilkins (2018)	T	Australia	Social interactions among Asian backpackers (*)	(Hinkin, Tracey, & Enz, 1997)	6	30	18	40.0
Busser and Shulga (2018)	T	US	Co-created value (CCV)	(Churchill, 1979; DeVellis, 2016)	5	129	25	80.6
Ceylan and Çizel (2018)	T	Turkey	Destination image scale (*)	Churchill (1979)	3	14	13	7.1
El-Adly and Abu Elsamen (2018)	H	UAE	Guest-based hotel equity (GBHE)	*	9	36	34	5.6
Ferreira, Morais, Pollack, and Bunds (2018)	T	US	The tourism E Microentrepreneurial self-efficacy scale (TeMSE)	(DeVellis, 1991)	5	34	13	61.8
Kim et al. (2018)	H	US	Customer perceptions of restaurant innovativeness (CPRI)	(Churchill, 1979; Hinkin, 1995)	4	42	17	59.5
Ko (2018)	H	Taiwan	Competence scale of food safety & hygiene for hospitality students (*)	*	2	72	29	59.7
Kumar and Nayak (2018)	T	India	Destination personality (*)	Churchill (1979)	6	92	23	75.0
Lee and Jan (2018)	T	Taiwan	Ecotourism behavior scale (*)	*	7	66	30	54.5
Luo (2018)	H	Macau	Corporate social responsibility in gambling industry (*)	Churchill (1979)	3	27	16	40.7

Table 1. (*Continued*)

Author(s) Year	Main Theme	Location	Scale Name and Purpose	Scale Guideline	Factors	Initial Item Pool	Final	Lost %
Ruiz-Molina et al. (2018)	T	Spain	Technological advancement in hotels from the guest perspective (ICT)	*	1	10	7	30.0
Taheri et al. (2018)	T	Turkey	Host sincerity (*)	(Churchill, 1979; Netemeyer et al., 2003)	2	25	10	60.0
Tsaur et al. (2018)	T	Taiwan	Tourist–resident conflict (*)	(Churchill, 1979; Wang, Hsieh, Chou, & Lin 2007)	4	27	14	48.1
Wen et al. (2018)	T	Netherlands	Drug tourism motivation of Chinese outbound tourists (*)	Churchill (1979)	6	43	21	51.2
Yen et al. (2018)	T	Taiwan	Tour leaders' job crafting (*)	(Churchill, 1979; Carlson et al., 2000)	4	24	30	23.1
Zeng, Liu, and Gong (2018)	T	China	Participating motivation scale (PMS)	*	5	75	21	72.0
Bozic, Jovanovic, Tomic, and Vasiljevic. (2017)	T	Serbia	Multi-attraction travel motivation scales (MATCS)	*	8	30 / 16	29 / 16	3.3 / 0.0
Cho et al. (2017)	T	US	Nostalgia scale for sport tourism (NSST)	(Menor & Roth, 2007)	5	69	30	56.5

Hahn et al. (2017)	H	Australia S. Korea	E-service quality (e-SQ)	*	6	97	24	75.3
Pijls et al. (2017)	H	Netherlands	Experience of hospitality scale (EH-Scale)	*	3	52	13	75.0
Taheri et al. (2017)	T	UK Iran China	Ceremonious politeness (C.P. scale)	(Churchill, 1979; DeVellis, 2003)	4	16	8	50.0
Tsai et al. (2017)	T	Taiwan	Students' career anxiety (*)	*	4	31	25	19.4
Bavik (2016)	H	New Zealand	Hospitality industry organizational scale (HIOCS)	Churchill (1979)	9	102	47	53.9
Choi et al. (2016)	T	Hong Kong	Shopping destinations trust (SDT)	(Churchill, 1979; Hinkinf, 1995)	9	48	42	12.5
Fatma et al. (2016)	T	India	Corporate social responsibility (CSR)	(Churchill, 1979; DeVellis, 1991)	3	46	18	60.9
Fetscherin and Stephano (2016)	T	US	Medical tourism index (MTI)	(Churchill, 1979; Rossiter, 2002)	4	58	34	41.4
Geus, Richards, and Toepoel (2016)	T	Netherlands	Event experience scale (EES)	Churchill (1979)	4	77	18	76.6
Liu and Arendt (2016)	H	US	Work motive measurement scale (WMMS)	DeVellis (2003)	4	22	22	0.0
	H	US	Hospitableness Scale (*)		3	46	10	78.3

Table 1. *(Continued)*

Author(s) Year	Main Theme	Location	Scale Name and Purpose	Scale Guideline	Factors	Initial Item Pool	Final	Lost %
Tasci and Semrad (2016)				(Churchill, 1979; DeVellis, 1991)				
Tsaur et al. (2016)	T	Taiwan	Destination brand identity (DBI)	(Churchill, 1979; Wang et al., 2007)	5	37	32	13.5
Wang (2016)	H	Taiwan	Green food & beverage literacy (GFBL)	(Churchill, 1979; DeVellis, 2003; Hinkin et al., 1997)	9	198	60	69.7
Chung and Petrick (2015)	T	S. Korea US	Price fairness (P.F.)	Netemeyer et al. (2003)	2	11	9	18.2
Kim and Heo (2015)	T	S. Korea	Scale for tourism facilitators (*)	*	3	15	13	13.3
Kim et al. (2015)	T	S. Korea	Scale of perceived social impacts (SPSI)	*	6	57	23	59.6
Kim (2014)	T	Taiwan	Memorable tourism experiences (MTEs)	Churchill (1979)	10	48	33	31.3
Lee et al. (2014)	T	S. Korea	Mega event expo quality (*)	(Churchill, 1979; DeVellis, 1991)	10	49	40	18.4
Liu et al. (2014)	H	Taiwan	Restaurant rating scale (*)	*	4	20	20	0.0
So, King, and Sparks (2014)	T	Australia	Customer engagement (C.E.)	(Churchill, 1979; Netemeyer et al., 2003)	5	34	25	26.5
Wong and Wan (2013)	T	Macau	Tourist shopping satisfaction (TSS)	(Churchill, 1979; Hair et al., 2006; Walsh & Beatty, 2007)	4	31	20	35.5

Study	Type	Location	Scale	References				
Wong & Fong (2012)	H	Macau	Casino service quality scale (CASERV)	(Churchill, 1979; DeVellis, 2003; Walsh & Beatty, 2007)	4	24	12	50.0
Ekiz, Au, and Hsu. (2012)	T	Hong Kong	Tourist complaint constraint (TCC)	(Churchill, 1979; DeVellis, 2003; Hinkin, 1995; Netemeyer et al., 2003)	5	61	15	75.4
Kim, Ritchie, and McCormick (2012)	T	US	Memorable tourism experiences (MTE)	(Churchill, 1979; DeVellis, 2003)	7	58	24	58.6
Dawson et al. (2011)	H	US	Hospitality culture scale (HCS)	(Clark & Watson, 1995; DeVellis, 2003; Hinkin, 1995)	10	55	22	60.0
Chu and Murrmann (2006)	H	US	Hospitality emotional labor scale (HELS)	(Churchill, 1979; DeVellis, 1991; Hinkin et al., 1997)	4	82	19	76.8
Petrick (2002)	H	Caribbean	Perceived value of a service (SERV-PERVAL)	(Lee & Crompton, 1992; Zaichkowsky, 1985)	5	52	25	51.9
Tepeci and Bartlett (2002)	H	Turkey US	Hospitality industry culture profile (HICP)	*	8	40	32	20.0
Ap and Crompton (1998)	T	US	Tourism impact scale (*)	(Churchill, 1979; DeVellis, 1991)	7	147	35	76.2
Lankford and Howard (1994)	T	US	Tourism impact attitude scale (TIAS)	Churchill (1979)	2	72	27	62.5

Notes: T = Tourism, H = Hospitality, * = Not specified.

Table 2. Evaluation of Scale Development Process Tourism and Hospitality Studies.

Author(s) and Year	Item Generation						Scale Development					Structural Validity		Confirmatory Factor Analysis Fit Indices Final Study		
				Pre-test				Sample (n)			Total	Overall				
	Item Generation	# Of Interviews	Expert Panel	Face Validity	Item Reduction	SDRB	Measure Type	Pilot	Main Study	Normality Test	Variance %>=0.50	α >=0.70	Estimation <0.85	RMSEA <=0.08	CFI >=0.90	NFI >=0.90
Choe and Kim (2019)	M	*	✓	✓	EFA	*	7-Point LS	400	870	✓	69.1	*	✓	0.06	0.95	0.93
Choi et al. (2019)		D	✓	✓	EFA	✓	5-Point LS	132	595	X	80.1	0.94	✓	0.06	0.96	0.94
Jorgenson et al. (2019)		D	X	✓	EFA	*	7-Point LS	1,000	704	*	66.0	*	*	*	*	*
Liu et al. (2019)	*	12	X	X	EFA	*	5-Point LS	226	253	X	64.6	*	✓	0.05	0.98	0.95
Lu et al. (2019)	M	10	✓	✓	EFA	*	7-Point LS	153	318 440 437	*	71.6	*	0.88 0.90	0.05	0.96	*
Omuris (2019)	M	17	✓	X	EFA	*	5-Point LS	514	621	✓	61.3	*	✓	0.06	0.98	0.97
Tsaur and Tu (2019)	I	20	✓	X	EFA	*	5-Point LS	321	284	X	70.0	*	✓	0.04	0.96	0.88
Ying and Wen (2019)	M	20	✓	X	EFA	*	7-Point LS	275	259	X	70.0	*	✓	0.06	0.94	0.90
Bui and Wilkins (2018)	M	31	X	X	EFA	*	7-Point LS	1,610	525	✓	60.2	*	✓	0.05	0.94	*
Busser and Shulga (2018)	M	*	✓	✓	EFA PCA	*	10-Point LS 7-Point LS	202	228	X	86.4	*	0.85	0.06	0.92	*
Ceylan and Çizel (2018)	M	*	✓	X	EFA	*	7-Point LS	52 58	1,495	X	68.7	0.89	✓	0.08	0.85	0.85
El-Adly and Abu Elsamen (2018)	M	*	✓	X	EFA	*	5-Point LS	166	182	X	80.3	*	0.86 0.86 0.87	0.06	0.92	0.92
Ferreira et al. (2018)		D	✓	✓	EFA	*	5-Point LS	116	300	X	70.7	✓	✓	0.07	0.96	*
Kim et al. (2018)	I	47	✓	X	EFA	*	7-Point LS	1,465	514	✓	65.0	✓	✓	0.08	0.94	0.93

Study	Type	D	No.	C1	C2	Method	C3	Scale	Sample	N	C4	Variance	C5	C6	AVE	CR	α
Ko (2018)	M		*	X	X	EFA	*	5-Point LS	100	504	X	*	✓	✓	0.05	0.95	0.98
Kumar and Nayak (2018)	M		12	X	*	EFA	*	5-Point LS	177	152	X	72.6	*	*	0.05	0.95	0.95
Lee and Jan (2018)		D		✓	X	EFA	*	7-Point LS	120	540	X	*	*	✓	0.05	0.91	0.97
Luo (2018)		D		✓	X	EFA	*	5-Point LS	150	302	X	*	*	*	0.07	0.92	0.88
Ruiz-Molina et al. (2018)		D		✓	✓	*	*	7-Point LS	*	197	X	*	*	✓	*	*	*
Taheri et al. (2018)	I		43	✓	✓	PCA	✓	7-Point LS	50	518 627	✓	81.5	*	✓	0.07	0.92	0.95
Tsaur et al. (2018)	I		21	✓	X	EFA	*	5-Point LS	50	265 264	✓	69.4	*	0.92 0.90 0.87	0.08	0.93	0.90
Wen et al. (2018)	I		55	✓	X	EFA	*	7-Point LS	*	346	X	69.4	0.86	✓	0.04	0.97	0.93
Yen et al. (2018)	M		17	✓	X	EFA	*	5-Point LS	268	253	X	*	0.91	0.93 0.93 0.87 0.85	0.07	0.92	0.90
Zeng et al. (2018)	M		*	X	X	EFA	*	5-Point LS	110	202	X	67.1	*	✓	*	*	*
Bozic et al. (2017)	M		*	✓	*	EFA	*	5-Point LS	273	281	X	61.0	*	✓	0.06	0.93	*
Cho et al. (2017)	M		21	✓	✓	EFA	✓	7-Point LS	157	1,000	✓	*	*	✓	0.06	0.93	*
Hahn et al. (2017)	M		24	✓	✓	EFA	*	7-Point LS	133	843	X	74.9	*	✓	0.07	0.94	0.91
Pijls et al. (2017)	M		24	✓	*	EFA PCA	*	5-Point LS	33	848 255	X	64	*	✓	0.07	0.96	*
Taheri et al. (2017)	M		23	✓	✓	PCA	*	7-Point LS	50	673 418	✓	93.1	*	✓	*	*	*
Tsai et al. (2017)	M		*	✓	✓	EFA	*	4-Point LS	50	479	X	53.9	0.89	✓	4.70	0.90	*
Bavik (2016)	M		18	✓	✓	EFA	✓	5-Point LS	130	281	✓	52.0	0.86	✓	0.06	0.83	0.80

Table 2. (Continued)

Author(s) and Year	Item Generation	# Of Interviews	Expert Panel	Pre-test Face Validity	Item Reduction	SDRB	Measure Type	Pilot	Main Study	Normality Test	Total Variance %>=0.50	Overall α >=0.70	Estimation <0.85	RMSEA <=0.08	CFI >=0.90	NFI >=0.90
Choi et al. (2016)	M	10	✓	✓	EFA	*	7-Point LS	*	708	X	85.1	*	✓	0.06	0.94	0.91
Fatma et al. (2016)	M	*	✓	✓	PCA	*	7-Point LS	*	833	X	68.7	*	✓	0.07	0.92	0.89
Fetscherin and Stephano (2016)	M	1FG	✓	✓	PCA	*	5-Point LS	394	801 800 3,000	✓	67.2	*	✓	0.07	0.93	0.91
Geus et al. (2016)	M	*	✓	✓	PCA	*	7-Point LS	*	565	X	61.7	*	✓	*	*	*
Liu and Arendt (2016)	M	11	✓	*	*	*	7-Point LS	94	388	X	*	*	✓	0.09	0.87	*
Tasci and Semrad (2016)	M	*	✓	✓	EFA	*	7-Point LS	70 253	623	✓	58.8	0.96	✓	0.04	0.98	0.97
Tsaur et al. (2016)	M	*	✓	✓	EFA	*	5-Point LS	251	272	X	53.2	*	✓	0.05	0.95	0.93
Wang (2016)	M	*	✓	*	EFA	*	5-Point LS	250	245	✓	*	*	✓	0.05	0.91	0.80
Chung and Petrick (2015)	M	*	✓	✓	EFA	*	5-Point LS	107	524	X	65.9	*	✓	0.06	0.99	*
Kim and Heo (2015)	D		X	*	*	*	5-Point LS	20	248	X	*	0.86	✓	✓	*	*
Kim et al. (2015)	M	*	✓	✓	EFA	*	*	50	1,567	✓	46.3	*	✓	0.04	0.95	*
Kim (2014)	M	93	✓	*	EFA	*	7-Point LS	311	265	X	71.6	*	✓	0.05	0.96	*
Lee et al. (2014)	M	6	✓	✓	EFA	*	5-Point LS	*	502	X	63.4	*	✓	0.04	0.91	*
Liu et al. (2014)	M	14	✓	*	EFA	*	5-Point LS	20	500	✓	62.4	0.92	✓	0.06	0.92	0.89

Study														
So et al. (2014)	M	*	*	EFA	*	7-Point LS	110	496	X	79.1	*	✔	0.08	0.95	0.92
Wong and Wan(2013)	M	54	*	EFA	*	5-Point semantic	✔	1,213	✔	66.1	*	✔	0.06	0.99	*
Wong and Fong (2012)	M	*	*	PCA	*	5-Point LS	*	238	*	71.5	*	✔	0.06	0.97	*
Ekiz et al. (2012)	M	15	X	EFA	✔	7-Point LS	155	1822	✔	55.3	0.85	✔	0.04	0.97	*
Kim et al. (2012)	M	62	*	EFA	*	5-Point LS	*	511	✔	75.8	*	✔	0.05	0.98	*
Dawson et al. (2011)	M	*	✔	PCA	*	7-Point LS	741	471	X	63.0	*	✔	*	*	*
Chu and Murrmann (2006)	M	3	✔	EFA	*	7-Point LS	117	317	X	62	*	*	*	0.91	*
Petrick (2002)	M	*	✔	EFA	*	10-Point LS	278	394 398	X	63.5	*	✔	*	0.90	0.90
Tepeci and Barlett (2002)	D	*	*	PCA	*	7-Point LS	150	182	X	65.0	*	*	*	*	*
Ap and Crompton (1998)	M	38	✔	PCA	✔	5-Point LS	416	958	X	68.0	*	*	*	*	*
Lankford and Howard (1994)	D	*	✔	PCA	✔	5-Point LS	385	1,436	X	51.4	0.96	✔	*	*	*

Notes: I = Inductive, X = No, EFA = Exploratory Factor Analysis, RMSEA = The Root Mean Square Error of Approximation, D = Deductive, ✔ = Checked, PCA = Principal Component Analysis, CFI = Comparative Fit Index, M = Mix, * = Not specified, LS = Likert scale, NFI = Normed Fit Index.

assess construct validity, the psychometric properties of the scales were evaluated by determining whether ta normality test was carried out and whether total variance, reliability (overall alpha), correlation estimations, and confirmatory fit indices were above or below the approved values. Table 3 summarizes the psychometric properties of the scales evaluated in terms of its content validity, criterion validity, and construct validity.

Limitations

The findings in this review are subject to at least four limitations. First, a traditional challenge when conducting systematic reviews is that we used the search terms in the title section, making it plausible that some relevant papers related to tourism and hospitality scales may not have been identified. Second, the Web of Science database was used to identify the tourism and hospitality scales, and some publications may have been overlooked. Third, another possible limitation may be that the sample size was only considered for the study, but not the characteristics of the sample. Lastly, in assessing structural validity, fit indices of the main study were limited to RMESA, CFI, and NFI. The priority and consideration of the fit indices such as the Comparative Fit Index (CFI), Degrees of freedom (D.F.), Incremental Fit Index (IFI), and Chi-Square may vary.

Results

General Results

An assessment and evaluation of the key characteristics of the developed scales in the tourism and hospitality field were conducted. Tables 1 and 3 summarize the main characteristics of the scales. Most of the scale studies evaluated were tourism, representing 68% of papers evaluated, while the remaining 32% were hospitality papers. A growing interest in industry-specific scales is also evident through the increased number of studies published over the past two decades. In this review, the first scale published by Lankford and Howard in 1994, the number of scale development slowly increased during the 1990s (e.g., Ap & Crompton, 1998) and gradually increased during the millennium (Chu & Murrmann, 2006; Petrick, 2002; Tepeci & Bartlett, 2002). It is worth highlighting that over 90% of the scales were developed in the last decade.

Based on the results, studies on scale development in tourism and hospitality were conducted in 10 countries (see Tables 1 and 3). Of the 56 scales reviewed, 15 were conducted in the United States, and 11 in Taiwan. Some researchers conducted their studies in multiple countries. For example, Choi et al. (2019) conducted their research in the two Asian countries of Thailand and South Korea. Other studies generated their samples from more distant countries such as Australia and South Korea (Hahn, Sparks, Wilkins, & Jin, 2017), Turkey, and the United States (Tepeci & Bartlett, 2002). Taheri, Jafari, and Okumus (2017) incorporated data from three countries, including the UK, Iran, and China, which are culturally and geographically diverse.

Table 5. Summary of Descriptive Characteristics and Psychometric Evaluation of Tourism and Hospitality ...

General Results (n = 56)						Summary of Psychometric Evaluation (n = 56)					
Descriptive Characteristics			**Item Generation**			**Scale Development**			**Structural Validity**		
Theme	F	%[a]	*Approach*	F	%[a]	*SDRB Check*	F	%[a]	*Normality Test*	F	%[a]
Tourism	38	68	Inductive	5	9	Yes	6	11	Yes	17	30
Hospitality	18	32	Deductive	9	16	No	50	89	No	39	70
Publication by year			Combined	42	75	*Item reduction method*			*Total variance explained (%)*		
1990-1999	2	4	*Target sample*			EFA	41	73	>= 50%	46	82
2000-2009	3	5	Students only	4	7	PCA	10	18	<50%	1	2
2010-2019	51	91	Non-students only	52	93	EFA & PCA combined	2	4	*	9	16
Country			*Expert panel &/or judges*			*	3	5	*Overall alpha report*		
Australia	2	4	Yes	47	84	*Measure type*			>=0.7	11	20
China	2	4	No	8	14	4-point-Likert-scale	1	2	*	45	80
Hong Kong	3	5	*	10	2	5-point-Likert-scale	26	46	*Estimation*		
India	2	4				7-point-Likert-scale	24	43	<=0.85	45	80
Macau	3	5	*Face validity pre-test*			Combined	2	4			

Table 3. (*Continued*)

General Results (n = 56)						Summary of Psychometric Evaluation (n = 56)					
Descriptive Characteristics			**Item Generation**			**Scale Development**				**Structural Validity**	
Theme	F	%#	*Approach*	F	%#	*SDRB Check*	F	%#	*Normality Test*	F	%#
Netherlands	3	5	Yes	26	46	Other	2	4	>0.85	5	9
S. Korea	3	5	No	16	29	*	1	2	*	6	11
Taiwan	11	20	*	14	25						
Turkey	3	5				*Pilot study*			*RMSEA critical*		
US	15	27				1 sample	47	84	<=0.08	43	77
Multiple countries	5	9				2 samples	1	2	>0.08	2	4
Other	4	7				3 samples	8	14	*		
Factors						*Main studies*			*CFI critical*		
Multi-dimensional	55	98				1 sample	49	88	>=0.9	43	77
Unidimensional	1	2				2 samples	5	9	<0.9	3	5
						3 samples	2	4	*	10	18
Lost percentage									*NFI critical*		
<25%	17	30							>=0.9	21	38
25%-50%	10	18							<0.9	7	12
>50%	29	52							*	28	50

Notes: * = Not specified, EFA = Exploratory Factor Analysis, RMSEA = The Root Mean Square Error of Approximation, # = % may exceed 100% due to rounding, PCA = Principal Component Analysis, CFI = Comparative Fit Index, F = Frequency, SBRB = Social Desirability Response Bias, NFI = Normed Fit Index.

It was found that various scale guidelines had been used to guide the scale development process. Notably, the most frequently used guidelines (i.e., mode) were those by Churchill (1979) and DeVellis (2003). Among these scale guidelines, researchers mostly prefer Churchill (1979) 33 studies (59%), De Vellis (2003) 14 studies (25%), and Hinkin (1995) seven studies (13%), while the other studies used different guidelines 31 studies (55%).

Regarding the number of factors, 99% of the scales were multi-dimensional ranging from two factors (Jorgenson et al., 2019; Ko, 2018; Lankford & Howard, 1994; Taheri, Gannon, Cordina, & Lochrie, 2018) to 10 (Dawson et al., 2011; Kim, 2014; Lee, Lee, & Park, 2014; Tsaur & Tu, 2019). While various factors were identified, one study presented a uni-dimensional scale (see Ruiz-Molina, Servera-Francés, Arteaga-Moreno, & Gil-Saura, 2018). It was found that four-factor scales were the most frequent with at least 25 items.

In addition to assessing the number of factors, the researchers examined the percentage of original items lost following purification of the scale. Consequently, it was found that just over half (52%) of the scales removed more than 50% of the generated items during the scale development procedure (see Table 3). For example, Busser and Shulga (2018) initially generated 129 items. Eventually, the authors removed 80% of the items.

Assessment of the Psychometric Properties of the Scales

Each scale's psychometric properties were assessed, and these were examined for item generation, scale development, and structural validity. Table 2 shows the descriptive characteristics of the scale development process, while Table 3 summarizes the psychometric evaluation of the tourism and hospitality scales.

It was found that during the item generation phase, most studies used a mix of inductive and deductive approaches. In terms of content validity, 84% of the studies sought the input of expert judges, while 14% did not. Consequently, nearly half of the developed scales (46%) reported on the pre-test face validation of the scale, while 29% of studies did not report using a pre-test to verify face validity. One quarter (25%) of the studies did not report any pre-test procedures.

The assessment of the scale development stage shows that most of the studies (89%) did not acknowledge any control for social desirability response bias (see Tables 2 and 3). In terms of the type of measures and response categories used, Likert scales were primarily adopted, with nearly half (46%) which used a five-point Likert scale followed by 43% of studies adopting a seven-point Likert scale. On the other hand, Tsai, Hsu, and Hsu (2017), for example, used a four-point Likert scale.

Table 3 also shows that most of the studies (84%) conducted a single sample for the pilot study. Ceylan and Çizel (2018) conducted two samples in their pilot, while eight studies (14%) of the studies collected three samples for the pilot study. Like the pilot study data collection, for the assessment of the main study, most of the studies (88%) collected one sample. Five studies were collected from two samples (Petrick, 2002; Pijls, Groen, Galetzka, & Pruyn, 2017; Taheri et al., 2017; Tsaur, Yen, & Teng, 2018), and only three studies collected data from three samples (Ap & Crompton, 1998; Fetscherin & Stephano, 2016; Lu, Cai, & Gursoy, 2019).

The 56 reviewed scales' sample size was further assessed in terms of the minimum sample size. For the pilot study, 51 scales displayed an adequate sample size of ≥50, whereas five studies reported a critical sample size of ≥50 (Kim & Heo, 2015; Kim, Jun, Walker, & Drane, 2015; Liu, Su, Gan, & Chou, 2014; Pijls et al., 2017; Taheri et al., 2017, 2018; Tsaur et al., 2018). Fifty-three studies were collected above the suggested number for the main study, whereas three studies did not have an adequate sample size for the main study with a sample less than 200. It is also worth noting that some studies generated a considerable sample size (Ap & Crompton, 1998; Ceylan & Çizel, 2018; Cho, Lee, Moore, Norman, & Ramshaw, 2017; Fetscherin & Stephano, 2016; Kim et al., 2015; Lankford & Howard, 1994; Lu et al., 2019; Taheri et al., 2018) most with a sample of nearly 1,000 respondents or more.

Nearly three-quarters of studies (73%) generated their items through exploratory factor analysis, with 18% ($n = 10$) conducting principal components analysis. Only two studies used mixed methods (Busser & Shulga, 2018; Pijls et al., 2017). It is worth highlighting that 70% of studies did not include a normality check. Except for Kim et al.'s (2015) study, 46 studies had acceptable levels (i.e., ≥50%) of total variance explained. Meanwhile, nine studies did not specify the explained variance. Internal consistency was assessed through reliability analysis, which was confirmed in 11 studies. However, 45 studies did not specify the overall Cronbach's alpha score.

Structural validity via structural equation modeling was successfully assessed in 45 studies. Except for Liu and Arendt (2016) and Tsai et al. (2017) all measures had an acceptable RMSEA $<=0.008$. However, absolute standards of good model fit Comparative Fit Index (CFI) > 0.90 and the Normed Fit Index NFI >0.90 were not assessed in five studies (Bavik, 2016; Ceylan & Çizel, 2018; Fatma, Rahman, & Khan, 2016; Liu & Arendt, 2016; Wang, 2016) while some studies had marginal results such as (Petrick, 2002; Tsaur et al., 2018; Yen, Tsaur, & Tsai, 2018). Discriminant validity was reported in four studies that showed correlations >0.85 (El-Adly & Abu Elsamen, 2018; Lu et al., 2019; Tsaur et al., 2018; Yen et al., 2018).

Discussion

This discussion is organized and based on the three stages of the scale development process (i.e., item generation and its content validity, scale development, and psychometric properties). Suggestions for best practices in future scale development studies are also provided.

It was found that tourism scales dominated the existing scale studies. Among these scales, the primary focus was on tourist perceptions such as local tourist interactions, participation, motivation, and memorable experiences (Choe & Kim, 2019; Wen, Meng, Ying, Qi, & Lockyer, 2018; Ying & Wen, 2019) as well as destination characteristics, including destination image, destination branding, and destination personality (Ceylan & Çizel, 2018; Choi & Chu, 2000; Kumar &

Nayak, 2018; Tsaur, Yen, & Yan, 2016). Four of these scales examined residents' perceptions of tourism and its impacts (Ap & Crompton, 1998; Choe & Kim, 2019; Lankford & Howard, 1994; Tsaur et al., 2018). It is commonly known that residents' perceptions and behaviors toward tourists in terms of the warmth of their welcome and friendliness are predictors for tourist satisfaction. Therefore, it is not surprising that some scales have been developed to address this particular aspect of tourism.

In the hospitality domain, existing scales have taken various research paths, yet the central focus has been paid to organizational characteristics, including organizational culture (Bavik, 2016; Dawson et al., 2011; Tepeci & Bartlett, 2002), workplace friendship (Omuris, 2019), and technological innovativeness (Kim, Tang, & Bosselman, 2018). Some hospitality researchers have focused on products such as restaurant rating, price, food safety, and green food (Chung & Petrick, 2015; Liu et al., 2014; Wang, 2016) as well as services such as host sincerity and hospitableness (Taheri et al., 2018; Tasci & Semrad, 2016). However, it has been noted by Liu and Arendt (2016) that there is a lack of studies on employee perceptions (e.g., work motivations), and there are opportunities to develop employee-oriented scales which can address some of the distinct characteristics of hospitality employment and its related stakeholder relationships.

One of the key research questions of this study was to identify and examine some of the common problems and pitfalls of the evaluated scales. It was found that none of the 56 evaluated scales had adhered to all the proper scale development procedures. Specifically, the scales were either psychometrically problematic or had some missing information regarding the procedures followed in their development. It is assumed that the researchers either did not utilize the required procedures or considered them too minor to report. Overall, many scales lacked the reporting of some procedures, which primarily revolved around issues pertaining to the number of interviews, pre-test of the scale, social desirability response bias, sampling, normality, estimations, overall reliability, and the confirmatory factor analysis (CFA) fit indices.

The results show that the face validity of the scales was partially established. Despite the interviews reviewed by the experts and/or judges, pre-test problems were noted at the item generation stage. Some studies reported below the recommended number of interviews (Choi et al., 2016; Chu & Murrmann, 2006; Liu & Arendt, 2016) (see Table 2). This finding has relevance for future scale development researchers, as the interviews seek to grasp and describe the true essence and meaning of the central themes of the construct whereby the number of interviews should cover and reflect original and genuine information about the phenomenon. The number of interviews contributes widely to increasing the scale's content validity and construct validity. Hence, it is suggested that future studies aim for a minimum of 15 interviews or when theoretical saturation has been achieved.

Notably, several studies failed to describe how they developed the pre-test measures explicitly. The process of face validation requires a pre-test to ensure that the measurement instruments are grasped and understood by the target population (Hinkin, 1995). It has been suggested by Schwab (1980) that construct validity includes the assessment of both content validity and face validity, which implies that any minor pitfall during this stage could potentially demonstrate a snowballing effect on the scale's overall construct validity. Therefore, it is suggested that all future scale studies establish face validity by administrating a questionnaire to a small group of people designed to enhance the survey instrument's readability, response format, and understandability. Consequently, the undertaking of pre-test procedures was found to be problematic. Nevertheless, overall, it was considered that all the scales had demonstrated a reasonable degree of content validity.

Two main shortcomings were identified and documented at the scale development stage. Firstly, and notably, a social desirability response bias check was not employed in most studies. As mentioned earlier, social desirability bias is regarded as a systematic error in scale development, leading to fallacious correlations among studied variables (King & Bruner, 2000). Hence, one aspect of construct validity, which should concern researchers, is the spillover effect of social-desirability response bias (Gove & Geerken, 1977). Future scale development attempts may adopt different ways to minimize and/or eliminate the abovementioned problems by using proxy subjects, the randomized response technique, selecting interviewers, the bogus pipeline, and forced-choice items to control social desirability bias (see Nederhof, 1985). The other notable concern is the sample size of the pilot and main studies in which some studies had sample sizes that were lower than the rule of thumb of around 200 valid respondents. Among the studies that used structural equation modeling, most had not indicated the fit indices problem that may arise due to the small sample size. Careful attention must be given to this matter. Otherwise, the findings may not completely postulate the target population. Consequently, future scale studies should not treat the rule of thumb for sample size as the maximum, but instead, researchers should aim to collect from a larger sample that treats minimum sample size as a means to increase the credibility of the results and provide a greater degree of precision for the scale.

It is also crucial to note that most items were generated through EFA (exploratory factor analysis). While some studies conducted PCA (principal components analysis), some used combined methods, namely EFA and PCA, indicating that different methods may be used. The two EFA methods that are recommended most often are maximum-likelihood (ML) estimation and principal axis factoring (PAF), with the latter being recommended when assumptions of data normality are "violated severely" (Sakaluk & Short, 2017, p. 3). Taken together, considering the nature of various item reduction techniques, it is suggested that future studies should employ EFA in cases where the underlying constructs cannot be measured directly and that one utilizes PCA when variables are highly correlated (see O'Rourke & Hatcher, 2013). Despite identifying multiple fit indices problems with some of the scales, it was found that, in general, the tourism and hospitality scales provided sufficient evidence to demonstrate that they were all psychometrically sound.

Nevertheless, it was found that the common elements of structural validity, such as the normality test and overall reliability score, were often ignored or not reported. As the overall reliability is associated with the homogeneity of the items, future studies should include the overall Cronbach's alpha scores as one of the main measurements of reliability. Future research regarding the normality test would be worth pursuing as excluding unnecessary items may not limit the generalizability of the findings (Nunnaly, 1978). However, unnecessary items may appear deceptive, with the resultant factor structure resulting in the ambiguity of construct validity. Consequently, it is suggested that future research focus on assessing normality and include tests for sampling adequacy.

This discussion has focused on examining the problems and weaknesses resulting from this evaluation. Despite this, one must also consider the context, level and extent of knowledge, and the time period when the respective scale development studies were developed. Given this, previous scale development efforts have met many of the standard criteria to assess the adequacy of the scale to varying degrees and one can conclude that these scales have been developed reasonably and in an acceptable manner. The deficiencies found in the reviewed scales certainly pose challenges for tourism and hospitality researchers. Without a doubt, addressing these challenges can ensure and enhance the overall quality, standard, and rigor of future scale development studies. Only with the passage of time will the tourism and hospitality field of study mature. Noting that 90% of scale development studies have been reported in the past decade and as time progresses into the twenty-first century, it is incumbent for tourism and hospitality researchers who embark upon scale development to address and report all the requirements as robustly and as rigorously as possible. It is acknowledged that some papers have not been reported as rigorously as possible, which may be due to factors such as deeming it to be a minor matter, addressing publisher word limits, or simply ignoring it. Failing to do so in future studies would serve as an indictment upon our field of study.

Conclusion

This study is the first to systematically evaluate the scales developed in tourism and hospitality scale development procedures and psychometric properties. The challenges and main limitations were identified, examined, and discussed. Noticeable methodological weaknesses were identified in the scale development process pertaining to such matters as the number of interviews, scale pre-tests, social desirability response bias check, and reporting of all the psychometric properties. It can be concluded that future studies need to improve the reporting of scale development procedures. The findings also highlight that the scales have been predominantly developed in limited regions and there is a need for such research to be conducted with more varied samples, populations, and countries. As Pattron (2002, p. 223), suggested: "there are always trade-offs to make in designing a study, due to limited resources, time, and human ability to grasp the complex nature of the social reality". As in all studies, there are some limitations and delimitations. The findings of this systematic review have pointed out the limitations, weaknesses, and challenges. Consequently, based on various scale development procedures, we offered holistic scale development guidelines (see Table 4) that can assist and guide

Table 4. Scale Development Guidelines and Procedures.

No	Stage	Action - Criteria	Reference(s)
1. Item Generation	Literature review	Systematic review for identifying existing scales and items	(PRISMA; Mother et al., 2011; Okoli & Schabram, 2010)
	Generating item pool	Information from the respondents (i.e., Interviews) From the literature	(Churchill, 1979; Hinkin, 1995; De Vellis, 2003, 2016)
	Formulation of interview questions	From the literature/self-generated	(Churchill, 1979; Hinkin, 1995; De Vellis, 2003, 2016)
	Interview sampling	Theoretical sampling/saturation 12–50 interviews	(Baker & Edwards, 2012; Creswell, 2009)
	Response of bias control	Common rater effects, item characteristic effects, item context effect, measurement context effects, social desirability. item priming effects, acquiescence biases (yea-saying and nay-saying), predictor and criterion variables measured in the same location, predictor and criterion variables measured using the same medium, transient mood state.	Podsakoff et al. (2012)
	Face validity/content validity	Expert panel/judges' assessment as appropriate (odd number)	(Hinkin, 1995; Netemeyer et al., 2003)
2. Scale Development	Sample size	In the pilot study, 50–150 respondents In the main study, 200 respondents	(DeVellis, 2003; Fowler, 1995; Hinkin, 1995, 1998)
	Sampling adequacy	The Kaiser-Meyer-Olkin Measure 0.60 Bartlett's Test of Sphericity 0.50	(Creswell, 2009; Hair et al., 2007)

Normality test	<2.00/Kurtosis <3.00	Nunnally (1978)
Identifying factors/ Item reduction	Exploratory Factor Analysis (EFA) Factor loading >0.30	(DeVellis, 2003; Fabrigar et al., 1999; Netemeyer et al., 2003)
Factor labeling	Unipolar/singular name (e.g., communication) Bipolar/multi-name (e.g., communication and innovation)	(Alexander, 1978; Tucker, McCoy, & Evans, 1990)
Type of measurement model	Formative – causality flows from the indicators to the construct Reflective – causality flows from the construct to the indicators	(Coltman et al., 2008; MacKenzie et al., 2005)
Dimensionality of factor(s) & the scale	Factor(s) – Internal reliability score >0.70 Scale – Overall reliability score >0.70	(Cronbach, 1951, 1972; Nunnally, 1978)
3. Scale Assessment *Convergent validity*	Average variance explained >0.050 Total variance explained >0.50	Fornell and Larcker (1981)
Discriminant validity	+/– two standard errors <0.85	(Fornell & Larcker, 1981; Gerbing & Anderson, 1988; Nunnally & Bernstein, 1994)
Construct validity	Confirmatory factor analysis Comparative Fit Index <0.90 Normed Fit Index <0.90 The root mean square error of approximation <0.90	(Fan & Sivo, 2005; Hu & Bentler, 1998; Vandenberg & Lance, 2000)

future researchers in enhancing the overall quality of tourism and hospitality scale measures as rigorously and robustly as possible to advance knowledge.

References

Alexander, M. (1978). *Organizational norms opinionnaire. The 1978 annual handbook for group facilitators* (pp. 81–88). La Jolla, CA: University Associates.

Ali, A. K. R., Bakhshi, E., Azarkeivan, A., & Biglarian, A. (2016). Bootstrap and jackknife resampling methods in survival analysis of patients with thalassemia major. *Iranian Journal of Epidemiology*, *12*, 56–63.

Ap, J., & Crompton, J. L. (1998). Developing and testing a tourism impact scale. *Journal of Travel Research*, *37*(2), 120–130.

Baker, S. E., & Edwards, R. (Eds.). (2012). *How many qualitative interviews is enough? Expert voices and early career reflections on sampling and cases in qualitative research*. National Centre for Research Methods. Retrieved from http://eprints. ncrm.ac.uk/2273/

Bavik, A. (2016). Developing a new hospitality industry organizational culture scale. *International Journal of Hospitality Management*, *58*, 44–55.

Bearden, W. O., Netemeyer, R. G., & Teel, J. E. (1989). Measurement of consumer susceptibility to interpersonal influence. *Journal of Consumer Research*, *15*, 473–481.

Bentz, V. M., & Shapiro, J. J. (1998). *Mindful inquiry in social research*. London: Sage Publications.

Berg, B. L. (2001). *Qualitative research methods for the social sciences*. Boston, MA: Allyn and Bacon.

Boley, B. B., Ayscue, E., Maruyama, N., & Woosnam, K. M. (2017). Gender and empowerment assessing discrepancies using the resident empowerment through tourism scale. *Journal of Sustainable Tourism*, *25*(1), 113–129.

Bollen, K. A. (1990). Overall fit in covariance structure models. Two types of sample size effects. *Psychological Bulletin*, *107*(2), 256.

Bollen, K., & Lennox, R. (1991). Conventional wisdom on measurement: A structural equation perspective. *Psychological Bulletin*, *110*(2), 305–314.

Bozic, S., Jovanovic, T., Tomic, N., & Vasiljevic, D. A. (1994). An analytical scale for domestic tourism motivation and constraints at multi-attraction destinations. The case study of Serbia's lower and middle Danube region. *Tourism Management Perspectives*, *23*, 97–111.

Brace, I. (2006). *An introduction to market & social research: Planning & using research tools & techniques*. London: Kogan Page Publishers.

Busser, J. A., & Shulga, L. V. (2018). Co-created value: Multi-dimensional scale and nomological network. *Tourism Management*, *65*, 69–86.

Bui, H. T., & Wilkins, H. C. (2018). Social interactions among Asian backpackers. *Current Issues in Tourism*, *21*(10), 1097–1114.

Ceylan, D., & Çizel, B. (2018). Testing destination image scale invariance among British, German and Russian tourists: A multigroup confirmatory factor analysis. *Advances in Hospitality and Tourism Research*, *6*(2), 119–146.

Chao, G. T., O'Leary-Kelly, A. M., Wolf, S., Klein, H. J., & Gardner, P. D. (1994). Organizational socialization: Its content and consequences. *Journal of Applied Psychology, 79*(5), 730–743.

Cheung, G. W., & Rensvold, R. B. (2002). Evaluating goodness-of-fit indexes for testing measurement invariance. *Structural Equation Modeling: A Multidisciplinary Journal, 9*(2), 233–255.

Choe, J. Y., & Kim, S. (2019). Development and validation of a multi-dimensional tourist's local food consumption value (TLFCV) scale. *International Journal of Hospitality Management, 77*, 245–259.

Choi, T. Y., & Chu, R. (2000). Levels of satisfaction among Asian and Western travellers. *International Journal of Quality & Reliability Management, 17*(2), 116–132.

Choi, H. M., Kim, W. G., Kim, Y. J., & Agmapisarn, C. (2019). Hotel environmental management initiative (HEMI) scale development. *International Journal of Hospitality Management, 77*, 562–572.

Choi, M., Law, R., & Heo, C. Y. (2016). Shopping destinations and trust-tourist attitudes. Scale development and validation. *Tourism Management, 54*, 490–501.

Cho, H., Lee, H. W., Moore, D., Norman, W. C., & Ramshaw, G. (2017). A multilevel approach to scale development in sport tourist nostalgia. *Journal of Travel Research, 56*(8), 1094–1106.

Chu, K., & Murrmann, S. (2006). Development and validation of the hospitality emotional labor scale. *Tourism Management, 27*(6), 1181–1191.

Chung, J. Y., & Petrick, J. F. (2015). Measuring price fairness: Development of a multi-dimensional scale. *Journal of Travel & Tourism Marketing, 32*(7), 907–922.

Churchill, G. A. (1979). A paradigm for developing better measures of marketing constructs. *Journal of Marketing Research, 16*(1), 64–73.

Clark, L. A., & Watson, D. (1995). Constructing validity: Basic issues in objective scale developmen. *Psychological Assessment, 7*(3), 309–319.

Coltman, T., Devinney, T. M., Midgley, D. F., & Venaik, S. (2008). Formative versus reflective measurement models: Two applications of formative measurement. *Journal of Business Research, 61*(12), 1250–1262.

Cooper, D. R., Schindler, P. S., & Sun, J. (1998). *Business research methods.* Burr Ridge, IL: Irwin; McGraw-Hill Burr Ridge, IL.

Creswell, J. W. (2009). *Research design: Qualitative, quantitative, and mixed methods approaches.* London: Sage Publications, Inc.

Creswell, J. W., & Clark, V. L. P. (2017). Designing and conducting mixed methods research. *Sage publications.*

Creswell, J. W., Plano Clark, V. L., Gutmann, M. L., & Hanson, W. E. (2003). Advanced mixed methods research designs. In *Handbook of mixed methods in social and behavioral research* (pp. 209–240).

Cronbach, L. J. (1951). Coefficient alpha and the internal structure of tests. *Psychometrika, 16*(3), 297–334.

Cronbach, L. J. (1972). *The dependability of behavioral measurements: Theory of generalizability for scores and profiles.* New York, NY: John Wiley & Sons.

Dawson, M., Abbott, J., & Shoemaker, S. (2011). The hospitality culture scale: A measure organizational culture and personal attributes. *International Journal of Hospitality Management, 30*(2), 290–300.

Denscombe, M. (2008). Communities of practice: A research paradigm for the mixed methods approach. *Journal of Mixed Methods Research*, *2*(3), 270–283.

De Witte, K., & Van Muijen, J. J. (1999). Organizational culture. *European Journal of Work & Organizational Psychology*, *8*(4), 497–502.

DeVellis, R. F. (1991).*Scale development: Theory and applications (Applied Social Research Methods Series, 26)*. Newbury Park, CA:Sage Publications.

DeVellis, R. F. (2003). *Scale development-theory and applications*. Thousand Oaks, CA: Sage Publications.

DeVellis, R. F. (2011). *Scale development: Theory and applications*. Thousand Oaks, CA: Sage Publications, Inc.

DeVellis, R. F. (2016). *Scale development: Theory and applications*. Thousand Oaks, CA: Sage Publications, Inc.

Diamantopoulos, A., & Winklhofer, H. M. (2001). Index construction with formative indicators: An alternative to scale development. *Journal of Marketing Research*, *38*(2), 269–277.

Ekiz, E., Au, N., & Hsu, C. (2012). Development of a tourist complaint constraint (TCC) scale. *Scandinavian Journal of Hospitality and Tourism, 12 No. 4*, pp. 373–299.

El-Adly, M. I., & Abu Elsamen, A. (2018). Guest-based hotel equity scale development and validation. *The Journal of Product and Brand Management*, *27*(6), 615–633.

Fabrigar, L. R., Wegener, D. T., MacCallum, R. C., & Strahan, E. J. (1999). Evaluating the use of exploratory factor analysis in psychological research. *Psychological Methods*, *4*(3), 272.

Fan, X., & Sivo, S. A. (2005). Sensitivity of fit indexes to misspecified structural or measurement model components: Rationale of two-index strategy revisited. *Structural Equation Modeling: A Multidisciplinary Journal*, *12*(3), 343–367.

Fatma, M., Rahman, Z., & Khan, I. (2016). Measuring consumer perception of CSR in tourism industry. Scale development and validation. *Journal of Hospitality and Tourism Management*, *27*, 39–48.

Ferreira, B. S., Morais, D. B., Pollack, J.M., & Bunds, K. S. (2018). Development and validation of the tourism e-microentrepreneurial self-efficacy scale. *Tourism Analysis*, *23*(2), 275–282.

Fetscherin, M., & Stephano, R. M. (2016). The medical tourism index. Scale development and validation. *Tourism Management*, *52*, 539–556.

Fornell, C., & Larcker, D. F. (1981). Structural equation models with unobservable variables and measurement error: Algebra and statistics. *Journal of Marketing Research*, *18*(3), 382–388.

Fowler, F. J. (1995). *Improving survey questions: Design and evaluation*. Thousand Oaks, CA: Sage Publications, Inc.

Gerbing, D. W., & Anderson, J. C. (1988). An updated paradigm for scale development incorporating unidimensionality and its assessment. *Journal of Marketing Research*, *25*, 186–192.

Geus, S. de, Richard, G., & Toepoel, V. (1995). Conceptualisation and operationalisation of event and festival experiences. Creation of an event experience scale. *Scandinavian Journal of Hospitality and Tourism*, *16*(3), 274–296.

Gove, W. R., & Geerken, M. R. (1977). The effect of children and employment on the mental health of married men and women. *Social Forces*, *56*(1), 66–76.

Hahn, S. E., Sparks, B., Wilkins, H., & Jin, X. (2017). E-Service quality management of a hotel website: A scale and implications for management. *Journal of Hospitality Marketing & Management*, *26*(7), 694–716.

Hair, J. F., Jr., Anderson, R. E., Tatham, R. L., & Black, W. C. (1998). *Multivariate data analysis (5th ed.)*. Upper Saddle River: NJ: Prentice Hall.

Hair, J. F., Money, A. H., Samouel, P., & Page, M. (2007). *Research methods for business*. West Sussex:John Wiley & Sons.

Hayes, J. R. (2012). Modeling and remodeling writing. *Written Communication*, *29*(3), 369–388.

Haynes, S. N., Richard, D., & Kubany, E. S. (1995). Content validity in psychological assessment. A functional approach to concepts and methods. *Psychological Assessment*, *7*(3), 238.

Hinkin, T. R. (1995). A review of scale development practices in the study of organizations. *Journal of Management*, *21*(5), 967–988.

Hinkin, T. R. (1998). A brief tutorial on the development of measures for use in survey questionnaires. *Organizational Research Methods*, *1*(1), 104–121.

Hinkinet, T. R., Tracey, J. B., & Enz, C. A. (1997). Scale construction: Developing reliable and valid measurement instruments.*Journal of Hospitality & Tourism Research*, *21*(1), 100–120.

Hooper, D., Coughlan, J., & Mullen, M. R. (2008). Structural equation modelling guidelines for determining model fit. *Journal of Business Research*, *6*(1), 53–60.

Hornby, P., & Symon, G. (1994). Tracer studies. *In C. Cassell & G. Symon (Eds.), Qualitative methods in organizational research: A practical guide. London: Sage Publications.*

Hu, L., & Bentler, P. M. (1998). Fit indices in covariance structure modeling: Sensitivity to under parameterized model misspecification. *Psychological Methods*, *3*(4), 424–453.

Johnson, R. B., Onwuegbuzie, A. J., & Turner, L. A. (2007). Toward a definition of mixed methods research. *Journal of Mixed Methods Research*, *1*(2), 112–133.

Jöreskog, K. G., & Sörbom, D. (1993). *LISREL 8 user's guide*. Chicago, IL: Scientific Software International.

Jorgenson, J., Nickerson, N., Dalenberg, D., Angle, J., Metcalf, E., & Freimund, W. (2019). Measuring visitor experiences. Creating and testing the tourism autobiographical memory scale. *Journal of Travel Research*, *58*(4), 566–578.

Kaiser, H. F. (1958). The varimax criterion for analytic rotation in factor analysis. *Psychometrika*, *23*(3), 187–200.

Kim, J. H. (2014). The antecedents of memorable tourism experiences. The development of a scale to measure the destination attributes associated with memorable experiences. *Tourism Management*, *44*, 34–45.

Kim, Y. G., & Eves, A. (2012). Construction and validation of a scale to measure tourist motivation to consume local food. *Tourism Management*, *33*(6), 1458–1467.

Kim, B. G., & Heo, J. (2015). Development of a scale for tourism facilitators. *Journal of Travel & Tourism Marketing*, *32*(5), 595–607.

Kim, W., Jun, H. M., Walker, M., & Drane, D. (2015). Evaluating the perceived social impacts of hosting large-scale sport tourism events. Scale development and validation. *Tourism Management*, *48*, 21–32.

Kim, J. H., Ritchie, J. R. B., & McCormick, B. (2012). Development of a scale to measure memorable tourism experiences. *Journal of Travel Research*, *51*(1), 12–25.

Kim, E., Tang, L., & Bosselman, R. (2018). Measuring customer perceptions of restaurant innovativeness. Developing and validating a scale. *International Journal of Hospitality Management, 74*, 85–98.

King, M. F., & Bruner, G. C. (2000). Social desirability bias: A neglected aspect of validity testing. *Psychology and Marketing, 17*(2), 79–103.

King, N., & Horrocks, C. (2010). *Interviews in qualitative research*. Thousands Oaks, CA: Sage Publications Ltd.

Ko, W.-H. (2018). The development of a competence scale of food safety and hygiene for hospitality students. *Journal of Food Safety, 38*(5), e12498.

Kumar, V., & Nayak, J. K. (2018). Destination personality: Scale development and validation. *Journal of Hospitality & Tourism Research, 42*(1), 3–25.

Lankford, S. V., & Howard, D. R. (1994). Developing a tourism impact attitude scale. *Annals of Tourism Research, 21*(1), 121–139.

Lee, T. H., & Crompton, J. (1992). Measuring novelty seeking in tourism. *Annals of Tourism Research, 19*(4), 732–751.

Lee, T. H., & Jan, F.-H. (2018). Development and validation of the ecotourism behavior scale. *International Journal of Tourism Research, 20*(2), 191–203.

Lee, J. S., Lee, C. K., & Park, C. K. (2014). Developing and validating a multi-dimensional quality scale for mega-events. *International Journal of Hospitality Management, 43*, 121–131.

Lin, J.-S. C., & Hsieh, P.-L (2011). Assessing the self-service technology encounters: Development and validation of SSTQUAL scale. *Journal of Retailing, 87*(2), 194–206.

Liu, Y. S., & Arendt, S. W. (2016). Development and validation of a work motive measurement scale. *International Journal of Contemporary Hospitality Management, 28*(4), 700–716.

Liu, C. H. S., Su, C. S., Gan, B., & Chou, S. F. (2014). Effective restaurant rating scale development and a mystery shopper evaluation approach. *International Journal of Hospitality Management, 43*, 53–64.

Liu, C. R., Wang, Y. C., Huang, W. S., & Tang, W. C. (2019). Festival gamification. Conceptualization and scale development. *Tourism Management, 74*, 370–381.

Lu, L., Cai, R. Y., & Gursoy, D. (2019). Developing and validating a service robot integration willingness scale. *International Journal of Hospitality Management, 80*, 36–51.

Luo, J.M. (2018). A measurement scale of corporate social responsibility in gambling industry. *Journal of Quality Assurance in Hospitality – Tourism, 19*(4), 460–475.

MacCallum, R. C., & Austin, J. T. (2000). Applications of structural equation modeling in psychological research. *Annual Review of Psychology, 51*, 201–226.

MacKenzie, S. B., Podsakoff, P. M., & Jarvis, C. B. (2005). The problem of measurement model misspecification in behavioral and organizational research and some recommended solutions. *Journal of Applied Psychology, 90*(4), 710–730.

Marsh, H. W., Wen, Z., & Hau, K.-T. (2004). Structural equation models of latent interactions: Evaluation of alternative estimation strategies and indicator construction. *Psychological Methods, 9*(3), 275–300.

Menor, L.J., & Roth, A.V. (2007). New service development competence in retail banking: Construct development and measurement validation. *Journal of Operations Management, 25*(4), 825–846.

Meredith, W. (1993). Measurement invariance, factor analysis and factorial invariance. *Psychometrika, 58*(4), 525–543.

Mick, D. G. (1996). Are studies of dark side variables confounded by socially desirable responding? The case of materialism. *Journal of Consumer Research, 23*(2), 106–119.

Moher, D., Altman, D. G., Liberati, A., & Tetzlaff, J. (2011). PRISMA statement. *Epidemiology, 22*(1), 128.

Narayanan, A. (2012). A review of eight software packages for structural equation modeling. *The American Statistician, 66*(2), 129–138.

Nederhof, A. J. (1985). Methods of coping with social desirability bias: A review. *European Journal of Social Psychology, 15*(3), 263–280.

Netemeyer, R. G., Bearden, W. O., & Sharma, S. (2003). *Scaling procedures: Issues and applications*. Thousands Oaks, CA: Sage Publications, Inc.

Nunnally, J. (1978). *Psychometric methods*. New York, NY: McGraw.

Nunnally, J. C., & Bernstein, I. H. (1994). *Psychometric theory*. New York, NY: McGraw.

Okoli, C., & Schabram, K. (2010). A guide to conducting a systematic literature review of information systems research. *Sprouts: Working Papers on Information Systems, 10*(26), 10–26.

Omuris, E. (2019). Workplace friendship in hospitality organizations a scale development. *International Journal of Contemporary Hospitality Management, 31*(3), 1390–1411.

Onwuegbuzie, A. J., & Johnson, R. B. (2006). The validity issue in mixed research.

O'Rourke, N., & Hatcher, L. (2013). *A step-by-step approach to using SAS for factor analysis and structural equation modeling*. Cary, NC: SAS Institute.

Pallant, J. (2007). SPSS survival manual: A step by step guide to data analysis using SPSS for windows (3rd Ed.). *New York: McGraw Hill Open University Press*.

Patton, M. Q. (2002). Two decades of developments in qualitative inquiry: A personal, experiential perspective. *Qualitative Social Work, 1*(3), 261–283.

Peter, J. P. (1981). Construct validity: A review of basic issues and marketing practices. *Journal of Marketing Research, 18*(2), 133–145.

Petrick, J. F. (2002). Development of a multi-dimensional scale for measuring the perceived value of a service. *Journal of Leisure Research, 34*, 119–134.

Pijls, R., Groen, B. H., Galetzka, M., & Pruyn, A. T. H. (2017). Measuring the experience of hospitality. Scale development and validation. *International Journal of Hospitality Management, 67*, 125–133.

Podsakoff, P. M., MacKenzie, S. B., Jeong-Yeon, L., & Podsakoff, N. P. (2003). Common method biases in behavioral research: A critical review of the literature and recommended redies. *Journal of Applied Psychology, 88*, 879–903.

Podsakoff, P. M., MacKenzie, S. B., & Podsakoff, N. P. (2012). Sources of method bias in social science research and recommendations on how to control it. *Annual Review of Psychology, 63*, 539–569.

Rossiter, J.R. (2002). *The C-OAR-SE procedure for scale development in marketing. International Journal of Research in Marketing, 19*(4), 305–335.

Ruiz-Molina, M.-E., Servera-Francés, D., Arteaga-Moreno, F., & Gil-Saura, I. (2018). Development and validation of a formative scale of technological advancement in hotels from the guest perspective. *Journal of Hospitality and Tourism Technology, 9*(3), 280–294.

Sakaluk, J. K., & Short, S. D. (2017). A methodological review of exploratory factor analysis in sexuality research: Used practices, best practices, and data analysis resources. *The Journal of Sex Research, 54*(1), 1–9.

Saxe, R., & Weitz, B. A. (1982). The SOCO scale. A measure of the customer orientation of salespeople. *Journal of Marketing Research, 19*(3), 343–351.

Schwab, D. P. (1980). Construct validity in organizational behavior. *Research in Organizational Behavior, 2*, 3–43.

Sireci, S. G. (1998). The construct of content validity. *Social Indicators Research, 45*(1), 83–117.

So, K. K. F, King, C., & Sparks, B. (2014). *Customer engagement with tourism brands. Scale development and validation. Journal of Hospitality – Tourism Research, 38*(3), 304–329.

Stening, B. W., & Zhang, M. Y. (2007). Methodological challenges confronted when conducting management research in China. *International Journal of Cross Cultural Management, 7*(1), 121–142.

Tabachnick, B. G., Fidell, L. S., & Osterlind, S. J. (2001). *Using multivariate statistics.* New York, NY: Pearsons.

Taheri, B., Gannon, M. J., Cordina, R., & Lochrie, S. (2018). Measuring host sincerity. Scale development and validation. *International Journal of Contemporary Hospitality Management, 30*(8), 2752–2772.

Taheri, B., Jafari, A., & Okumus, B. (2017). Ceremonious politeness in consuming food in VFR tourism. Scale development. *Service Industries Journal, 37*(15–16), 948–967.

Tasci, A. D. A., & Semrad, K. J. (2016). Developing a scale of hospitableness. A tale of two worlds. *International Journal of Hospitality Management, 53*, 30–41.

Tashakkori, A. (2006). *Mixed methodology: Combining qualitative and quantitative approaches.* Thousand Oaks, CA: Sage.

Tepeci, M., & Bartlett, A. B. (2002). The hospitality industry culture profile: A measure of individual values, organizational culture, and person–organization fit as predictors of job satisfaction and behavioral intentions. *International Journal of Hospitality Management, 21*(2), 151–170.

Thompson, B. (2004). *Exploratory and confirmatory factor analysis: Understanding concepts and applications.* Washington, DC: American Psychological Association.

Tsai, C. T., Hsu, H., & Hsu, Y. C. (2017). Tourism and hospitality college students' career anxiety. Scale development and validation. *Journal of Hospitality and Tourism Education, 29*(4), 158–165.

Tsaur, S. H., & Tu, J. H. (2019). Cultural competence for tour leaders. Scale development and validation. *Tourism Management, 71*, 9–17.

Tsaur, S.-H., Yen, C.-H., & Chen, C.-L. (2010). *Independent tourist knowledge and skills. Annals of Tourism Research, 37*(4), 1035–1054.

Tsaur, S. H., Yen, C. H., & Teng, H. Y. (2018). Tourist-resident conflict. A scale development and empirical study. *Journal of Destination Marketing & Management, 10*, 152–163.

Tsaur, S. H., Yen, C. H., & Yan, Y. T. (2016). Destination brand identity. Scale development and validation. *Asia Pacific Journal of Tourism Research, 21*(12), 1310–1323.

Tucker, R. W., McCoy, W. J., & Evans, L. C. (1990). Can questionnaires objectively assess organisational culture? *Journal of Managerial Psychology, 5*(4), 4–11.

Vandenberg, R. J., & Lance, C. E. (2000). A review and synthesis of the measurement invariance literature: Suggestions, practices, and recommendations for organizational research. *Organizational Research Methods, 3*(1), 4–70.

Wang, Y. F. (2016). Development and validation of the green food and beverage literacy scale. *Asia Pacific Journal of Tourism Research, 21*(1), 20–56.

Wang, K.-C., Hsieh, A.-T.,Chou, S.-H., & Lin, Y.-S. (2018). *GPTCCC: An instrument for measuring group package tour service. Tourism Management, 28*(2), 361–376.

Wong, I.A., & Fong, V.H. (2012). *Development and validation of the casino service quality scale: CASERV. International Journal of Hospitality Management. 31*(1), 209–217.

Wong, I.A., & Wan, Y.K.P. (2013). *A systematic approach to scale development in tourist shopping satisfaction. Linking Destination Attributes and Shopping Experience. Journal of Travel Research, 52*,(1) 29–41.

Wen, J., Meng, F., Ying, T. Y., Qi, H. X., & Lockyer, T. (2018). Drug tourism motivation of Chinese outbound tourists. Scale development and validation. *Tourism Management, 64*, 233–244.

Wu, A. D., Li, Z., & Zumbo, B. D. (2007). *Decoding the meaning of factorial invariance and updating the practice of multi-group confirmatory factor analysis: A demonstration with TIMSS data.* Amherst, MA: University of Massachusetts.

Yen, C. H., Tsaur, S. H., & Tsai, C. H. (2018). Tour leaders' job crafting. Scale development. *Tourism Management, 69*, 52–61.

Ying, T. Y., & Wen, J. (2019). Exploring the male Chinese tourists' motivation for commercial sex when travelling overseas. Scale construction and validation.*Tourism Management, 70*, 479–490.

Zaichkowsky, J. L., (1985). Measuring the involvement construct. *Journal of Consumer Research, 12*(3), 341.

Zeng, X.Q., Liu, R., & Gong, H. (2018). *Motivations of adventure recreation in an emerging market. scale development and an empirical study on mainland Chinese enthusiasts. Asia Pacific Journal of Tourism Research, 23*(6), 600–612.

Zikmund, W. G., & Babin, B. J. (2009). *Essentials of marketing research.* Southampton: South-Western Pub.

Chapter 5

Using Neuromarketing Tools in Hospitality and Tourism Research

Hakan Boz and Erdogan Koç

Abstract

This chapter explains and discusses the role and potential of psychophysiological tools of research in tourism and hospitality. As tourism and hospitality services are in general inseparable, i.e. the delivery and the consumption of the service mostly take place at the same time, they tend to involve service encounters which intense and frequent contact and social interactions between the customers and the service providers. These intense and frequent contact and social interactions during service encounters may determine the satisfaction and dissatisfaction of the customers. Hence, the measurement of actual emotions to understand the reactions of customers to various aspects of the service is of paramount importance. Psychophysiological tools, often referred to as neuromarketing tools, allow the collection of realistic data regarding the emotions of the customers. Based on the above background, this chapter explains and discusses the use of tools such as the EEG, Eye Tracker, Galvanic Skin Response, and Facial Expression Recognition in understanding tourism and hospitality customers' reactions and emotions to various aspects of the service.

Keywords: Neuromarketing; EEG; eye tracking; heart rate; galvanic skin response; facial expression recognition

Introduction and the Rationale of Neuromarketing

Tourism industry can be considered as one of the largest industries in the world in terms of its contribution to total world employment and income (UNWTO, 2020). Moreover, tourism is an important source of foreign exchange earnings (Dehnavi, Amiri, DehKordi, & Heidary, 2012; Kumar & Singh, 2019). In 2019, tourism industry revenues accumulated to $1.7 trillion in 2019 with the participation of about 1.5 billion international tourists (UNWTO, 2020). The revenues

Advanced Research Methods in Hospitality and Tourism, 87–109
Copyright © 2023 Hakan Boz and Erdogan Koç
Published under exclusive licence by Emerald Publishing Limited
doi:10.1108/978-1-80117-550-020221005

directly earned in the tourism industry in the world reached to $1.7 trillion in 2019 with the participation of about 1.5 billion global tourists (UNWTO, 2020). It must be also borne in mind that the above figures have been arrived at with the participation of 7% of the world's population (UNWTO, 2020). In line with the economic growth in the world and the increasing proportion of people partici- pating in tourism activities, there is a significant further growth potential of the international travel and tourism industry in the world.

In line with the growth of the tourism industry the competition, both at the macro-level (country and regional level) and micro-level (travel, tourism, and hospitality businesses) there is a need to design and implement activities based on an actual understanding of the customers. The survival and growth of tourism and hospitality businesses and the destinations largely depend on the establish- ment of competitive advantage (Koc, 2020), which largely depends on a better understanding of customers (Charles, Joel, & Samwel, 2012; Chow, Lo, Sha, & Hong, 2006; Koc & Boz, 2018; Powers et al., 2020). Research shows about 80% of new products/services fail within their first three years after their launch (Căpățînă & Drăghescu, 2015; Pradeep, 2010). Research by Oh and Schuett (2010) showed that 75% of small businesses went bankrupt within the first three years of their operation. In the hospitality sector, it was seen that 5–50% of all restaurants go of business every as they are unable to understand customers better and establish competitive advantage (Gumenyuk, 2020; Luca, 2016; Rothbart et al., 2019).

Tourism and hospitality businesses need to accurately identify the needs and of customers so as to be able to design and implement appropriate marketing mix decisions (Koc, 2021; Koc & Boz, 2018; Oh & Schuett, 2010). As tourism and hospitality services are experiential in nature.

However, tourism and hospitality are experiential services by nature, under- standing feelings and emotions tend to be significantly more important (Boz & Koc, 2019; Decrop & Snelders, 2004; Pearce & Gretzel, 2012). The use of traditional research methods such as surveys tends to fail in uncovering the real truth regarding feelings and emotions due to a number of reasons. For instance, participants in surveys may be biased as they (1) may engage in impression management when responding to the survey questions, (2) may have hidden motives, which they may be unaware of, and (3) may have memory problems and cannot remember how they thought and felt (Hall, Johansson, Tärning, Sikström, & Deutgen, 2010; Johansson, Hall, Sikström, & Olsson, 2005; Koc & Boz, 2014a, 2014b). Braidot (2005) argues that traditional data collection methods such as the surveys are not suitable for measuring emotions and feelings (e.g. happiness, anger, arousal, contempt, disgust, stress, embarrassment, excitement, frustration, fear, guilt, pride, joy, relief, satisfaction, and shame.

The criticisms relating to the limitations of traditional data collection methods have further increased in recent years. These criticisms and the limitations of the traditional data collections methods are shown in Table 1 (Boz, 2015; Boz, Arslan, & Koc, 2017; Cooper, 1981; Dawes & Smith, 1985; Koc & Boz, 2014a; Newstead & Collis, 1987; Rosenthal & Rosnow, 2008; Whitley, 2002). The use of more than one data collection method (triangulation) may help researchers overcomes some of the limitations of traditional data collection methods (Greene,

Table 1. Limitations of Frequently Used Traditional Data Collection
Methods.

Data Collections Methods	Limitations
Survey	• *Developmental issues of measurement instrument* (such as validity and reliability) • The fact that participants from different education and socio-economic levels cannot understand the language of survey • *Scale ambiguity* (For instance in Likert type measurements, people can evaluate the item/question relative amount to their standard), • *Social desirability response bias* (Tendency of participants to give responses found desirable by the society), • *Acquiescence response bias* (Tendency of participants to prefer "I agree" or "I do not agree" to generally all questions), • *Extremity response bias* (Tendency of participants to prefer "I definitely agree" or "I definitely do not agree" to generally all questions), • *Halo and Leniency bias* (For the person to have a positive or negative bias to the researched topic beforehand) • *Question order/Order effect* (Asking private information that may expose the identity of the person beforehand like their department, gender or age may prevent them from providing correct information).
Self-report	• *Developmental issues of measurement instrument* (such as validity and reliability) • *Social desirability response bias* • *Invasion of privacy* • *Interpreting Responses* • Participants may have hidden motives, desires, etc. (Koc & Boz, 2018). • Participants of the research may not remember the answer of the questions. • Participants may engage in impression management, • Participants may not remember correctly due to the memory problems.
Focus Group	• *Developmental issues of measurement instrument* (such as validity and reliability) • The responses of the people who participated in the study may be influenced and hence be biased due to the existence of dominant group members, time and other factors (Koc & Boz, 2018).

Table 1. *(Continued)*

Data Collections Methods	Limitations
Interview	• Participants may engage in impression management, • *Interpreting Responses* • *Developmental issues of measurement instrument* (such as validity and reliability) • *Invasion of privacy* • Participants may engage in impression management, • *Halo and Leniency bias* (For the person to have a positive or negative bias to the researched topic beforehand or to be affected by the interviewer (charm, clothing, ethnicity etc. or characteristics of the interviewer's style) • *Participant's or respondents' bias* • *Interpreting Responses*

Caracelli, & Graham, 1989; Koc, 2021; Koc & Boz, 2014a, 2014b). However, resorting to triangulation by researchers tends to be rather rare. For instance, Koc and Boz's (2014b) bibliometric study showed that fewer than 3 of the 1964 papers published in top-tier tourism and hospitality journals resorted to triangulation.

The limitations of traditional data collection methods (Table 1) have led to the search for new alternative approaches in research methods. Koc and Boz (2014a) propose a new approach, called *psychoneurobiochemistry* in tourism and hospitality marketing. According to the psychoneurobiochemistry perspective, a better understanding of consumers may require combining the aspects of psychology, neurology, biology, and chemistry in research (Fig. 1). Boz (2015) compared the findings of traditional and psychophysiological tools in the study and showed how psychophysiological tools can enable the collection of more realistic data about tourism and hospitality customers' emotions and feelings.

Additionally, research on human brain and decision-making years (Damasio, 1994; Damasio & Carvalho, 2013; Gladwell, 2005; Kahneman, 2003; Kahnemann & Tversky, 1979; Kahneman & Tversky, 2000; Lindstrom, 2011; Mihic &

Fig. 1.   Psychoneurobiochemistry of Marketing.

Kursan, 2010) showed that as much as 90% of the purchasing decisions are affected by unplanned and unconscious and subconscious processes, (Boz, 2015; Koc & Boz, 2014a; Mihic & Kursan, 2010; Zurawacki, 2010). Based on the above, it is seen that a better understanding of the use of psychophysiological tools is essential for both tourism and hospitality practitioners and researchers.

Based on the above background, this chapter explains and discusses the role and potential of neuromarketing tools such as the EEG, Eye Tracker, Galvanic Skin Response, and Facial Expression Recognition in identifying and tourism and hospitality customers' reactions and emotions to various aspects of the service. Following the Introduction section, the chapter first provides an overview of the concept of neuromarketing. After the overview of neuromarketing, the use of each marketing tool (fMRI, EEG, Eye Tracing, and Facial Recognition) is explained in terms of what and how they measure. Then, the specific use of neuromarketing tools is explained with specific examples relating to various aspects of tourism and hospitality are explained. The chapter ends with conclusions.

Neuromarketing

The limitations of the traditional research methods (Table 1) and breakthrough developments in the areas of human behavior and medical technologies have increased by the importance of psychophysiological data collection methods (Bastiaansen et al., 2018). The new understanding in which psychophysiological data collection methods are integrated into marketing is called neuromarketing (Boz, 2015; Boz et al., 2017). Neuromarketing is a branch of neuroscience that allows a better understanding of consumers by identifying and measuring their preferences, attitudes, motivations, and expectations toward any marketing stimuli (Boz, 2015; Boz et al., 2017).

According to the data provided in Fig. 2, the literature pertaining to neuromarketing has shown major growth over the past decade. It can be seen that more than 2,000 studies tend to be published in neuromarketing annually in recent years. In 2019, 2,400 studies were conducted in this field. A further study of the publications shows that a significant proportion of neuromarketing studies were carried out in social sciences. Fig. 3 shows data on neuromarketing research relating to tourism and hospitality. The figure shows that neuromarketing studies in tourism and hospitality are extremely limited in terms of the number of publications published in these fields.

Some of the reasons that can be offered to explain the low number of neuromarketing studies in social sciences in general, and in tourism and hospitality, in particular, are as follows (Boz, 2019, pp. 178–179);

(1) Psychophysiological data collection devices used in neuromarketing studies are relatively expensive,
(2) Neuromarketing studies are labor intensive.
(3) Neuromarketing studies require longer periods in terms of research design, implementation, analysis, and interpretation of the findings.

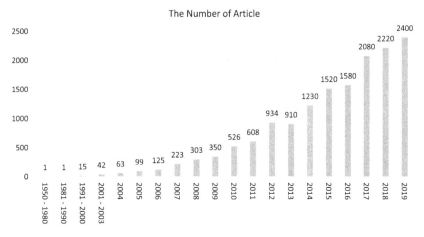

Fig. 2.   Development of Neuromarketing Literature.

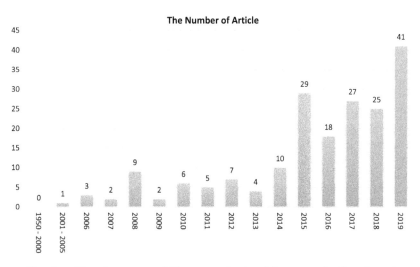

Fig. 3.   Development of Neuromarketing Literature in Tourism &
Hospitality.

(4) Neuromarketing studies may require the cooperation of researchers from
different disciplines.
(5) Neuromarketing studies require the researchers to have an in-depth knowledge of statistics, software, and coding.

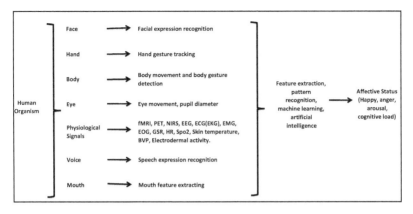

Fig. 4. Psychophysiological/Neuromarketing Data Collection Methods. *Source:* Adapted from Wu, Huang, & Hwang (2015); Boz, Arslan, & Koc (2017); Koc, & Boz (2018, p. 136); Boz (2019, p. 180).

However, despite the above difficulties, it needs to be kept in mind that psychophysiological data collection methods provide an opportunity to explore hidden drives behind the purchasing decisions of consumers, without the limitations of the traditional data collection methods (Tao & Tan, 2005; Koc & Boz, 2018, p. 136). Neuromarketing tools allow the collection of more solid and objective data and help researchers avoid the influences of various cognitive biases of consumers cased caused by the social desirability constraints and differences in their mental processing (Paulhus, 2002).

Fig. 4 depicts psychophysiological data collection methods used in neuromarketing. According to Fig. 4, there are numerous psychophysiological data collection methods allowing data collection from different parts of the human body such as from hands, face, bodily movements (like feet and arm movements), eyes, brain, sound, and mouth.

The most frequently used psychophysiological data collection methods are electroencephalography (EEG), facial expression recognition, eye tracker, heart rate, galvanic skin response, and functional magnetic resonance imaging (fMRI) (Wu, Huang, & Hwang, 2015).

Functional Magnetic Resonance Imaging

fMRI is not one of the first neuroimaging techniques that come to mind when neuromarketing studies are discussed. fMRI measures the direct modulation of brain activity by detecting fluctuations in blood-oxygenation-level-dependent (BOLD) signal (Wong et al., 2014). Al-Kwifi (2015) is one of the most prominent researchers who carried tourism and hospitality research by using fMRI. Al-Kwifi (2015) analyzed the influence of destination images on tourists' future destination preferences. Research shows that ventromedial prefrontal cortex (vmPFC) activity in the brains of the subjects increased when the destination images the participants exposed to were more attractive. The results of Al-Kwifi's (2015) study showed that when the marketing communication visual was positive for the participants t there was an increase in the activity of the ventromedial prefrontal cortex (vmPFC) in their brains.

However, despite recent advances in neuroimaging technology, and particularly in the fMRI technology, fMRI is not an easy-to-use device both for the users and for the participants. For instance, the fMRI systems may weigh between 4,5 and 10 tonnes. They are expensive to use and social can have access to fMRI machines only in hospitals or research laboratories. Also, a significant number of fMRI participants develop claustrophobia during scanning as their heads, arms, and legs are placed between the fasteners to prevent movement when the fMRI machine works noisily (Szameitat et al., 2009). Hence, although people may be more willing toward fMRI scans when the matter is their health, they may not be so keen to have an fMRI scan to take part in a study. Due to the above disadvantages, the use of fMRI in social research, and tourism and hospitality are extremely rare. The advantages and the disadvantages of fMRI can be summarized as follows:

General advantages of fMRI

- Allows opportunity to draw a picture of deep brain structures
- Allows opportunity to measure emotional activations in the limbic system
- No major physiological side effects other than claustrophobia.

General disadvantages of fMRI

- Expensive
- Requirement of advanced expertise
- Labor-intensive
- Allows measurements only with a limited number of subjects
- The feeling of claustrophobic may deter participants to take part in the study and some instances may cause deviations in results.

Electroencephalography (EEG)

Electroencephalography (EEG) is one of the most frequently used psychophysi-ological data collection methods (Lopez et al., 2020). EEG scan is implemented through the placement of metal electrodes on the subject's scalp to measure the small electrical potentials depending on the real-time fluctuations in voltage, caused by the brain activity (Koc & Boz, 2018, p. 137). As the oldest brain scanning method, EEG measures five different waves as alpha, beta, delta, theta, and gamma. EEG is a highly sensitive tool used for measuring the current in the top layer of the cerebral cortex. Despite that, EEG does not provide information about the subcortical brain activity such as the limbic system and brain stem

(Charron, Fuchs, & Oullier, 2008). EEG studies are usually carried out between 10 and 40 participants (Boz, 2015; Ruff & Huettel, 2014; Taşkın, Koç, & Boz, 2017). In one of the EEG studies applied in tourism Taskin et al. (2017) measured tourists' reactions toward conflict-ridden destinations by using EEG together with an eye tracker. Taskin et al. (2017) showed that the level of risk motivated tourists to pay more attention to the verbal cues, as opposed to the visual cues tourists tend to pay attention to normally. In another study, Boz (2015) used EEG, GSR, HR, Eye Tracking tools to measure the influence of refund options on the purchase of package holidays. The study showed that refund opportunities reduced tourists' perception of risk and increased their likelihood to make a purchase.

The EEG method has several advantages which researchers need to take into account. The advantages of EEG are as follows (Nagyová et al., 2014):

- Low cost
- Allows high precision time measurements
- Availability of wide scientific literature pertaining to various fields
- Allows results in a single millisecond
- Does not require other specific equipment or a laboratory.

The disadvantages of EEG are as follows (Nagyová et al., 2014):

- The inability of the EEG to measure the electrical activity in the subcortical brain
- The need for specialized staff for interpreting the results
- A large number of trials may be re required
- Electrical conductivity varies between participants, hence variations in measure durations between the participants
- May be difficult to discern whether the activation in the brain of participants results from the visuals they have been exposed to or from another visual that may have come to their mind.

Galvanic Skin Response (GSR) and Heart Rate (HR)

Galvanic skin response (GSR), also known as electro-dermal activity (EDA), is an important data collection method used to measure participants' level of arousal. EDA is measured in micro siemens (μS) (Li, Walters, Packer, & Scott, 2018). GSR is one of the most sensitive markers for emotional arousal. GSR measures the amount of sweat secretion from sweat glands (Boz, 2019). The skin conductions changes such as the level of secretion in palms or on foot may be triggered significantly by emotional stimulation/arousal (Boucsein, 2012). Galvanic skin response measures the activation of the autonomic nervous system (ANS), and it measures arousal in a valid and reliable manner (Klebba, 1985; Kroeber-Riel, 1979). The autonomic nervous system is also called the "involuntary nervous system" controlling the system that acts predominantly unconsciously and regulates bodily functions such as the HR, respiratory rate, pupil response, and arousal (Schmidt & Thews, 1989).

The sympathetic nervous systems of individuals are activated when they are exposed to visual stimuli they find exciting. This increases the movement in their sweat glands, causing an increase in skin conductivity (Grabe, Lang, Zhou, & Bolls, 2000). Although it is possible to measure many feelings with GSR, arousal is the most accurately measured emotional state (Klebba, 1985).

Heart rate is also one other most frequently used method in social sciences research together with GSR (Wu, Huang, & Hwang, 2015). Heart rate measures the number of heartbeats in a certain period (Ravaja, 2004). Heart rate is generally used to measure consumers' attention, arousal level, and emotional valence (Boz, 2015, 2019; Koc & Boz, 2018). The increase in heart rate is associated with arousal (Boz, 2015). HR and GSR are generally used together with EEG and eye-tracking devices. In a study conducted by Raudenbush and Capiola (2012) where data were collected via GSR and HR, a positive correlation was found between the heartbeat rate, sweat secretion, and food neophobia. Heartbeat and sweat secretion increased as their neophobia levels increased when participants were exposed to a new food (Drachen, Nacke, Yannakakis, & Pedersen, 2010). GSR and HR methods have the following advantages and disadvantages:

The advantages of GSR and HR are (Cartocci et al., 2017):

- Low cost
- Availability of wide scientific literature pertaining to various fields
- The availability of experiments in the real environment

The disadvantages of GSR and HR are (Cartocci et al., 2017):

- The need for specialized staff to interpret the results
- Large number of trials may be required
- Level of heartbeat and sweat secretion variations among participants

Eye Tracking and Facial Expression Recognition

Although eye-tracking has been available as a data collection technique for a period of almost a century, its use in areas of marketing, tourism, and hospitality has been rather recent following the latest technological developments.

By measuring eye movements and pupil dilation through eye-tracking, the areas which the participant focused on in the visual exposed can be detected. Eye-tracking is generally used to measure consumers' interest, focusing level, and cognitive load 1 toward a particular visual material (Boz, 2015; Scott, Green, & Fairley, 2016). Levels of arousal can also be measured by using an eye tracker based on pupil dilation and eye movement data (Bradley, Miccoli, Escrig, & Lang, 2008).

As eye tracking the use of facial expression recognition has increased significantly over the past few years. Consumers' positive and negative feelings or emotions such as astonishment, anger, sadness, disgust, fear, happiness, as well as neutrality, can be measured concurrently through facial expression and facial muscles (zygomaticus minor and major muscles) (Boz, 2019). The measurement of numerous feelings and emotions through eye tracking and facial expression has contributed to the increasing use of these methods in research studies over the past few years. The advantages of eye tracking and facial expression are as follows (Boz, 2019):

- The best method to measure cognitive load with eye tracker
- Facial expression recognition can measure micro facial movements with high accuracy
- The visuals that the consumers paid attention to can be measured easily through an eye tracker.

However, eye tracking and facial recognition may have a number of disadvantages such as the following (Boz, 2019):

- They are expensive
- Studies may take long periods
- Researchers need to have expert knowledge in the use of these tools in research.

In a study conducted by Slanzi, Balazs, and Velasquez (2017), pupil dilations of customers were detected while they were making purchasing decisions. Slanzi et al.'s (2017) shed light on how consumers made their chokes. In a study carried out by Boz (2015) tourists who were exposed to holiday, adverts tended to focus more on people's faces and the discount rates, rather than the actual price information. It was seen that while tourists, in general, tended to read information written in bullet point form, they avoided reading texts written in long paragraphs.

In another study by Koc, Boz, and Boz (2019) that collected data by using eye-tracking and facial expression recognition, it was found that customers had a more positive attitude toward service failures rendered by more attractive tourism and hospitality staff.

Eye-tracking can also be used in other areas of business and management research such as human resource management and organizational behavior. A study by Boz and Yılmaz (2017) which eye-tracking and facial expression recognition found that when making recruitment decisions managers tended to concentrate more on photos of the candidates than information relating to their experience and skills.

The Use of Neuromarketing Tools in Hospitality and Tourism Research

This section explains how neuromarketing tools are used in tourism and hospitality settings by providing specific examples and applications. For the sample neuromarketing application in the study, www.tatilbudur.com (an online travel agency in Turkey) was used based on the permission granted by the business.

Fig. 5.   tatilbudur.com Web Site Header Banner -1- Heat Map and
Scan Path Analysis.

Fig. 5 shows the visual of the scan path and attention/heat map obtained via an eye-tracking device. A heat map in marketing research is used to identify where the participants in the study focused more intensely on the visual material. According to the example shown in Fig. 5, the viewers concentrated most intensively on the expression *"koşulsuz iptal (opportunity to cancel with no fees/ fines)"*.

In marketing research, a scan path analysis is usually used to measure the flow of the eye movements of the people who are exposed to visual stimuli. Accordingly, scan path analysis provides the sequence of the areas the viewers looked at in the visual stimuli. In the example (Fig. 5) the viewers first glanced at the center of the visual material. Later on, the third, fourth, fifth, sixth, seventh, eighth, and ninth glances moved around the *"45% discount/%45 indirim"* statement. As for the 10th glance, they moved around the *"last minute discount/son dakika indirim"* statement. The 11th and the 12th scan path movements, however, were on *koşulsuz iptal (opportunity to cancel with no fees/fines)* for a long period of time. However, it needs to be noted that about nearly 70% of the visual material was almost totally ignored. The watermelon visual in the visual material did not attract any attention. By examining the results of both scan path and heat map it may be recommended that the watermelon visual needs to be changed. Besides, since the center of the visual is viewed first, it is clear that moving the verbal statements toward the center of the visual could make perception the easier. In the meantime, since the *"opportunity to cancel with no fees/fines/koşulsuz iptal"* statement attracted a significant level of attention it may be helpful to use in other package holiday marketing communications materials as well. It can be seen that

Fig. 6.   tatilbudur.com Web Site Header Banner -2- Heat Map and
Scan Path Analysis.

the viewers of the visual spent most of their time on the "*koşulsuz iptal (oppor-tunity to cancel with no fees/fines)*" statement after examining the visual in 12 glances.

Fig. 6 demonstrates the visual of the scan path and attention/heat map obtained via an eye-tracking device. According to the test study, the areas where attention is most intense are the areas that contain the statements "last minute" and "50% discount" As for the third most attractive point, it is the visual of the rainbow-colored www.tatilbudur company logo. As a matter of fact, looking at the scan path analysis it is clear that the visual of the rainbow-colored www.ta-tilbudur logo appears to be the first visual element to attract people's attention. Hence, the bringing of the two centers of attention in the marketing stimuli may be recommended to increase the impact of the message conveyed.

In Fig. 7, the visual of scan path and attention/heat map obtained after showing the hotel advertisements on www.tatilbudur.com web site to viewers by using an eye-tracking device.

According to the scan path movements in the application, the attention of the viewers is scattered. According to the heat map and scan path movements, it can be seen that the advertisement at the bottom left corner of the visual was completely ignored as this advertisement did not contain any info on discounts. This means that discounts attract the attention of the customers. The heat map results show that discount rate information is the top criteria when comparing holiday advertisements. Again, as seen in the above visuals, the first thing the viewers were attracted to was the center of the visual material.

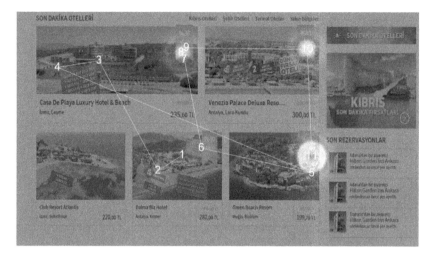

Fig. 7.   tatilbudur.com Web Site Hotel Comparison Heat Map and
Scan Path Analysis.

In Fig. 8 the scan path and attention/heat map of a hotel room are shown obtained by using an eye-tracking device. According to the scan path movements it can be seen that although the attention of the viewers is scattered over a large area, the outside view attracts more attention than the room itself. Also, the viewers' attention tends to focus on the lighting in the room as it is on, as opposed to the lighting in Fig. 9. The analysis of the scan path and attention/heat map

Fig. 8.   Hotel Room -1- Heat Map and Scan Path Analysis/
tatilbudur.com.

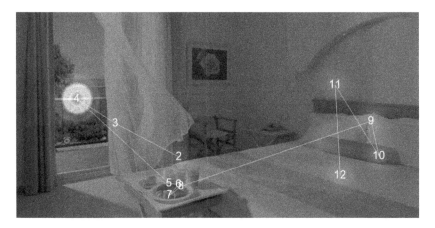

Fig. 9.   Hotel Room -2- Heat Map and Scan Path Analysis/
tatilbudur.com.

shows that the outside view is important, as viewers pay attention to pay more attention to the outside than the room itself. The hotels tend to spend a significant amount of money on the interiors of rooms. However, as the view from the room attracts more attention of the tourists, they need to need to make sure that the view from the room needs to be a nice one as well.

Fig. 9 shows the scan path and attention/heat map for another hotel room visual obtained by using an eye-tracking device. As in the above example (Fig. 8) the outside of the room attracted more attention than the room itself. The center of attention (heat map center) is the sea view. Also, the food and drinks appear to attract attention in the room. The remaining visual elements do not tend to attract the attention of the viewers.

In Fig. 10, there are written explanations regarding the details of services the hotel offers on the www.tatilbudur.com website. By looking at the data of the scan path and heat map movements, it can be seen that the attention of the viewers tends to be locked on the left-hand sand on a narrow strand. The analysis also shows while the viewers do not pay attention to texts written in paragraph form, they tend to pay attention to texts in bullet point form. Based on these visual proofs it may be recommended that the texts should be provided in short bullet points form, not in long paragraph form.

Fig. 11 shows the scan path and attention/heat map on a visual containing written statements. It can be seen that the attention of the viewers moves on a horizontal axis. According to the heat map and scan path movements, it is seen that the viewers looked at the general service evaluation score of the hotel (8.3 out of 10). At the opposite end of the visual material, "price/performance" score (75/100) of the hotel appears to attract a significant level of attention. However, it is interesting to see that the comments made by previous customers on the left were overlooked. This means that customers are interested in having short cuts in making their decisions.

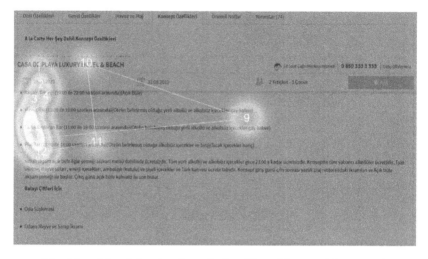

Fig. 10.   Hotel Service Description Heat Map and Scan Path
Analysis/tatilbudur.com.

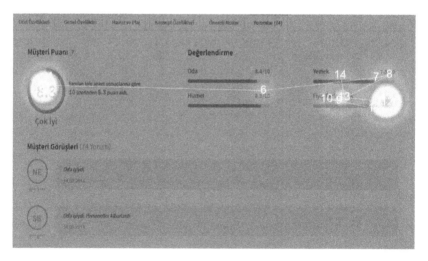

Fig. 11.   Hotel Service Description Heat Map and Scan Path
Analysis/tatilbudur.com.

Fig. 12 shows that the viewers mainly paid attention to the woman in the bikini in the visual holiday material. According to the heat map and scan path movements, the second attention-attracting stimulus is the "45% discount" statement on the top right corner of the visual. However, this time *"koşulsuz iptal (opportunity to cancel with no fees/fines)"* statement needs to be ignored.

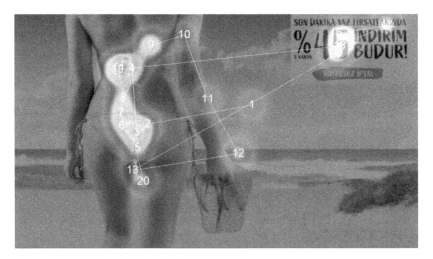

Fig. 12.　A Holiday Campaign Visual Heat Map and Scan Path
Analysis/freepic.com & tatilbudur.com.

Fig. 13 shows the results of the Area of Interest (AOI) analysis of a package holiday advertisement visual. In the AOI analysis, a visual is divided into parts and each part is analyzed separately in terms of the level of attention each part

Fig. 13.　A Holiday Campaign Visual Area of Interest Analysis/
freepic.com & tatilbudur.com.

attracts. The visual was viewed by the participants for a duration of 10 seconds in total. According to the analysis the female figure in the visual was viewed for 4.39 seconds (44% of the total time), while the visual on the top left corner was viewed for less than 1 second As for the remaining 5 seconds in the process of viewing it is noticed that there was no focusing on any item but a continuation of searching for information. By examining the analysis results it may be concluded that the sexy female figure took precedence over the message which was intended to be given. Therefore, it is recommended that the female figures need to be shown carefully in advertisements so as not to cause wastage in the advertisement budget.

Fig. 14 provides the AOI analysis results of the banner on the www.tatilbudur.com holiday website. It can be noticed that the "cancellation opportunity without no cancellation fees" statement was focused on for a period of 35 secs (35% of the total time) "45%, this is called discount" statement was focused for 24 secs (24% of the total time). On the other hand, while "last-minute discount" got 1.5-second attention, the watermelon and search for hotels sections in the visual were totally ignored. According to the results of this analysis, it would be useful to change places of the watermelon visual as well as the hotel search menu. Also, the color of the search button (yellow) (ARA) at the bottom right could be changed, as it did not seem to attract attention.

Fig. 15 shows the facial expression recognition, galvanic skin response, and heart rate data analysis results for three advertisement visuals. The analysis of the study shows that compared with the other two visuals the visual with the woman figure attracted more arousal and positive feelings.

Fig. 14.   tatilbudur.com Web Site Header Banner -1- Area of Interest Analysis.

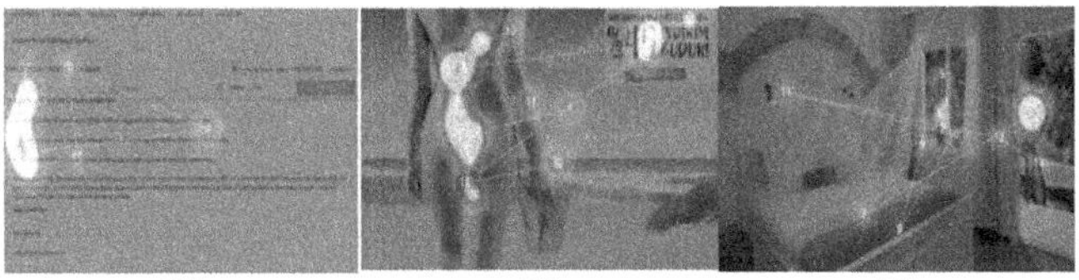

	Ad 1	Ad 2	Ad 3
Negative Feelings (Facial Expression Recognition)	0,11	0,37	0,22
Positive Feelings (Facial Expression Recognition)	0,16	0,08	0,09
Galvanic Skin Response (µS)	0,12	0,56	0,19
Heart Rate (Beat per min)	78	103	94

Fig. 15.   Facial and Vocal Expression Recognition Analysis. *Source:* freepic.com & tatilbudur.com.

When the results are examined it becomes clear that compared to the other two visuals, the visual with the woman aroused much more positive feelings. Also, there is similarity/consistency among the results obtained from all data collection methods.

Conclusions

As explained in the chapter traditional research methods such as surveys have important shortcomings and limitations, especially in the measurement of emotions and feelings. The chapter provided a basic framework on the most frequently used psychophysiological tools of research for researchers and practitioners interested in using methods other than the traditional methods. As explained above gleaning more realistic data about customers could help tourism and hospitality businesses to establish a competitive advantage.

This chapter has provided a basic framework for researchers and practitioners to understand neuromarketing applications in tourism and hospitality. The specific examples showed the outcomes produced by the neuromarketing and how they can be interpreted. However, despite their advantages, it needs to be kept in mind the neuromarketing tools have a number of disadvantages as well such as their cost, the level of expertise required to use these tools, and the limited number of subjects the applications could be used on.

Acknowledgments

The authors would like to thank free photo sharing websites of freepic.com (nensuria) "<a   href="https://www.freepik.com/free-photos-vectors/people">People   photo created by nensuria - www.freepik.com</a>" and pixabay.com for making photo available for free use. The authors also would like to thank HBlab for use of the neuromarketing devices and tools and General Manager Assistant of tatilbudur.com Mr Mustafa Kemal ÇUBUK.

References

Al-Kwifi, O. S. (2015). The impact of destination images on tourists' decision making. *Journal of Hospitality and Tourism Technology*, 6(2), 174–194.

Bastiaansen, M., Straatman, S., Driessen, E., Mitas, O., Stekelenburg, J., & Wang, L. (2018). My destination in your brain: A novel neuromarketing approach for evaluating the effectiveness of destination marketing. *Journal of Destination Marketing & Management*, 7, 76–88.

Boucsein, W. (2012). *Electrodermal activity* (2nd ed.). New York, NY and Berlin: Springer.

Boz, H. (2015). *Turistik ürün satın alma karar sürecinde itkiselliğin rolü: Psikonörobiyokimyasal analiz.* Unpublished Doctoral Thesis. Balikesir University, Institute of Social Sciences, Balikesir, Turkey.

Boz, H. (2019). Anchoring effect: A myth or reality?. *Ekonomik ve Sosyal Araştırmalar Dergisi*, 15(1), 33–47.

Boz, H., Arslan, A., & Koc, E. (2017). Neuromarketing aspect of tourism pricing psychology. *Tourism Management Perspectives*, 23, 119–128.

Boz, H., & Koc, E. (2019). Service quality, emotion recognition, emotional intelligence and Dunning Kruger syndrome. *Total Quality Management and Business Excellence*, 1–14.

Boz, H., & Yılmaz, Ö. (2017). An eye tracker analysis of the influence of applicant attractiveness on employee recruitment process: A neuromarketing study. *Ecoforum Journal*, 6(1), 1–6.

Bradley, M. M., Miccoli, L., Escrig, M. A., & Lang, P. J. (2008). The pupil as a measure of emotional arousal and autonomic activation. *Psychophysiology*, 45(4), 602–607.

Braidot, N. (2005). *Neuromarketing/neuroeconomia y negocios.* Madrid: E Puerto NORTE-SUR.

Căpătînă, G., & Drăghescu, F. (2015). Success factors of new product launch: The case of the iPhone launch. *International Journal of Economics and Finance*, 7(5), 61–70.

Cartocci, G., Caratù, M., Modica, E., Maglione, A. G., Rossi, D., Cherubino, P., & Babiloni, F. (2017). Electroencephalographic, heart rate, and galvanic skin response assessment for an advertising perception study: Application to anti-smoking public service announcements. *Journal of Visualized Experiments*, 126, e55872.

Charles, L., Joel, C., & Samwel, K. C. (2012). Market orientation and firm performance in the manufacturing sector in Kenya. *European Journal of Business and Management*, 4(10), 2222–2839.

Charron, S., Fuchs, A., & Oullier, O. (2008). Exploring brain activity in neuro-economics. *Revue d'Économie Politique*, 118(1), 97–124.

Chow, I. H. S., Lo, T. W. C., Sha, Z., & Hong, J. (2006). The impact of developmental experience, empowerment, and organizational support on catering service staff performance. *International Journal of Hospitality Management, 25*(3), 478–495.

Cooper, W. H. (1981). Ubiquitous halo. *Psychological Bulletin, 90*(2), 218–244.

Damasio, A. (1994). *Descartes' error: Emotion, reason, and the human brain.* New York, NY: Grosset/Putnam.

Damasio, A., & Carvalho, G. B. (2013). The nature of feelings: Evolutionary and neurobiological origins. *Nature Reviews Neuroscience, 14,* 143–152.

Dawes, R. M., & Smith, T. L. (1985). Attitude and opinion measurement. In G. Lindsay & E. Aronson (Eds.), *Handbook of social psychology* (3rd ed., Vol. 1, pp. 509–566). New York, NY: Random House.

Decrop, A., & Snelders, D. (2004). Planning the summer vacation: An adaptable process. *Annals of Tourism Research, 31*(4), 1008–1030.

Dehnavi, A., Amiri, M., DehKordi, P. H., & Heidary, A. (2012). On the multidimensionality of sport tourism: Challenges and guidelines. *International Journal of Academic Research in Business and Social Sciences, 6,* 105–110.

Drachen, A., Nacke, L. E., Yannakakis, G., & Pedersen, A. L. (2010, July). Correlation between heart rate, electrodermal activity and player experience in first-person shooter games. In *Proceedings of the 5th ACM SIGGRAPH symposium on video games* (pp. 49–54). Los Angeles, CA: Association for Computing Machinery (ACM).

Gladwell, M. (2005). *The power of thinking without thinking.* New York, NY: Little, Brown and Cie.

Grabe, M. E., Lang, A., Zhou, S., & Bolls, P. D. (2000). Cognitive access to negatively arousing news: An experimental investigation of the knowledge gap. *Communication Research, 27*(1), 3–26.

Greene, J. C., Caracelli, V. J., & Graham, W. F. (1989). Toward a conceptual framework for mixed-method evaluation designs. *Educational Evaluation and Policy Analysis, 11*(3), 255–274.

Gumenyuk, Y. (2020). Prospects for development of restaurant business in agrarian and industrial state. *Journal of European Economy, 18*(4), 466–477.

Hall, L., Johansson, P., Tärning, B., Sikström, S., & Deutgen, T. (2010). Magic at the marketplace: Choice blindness for the taste of jam and the smell of tea. *Cognition, 117*(1), 54–61.

Johansson, P., Hall, L., Sikström, S., & Olsson, A. (2005). Failure to detect mismatches between intention and outcome in a simple decision task. *Science, 310*(5745), 116–119.

Kahneman, D. (2003). Maps of bounded rationality: Psychology for behavioral economics. *The American Economic Review, 93*(5), 1449–1475.

Kahneman, D., & Tversky, A. (2000). *Choice, values, frames.* Cambridge: Cambridge University Press.

Kahnemann, D., & Tversky, A. (1979). Prospect theory: An analysis of decision under risk. *Econometrica, 47*(2), 263–291.

Klebba, J. M. (1985). Physiological measures of research: A review of brain activity, electrodermal response, pupil dilation, and voice analysis methods and studies. *Current Issues and Research in advertising, 8*(1), 53–76.

Koc, E. (2020). *Cross-cultural aspects of tourism and hospitality: A services marketing and management perspective.* London: Routledge.

Koc, E. (2021). Intercultural competence in tourism and hospitality: Self-efficacy beliefs and the Dunning Kruger effect. *International Journal of Intercultural Relations, 82*, 175–184.

Koc, E., & Boz, H. (2014a). Psychoneurobiochemistry of tourism marketing. *Tourism Management, 44*, 140–148.

Koc, E., & Boz, H. (2014b). Triangulation in tourism research: A bibliometric study of top three tourism journals. *Tourism Management Perspectives, 12*, 9–14.

Koc, E., & Boz, H. (2018). How can consumer science Be used for gaining information about consumers and the market?: The role of psychophysiological and neuro-marketing research. In *Case studies in the traditional food sector* (pp. 129–152). Cambridge: Woodhead Publishing.

Koc, E., Boz, H., & Boz, B. (2019). The influence of employee attractiveness on service recovery paradox: facial recognition and eye tracker analyses. *BRAIN. Broad Research in Artificial Intelligence and Neuroscience, 10*(3), 96–105.

Kroeber-Riel, W. (1979). Activation research: Psychobiological approaches in con-sumer research. *Journal of Consumer Research, 5*(4), 240–250.

Kumar, A., & Singh, G. (2019). Seasonal effect on tourism in India. *Journal of Finance and Economics, 7*(2), 48–51.

Lindstrom, M. (2011). *Buyolog: Satın Almaya Dair Bildiğimiz Her Şey Neden Yanlış?* İstanbul: Optimist Yayınları.

Li, S., Walters, G., Packer, J., & Scott, N. (2018). Using skin conductance and facial electromyography to measure emotional responses to tourism advertising. *Current Issues in Tourism, 21*(15), 1761–1783. Journal of Consumer Research.

Lopez, C. A. F., Li, G., & Zhang, D. (2020). Beyond technologies of electroencephalography-based brain-computer interfaces: A systematic review from commercial and ethical aspects. *Frontiers in Neuroscience, 14*, 1–23.

Luca, M. (2016, March 15). *Reviews, reputation, and revenue: The case of Yelp.com. Com* (pp. 12–16). Harvard Business School NOM Unit Working Paper.

Mihic, M., & Kursan, I. (2010). Assessing the situational factors and impulsive buying behavior: Market segmentation approach. *Journal of Management, 15*(2), 47–66.

Nagyová, Ĺ., Horská, E., Kretter, A., Kubicová, Ĺ., Košičiarová, I., Récky, R., … Holienčinová, M. (2014). *Marketing* (p. 460). Nitra: Slovak University of Agriculture.

Newstead, S. E., & Collis, J. M. (1987). Context and the interpretation of quantifiers of frequency. *Ergonomics, 30*(10), 1447–1462.

Oh, J. Y., & Schuett, M. A. (2010). Exploring expenditure-based segmentation for rural tourism: Overnight stay visitors versus excursionists to fee-fishing sites. *Journal of Travel & Tourism Marketing, 27*(1), 31–50.

Paulhus, D. L. (2002). Socially desirable responding: The evolution of a construct. In H. I. Braun, D. N. Jackson, & D. E. Wiley (Eds.), *The role of constructs in psy-chological and educational measurement* (pp. 49–72). London: Routledge.

Pearce, P. L., & Gretzel, U. (2012). Tourism in technology dead zones: Documenting experiential dimensions. *International Journal of Tourism Sciences, 12*(2), 1–20.

Powers, T. L., Kennedy, K. N., & Choi, S. (2020). Market orientation and perfor-mance: Industrial supplier and customer perspectives. *Journal of Business & Industrial Marketing.* Article in Press.

Pradeep, A. (2010). *The buying brain: Secrets for selling to the subconscious mind.* Hoboken, NJ: Wiley & Sons, Inc.

Raudenbush, B., & Capiola, A. (2012). Physiological responses of food neophobics and food neophilics to food and non-food stimuli. *Appetite*, *58*(3), 1106–1108.

Ravaja, N. (2004). Contributions of psychophysiology to media research: Review and recommendations. *Media Psychology*, *6*(2), 193–235.

Rosenthal, R., & Rosnow, R. L. (2008). *Essentials of behavioral research: Methods and data analysis* (3rd ed.). Boston, MA: McGraw-Hill.

Rothbart, M. W., Schwartz, A. E., Calabrese, T. D., Papper, Z., Mijanovich, T., Meltzer, R., & Silver, D. (2019). What a difference a grade makes: Evidence from New York city's restaurant grading policy. *Public Administration Review*, *79*(5), 651–665.

Ruff, ChC., & Huettel, S. A. (2014). Experimental methods in cognitive neuroscience. In P. W. Glimcher & E. Fehr (Eds.), *Neuroeconomics: Decision making and the brain* (pp. 77–108). London: Academic Press.

Schmidt, A., & Thews, G. (1989). Autonomic nervous system. In W. Janig (Ed.), *Human physiology* (2 ed., pp. 333–370). New York, NY: Springer-Verlag.

Scott, N., Green, C., & Fairley, S. (2016). Investigation of the use of eye tracking to examine tourism advertising effectiveness. *Current Issues in Tourism*, *19*(7), 634–642.

Slanzi, G., Balazs, J. A., & Velásquez, J. D. (2017). Combining eye tracking, pupil dilation and EEGanalysis for predicting web users click intention. *Information Fusion*, 35, 51–57.

Szameitat, A. J., Shen, S., & Sterr, A. (2009). The functional magnetic resonance imaging (fMRI) procedure as experienced by healthy participants and stroke patients–A pilot study. *BMC Medical Imaging*, *9*(1), 1–11.

Tao, J., & Tan, T. (2005). Affective computing: A review. In J. Tao, T. Tan, & R. Picard (Eds.), *Affective computing and intelligent interaction* (pp. 981–995). Berlin, Heidelberg: Springer.

Taşkın, Ç., Koç, E., & Boz, H. (2017). Perceptual image of conflict-ridden destinations: An EEG and eye tracker analysis. *Business and Economics Research Journal*, *8*(3), 533–553.

UNWTO. (2020). International tourism growth continues to outplace the global economy. Retrieved from https://unwto.org/international-tourism-growth-continues-to-outpace-the-economy

Whitley, B. E., Jr. (2002). *Principles of research in behavioral science* (2nd ed.). New York, NY: McGraw-Hill.

Wong, C. W., Olafsson, V., Plank, M., Snider, J., Halgren, E., Poizner, H., & Liu, T. T. (2014). Resting-state fMRI activity predicts unsupervised learning and memory in an immersive virtual reality environment. *PLoS One*, *9*(10), e109622.

Wu, C. H., Huang, Y. M., & Hwang, J. P. (2015). Review of affective computing in education/learning: Trends and challenges. *British Journal of Educational Technology*, *46*(5), 1–20.

Zurawicki, L. (2010). *Neuromarketing: Exploring the brain of the consumer*. Boston, MA: Springer Science & Business Media.

Chapter 6

Using Archival Material in Tourism, Hospitality, and Leisure Studies: Beauty and the Beast

Parisa Saadat Abadi Nasab, Neil Carr and Trudie Walters

Abstract

The aim of this chapter is to emphasize the importance of archival material and how, despite its secondary nature, it is capable of providing first-hand information for researchers. By providing a variety of examples from tourism, hospitality and leisure, this chapter demonstrates how this under-used data can be a valuable resource for these areas of study. In order to illustrate how to use archival material as data, a step-by-step process to analyzing archival photographs is provided. The chapter discusses the challenges and ethical considerations associated with using archival material while also providing suggestions for the use of this data source in future studies.

Keywords: Archival data; tourism; hospitality; leisure; photographs; ethics

Introduction

Archival research utilizes secondary data that may not have been developed for the specific purpose of a particular study (Jackson, 2006; Timothy, 2012). This means that archival research can be viewed as the recycling of existing data (Power, 2018) or the transformation of material into data. Conducting archival-based research is not a new trend. Rather, historians and researchers in other fields have used this type of material for research purposes for a long time. Although archival material is mainly associated with historical studies, archive-based studies are becoming more prevalent in multiple academic fields (Timothy, 2012), including tourism, hospitality, and leisure studies. It is important to recognize that historians identify archival material as primary, rather than

Advanced Research Methods in Hospitality and Tourism, 111–125
Copyright © 2023 Parisa Saadat Abadi Nasab, Neil Carr and Trudie Walters
Published under exclusive licence by Emerald Publishing Limited
doi:10.1108/978-1-80117-550-020221006

secondary, data. This highlights a blurred division between the two types of data, something that tends not to be acknowledged in social science studies.

Archival material appears in various shapes, such as diaries, postcards, birthday cards, newspapers, magazines, CD tracks, records, photographs, reports, social surveys, articles, memorabilia, scrapbooks, advertising materials, census records, business and national accounting records, TV broadcasts, letters, oral narratives, guidebooks, travel journals, and brochures, among others. Looking through these diverse information sources has the potential to enable us to understand historical problems, unfold important events, understand people's lives, and narrate stories (Timothy, 2012). Archival research is not about understanding the past. Instead, it can be argued that by developing understandings of the past we can aid predictions of the future and understandings of contemporary events and issues.

Despite popular belief, archival materials are not just dusty documents in dark and old libraries. Rather, it could simply be a photo from a happy group of friends shared in Instagram yesterday. Viewed from this perspective, archival materials could provide us with a myriad of opportunities. With specific reference to photographs, there is a vast archive of them available in hard and, increasingly, digital form in libraries and museums around the world waiting to be discovered. Aside from traditional sources, many photographs are now available online as people share their photographs in popular social network platforms such as Instagram and Facebook every day. In this context, it is important to recognize the social e-networks as an enormous repository of archival material, one which researchers are only just beginning to explore but have generally failed to recognize as being archival.

Partially as a consequence of the digitization of archival records and with the internet being a "virtual archive" (Margolis & Zunjarwad, 2018, p. 1072), archival research is being "discovered" by researchers from beyond the boundaries of history departments and related disciplines (Timothy, 2012). The beauty of working on archival material is the fact that, while not necessarily produced for the purpose of research, it has the potential to provide very important and interesting information for curious researchers interested in novelty and pushing the boundaries of knowledge. However, as Power (2018) points out, "archival research is a much underused yet tremendously attractive research strategy for qualitative tourism and hospitality research" (p. 231). As a result, the aim of this chapter is to take a critical look at archival material as a useful and interesting source of data in tourism, hospitality and leisure studies.

The chapter's main focus is on visual data (e.g., film, photography, and drawings), since the multidimensionality of such data makes it an even richer source than mere textual data. Despite the ubiquitous use of photography in tourism and hospitality, by all stakeholders, "current tourism research remains predominantly textocentric" (Balomenou & Garrod, 2019, p. 201). In order to gain a more comprehensive and nuanced understanding of the tourist experience, it is essential to use other sources of data. In this chapter, we present an overview of archival research in tourism, hospitality and leisure studies. The challenges and ethical considerations of this method are then discussed followed by a case study which acts as a "how-to" guide for analyzing visual archival material. Avenues for future research using visual archival material is also presented in the final section.

A Review of Tourism, Hospitality, and Leisure Studies Using Archival Material

In the last two decades, a growing number of researchers have used a variety of types of archival material to study tourism, hospitality and leisure. Using archival data in historical studies is a common way of thinking of archival research. There are also several tourism, hospitality, and leisure researchers who have adopted a historical approach, employing a series of documents available in libraries, museums, and other archives as their data source. For example, McAvoy, McDonald, and Carlson (2003) used documents in the British Columbia Provincial Archives located in Victoria, Canada, to describe historical relationships that the Nuu-chah-nulth people have with the parks and protected lands surrounding their communities and the governmental agencies that control these lands.

By focusing on the first two decades of the Gay Games (1982–1998), Davidson (2014) discussed how the early Games are a homonormative leisure formation seeking mainstream acceptance. Broadcast and print media are also a rich type of archival material which have the potential of being a useful source to study tourism and hospitality. They encompass the back issues of the world's newspapers and magazines that cover everything from ones about homes, fashion, hobbies, and sport, to sexual gratification (Walters & Duncan, 2015). Todorović and Bakir (2005), for instance, have used newspaper articles, web forums and television documentaries to focus on the *Academy* nightclub, its transformations and long-term impact on the Belgrade scene. In another study, Walters and Carr (2015) analyze both text and photographs in a New Zealand architecture and lifestyle magazine between 1936 and 2012 to assess the validity of traditional definitions of second homes. They found that second homes in New Zealand have always been a site for the consumption of luxury.

Using data from organizations and companies' archives is yet another type of archival research. This type of research tends to be quantitative and based on numerical annual reports. Almeida, Costa, and Nunes da Silva (2017) provide a documentary analysis of the Troia-Melides coastline to understand the tourism development versus land use planning conflicts. After analyzing data using content analysis, they were able to categorize conflicts in order to develop appropriate strategies for the purpose of conflict management. In another example, Connolly and Smale (2001) examined trends in financing for local recreational and cultural services between 1988 and 1996 in 19 municipalities in Ontario, Canada. Reis, Sousa-Mast, and Vieira (2013) used publicly available policy and planning documents from the websites of Brazilian ministries and departments which showed public policies play a role in facilitating access to sport and physical activities.

According to Jackson (2006), in general terms, archival material is a type of data which already exists before a given research project is started. In other words, it is not something the researcher collected themselves. Yet such a definition is stretched to breaking point when we realize how researchers are now utilizing ethnographic archival data. Kavanagh, Jones, and Sheppard-Marks (2016) used online ethnography, also known as netnography, for their research by examining a collection of existing tweets to find different types of abuse present in online environments. Markwell (2019) also explored his lifelong interest in amateur herpetology, a branch of zoology concerned with the study of amphibians, using an autoethnographic methodology by employing his own personal archive of photographs, letters, birthday cards, notebooks, newspaper clippings, and his short articles for newspapers and magazines that he wrote when he was a child.

Here we see the potential for the blurring of the distinction between archival material and the creation of new material that can potentially occur as archival material is transformed into data through the collection process. In this process, the physical nature of the material may not change, but the implied meaning of the data may. Jones and Denison (2019) narrative approach, based on stories written by the first author, a former football player, to provide a sociocultural reading of various challenges involved in the transition from exercise as a vocation to a leisure activity could also be considered as archival research. This is because those narratives already existed and were not specifically written for any research.

Oral history can be defined as knowledge about the past that is transferred from one generation to another through the use of word of mouth and/or recordings (Reilly, Freund, & Llewellyn, 2015). It can be focused around individuals, groups, societies, or lifestyles. Since it is a knowledge about the past and life histories coming from an "archival memory" (Cave, 2015, p. 96), oral history is also considered a type of archival material for research purposes. Such material has been utilized in tourism, hospitality, and leisure studies. For example, in conducting an oral testimony, Hodson (2018) attempted to broaden knowledge about post-war holidaymaking (c. 1950–1980) by studying the Isle of Man, a popular holiday resort from the late nineteenth century. Brydon, Jenzen, and Nourse (2019) also used oral history narratives, among other materials, to examine how British coastal resorts were not only important for tourists but also for the leisure activities of the young local population in the postwar era.

Other types of archival material which may be useful for researchers but have been less commonly utilized are CD tracks (Lashua, 2007), dance records (Snape, 2009), historical maps (Lashua, 2011), social media content (Navarro, Tschöke Santana, & Rechia, 2018), and guidebooks, travel journals, and postcards (Cleave, 2019) for example. Other types of archival material which may be useful for researchers but have been less commonly utilized are CD tracks (Lashua, 2007), dance records (Snape, 2009), historical maps (Lashua, 2011), guidebooks, and travel journals.

Yet it is necessary to recognize that the archival material collection process can in itself become a data source, questioning whether archival research can only be based on material that has been collected prior to the beginning of the research. In relation to this, and in tourism, hospitality and leisure context, family history enthusiasts spend significant amounts of time searching through and for archival material. One of the most useful and underused types of archival material is family album. Photographs are not just images, they are "social objects" (Edwards, 2005, p. 27). As such, they can provide social evidence and tell stories of human life that aid attempts to unearth the underlying meanings of events. One of the main reasons photographs may be of interest to researchers is what they can reveal about families (Bryman, 2012). Despite all these potential benefits, most archival family photographs (here family albums) remain untouched by researchers in general and tourism, hospitality and leisure researchers in particular. In the next section, challenges and ethical considerations for conducting archival material is presented in details.

Challenges and Ethical Considerations for Visual Archival Research

Each research brings its own challenges for the researcher and archival research is no exception. Using secondary data has some advantages for the researcher, such as potentially saving time and money (Bryman, 2012; Power, 2018; Saunders, Lewis, & Thornhill, 2012; Timothy, 2012), not being involved with participants (Power, 2018; Timothy, 2012), and the possibility of unforeseen discoveries (Saunders et al., 2012). However, there are many difficulties that researchers have to consider before, during and after data collection, and these are discussed below.

Before Data Collection

When deciding to work with archival material, researchers have to consider accessibility issues (Power, 2018; Saunders et al., 2012; Timothy, 2012), in terms of archives being open to the public (e.g., opening hours) and the restrictions on some materials. Therefore, researchers need to get the necessary permissions to access some data (e.g., restricted photographs) and adjust their time to the archives' opening hours. Another consideration is probable charges data owners may be make (Power, 2018; Saunders et al., 2012). Therefore, researchers need to ensure they have enough funds and time to conduct archival research. There is also, as noted earlier in this chapter, the need to recognize that no matter how well you prepare, it is only when you are actually in an archive that you will find what is actually in there. Records in many archives are inaccurate and incomplete. This is not a critique of archivists but a recognition of the underfunded nature of many archives.

During Data Collection

With the possibilities digitization brings, some archives are attempting to provide detailed information of their material online. Although this provides many opportunities, there is also a possibility of mismatching the available online data with the exact material at the archive. As a result, you have to be aware of what you are dealing with and make your final judgment when you are looking at the actual material. Remember that when you are working with old material in libraries, museums or other archives, they are most likely fragile objects. Therefore, you have to be extremely careful while touching and/or reproducing them.

After Data Collection (During Data Analysis)

The unknown world behind photographs and other archival material or, in other words, the lack of familiarity with data (Bryman, 2012) is a major challenge you have to deal with after your data collection phase. Although you may be aware of the general content of archival material, you may not be familiar with details. Therefore, you may have to spend extra time to become familiar with data. In relation to older material there may be no possibility of learning about it from those who produced it as they may have died or moved on. Even in the case of more contemporary archival material, the creator/s are often unknown and/or uncontactable. Quality of data may be a challenge for reading archival material, whether it be handwritten material or faded photographs or cine films. Old photographs were taken with primitive cameras and as producing photographs used to be an expensive procedure, people tended to keep all the photographs they took. Therefore, all photographs, regardless of their quality, were considered as precious objects. The interpretation of such photographs may be further hampered by the quality of captions associated with them. Deterioration in the quality of photographs and associated captions occurs over time because of chemical interactions between the photo paper, ink, and general environment.

Because of the subjectivity of archival data interpretation, which (Timothy, 2012) considers to be a disadvantage of using this type of data, researchers need to employ necessary procedures to ensure rigor of their analysis while avoiding any bias. Yet such procedures are arguably no different from those required of any qualitative study. Indeed, even quantitative research based on positivistic foundations is not immune to problems of rigor and bias.

Data protection considerations (Power, 2018) are another element you have to be mindful of before, during and after data collection. Such considerations are especially important when working with archival materials, which are sensitive either in terms of physical properties (e.g. old and fragile photographs) or their content (e.g. photographs of children). This leads to ethical considerations.

Ethical Considerations

Being ethical when using archival material is very important, especially when people are represented in them. In some instances, archival photographs may be unpublished. Thus, there is a need for the researcher to maintain confidentiality. Even when the material is published we must consider whether using it for a different purpose (e.g., research) absolves researchers of the need to preserve confidentiality. While not an ethical consideration, researchers must also be mindful of copyright when using photographs or other archival materials. When researchers have decided to collect archival material from libraries and public archives, there is a need to discuss all considerations with the curators and obtain all necessary permissions.

Ethical considerations can appear to be even trickier when collecting material from personal archives. Here there is no archival curator to advise researchers and enforce rules. Specifically, as family photographs are an important part of every family, and for some the most important treasure, researchers must be extremely careful about how to collect, preserve and use such data. The first step is to reassure the research participants or the owners of photographs, or other archival material such as diaries, that their assets will be taken care of during the data collection and analysis process. Also, after the data collection phase, preserving any reproduced materials, often as digital files, is highly important. The researcher needs to assure participants that confidentiality will be maintained throughout all research stages. Informed consent should be obtained about the possibility of any other use of photographs, such as publication in journal articles in the future. Researchers also have to remind participants that the anonymity of any people captured in the photographs, or other archival material, will be guaranteed. Yet this process is not without complications – the people who created the material or are featured in it may no longer be alive or may not, if very young, be in a position to give permission to use, or not use, the material. Such discussions are being undertaken in relation to the rights and empowerment of children in research in general and family studies in particular (see Carr (2011) for a discussion of this issue).

There are ample opportunities to study many types of archival material, including family photographs. However, alongside these opportunities are responsibilities, especially when photographs include sensitive material, such as depictions of children. Researchers must ensure that these photographs and the albums in which they are situated are archived safely, in a way that ensures they can only be accessed in a responsible manner. Responsibility is, therefore, key in this discussion of ethical consideration. As archivists and researchers, we have a strong responsibility to those who donate their archival material to us and to those who appear in it. How we store and enable access to this material, how we interpret it, and how we, as researchers, utilize it in our research outputs is crucial. Irrespective of whether the owner of, or the people in, the material are still alive, we have a responsibility to take care of the material. We must also cause no harm through our distribution and use of the material.

In the next section, we provide an example of a longitudinal study using thematic analysis to analyze family albums in order to examine changes in family relationships and functioning within the leisure context. The study was conducted between 2017 and 2021. Family albums were collected from the Hocken Library archive in Dunedin (1896–1955) and private family albums (1955–2018). After excluding irrelevant photographs, 4,700 images were analyzed. Recognizing the importance of family and how families function within the context of leisure, this research provides a nuanced way to examine family relations by using archival family photographs, acknowledging the usefulness of archival material and family photographs. It is worth mentioning that although this example focuses on the leisure context, the method is equally applicable to studies within the fields of tourism and hospitality.

Analyzing Archival Photographs Using Visual Thematic Analysis: A Stepwise Example

Phase One: Simultaneous Data Collection and Data Analysis to Be Familiar with Data

Data collection and data analysis were conducted simultaneously (Sather-Wagstaff, 2011). Interesting points about family activities in their leisure time, such as horseback riding, skating, skiing, picnicking, hunting, mountaineering, being at the beach, traveling, and walking, were written down in a notebook in bullet points as a first step toward familiarization with the data. The purpose of the research necessitated a historical look at the data. Therefore, data and all related interesting points were purposefully categorized into different decades (e.g. 1900s, 1910s, etc.). Later, these notes were transferred into a Word document to make working with them easier in later stages of analysis (see Table 1 for an example).

A thematic analysis approach was adopted. The essential purpose of thematic analysis is to search for patterns or themes within the dataset. It offers a systematic yet flexible approach to analyzing qualitative data (Braun & Clarke, 2006). As it provides an orderly and logical process to analyze qualitative data it can be used to analyze large qualitative datasets, which makes it an appropriate tool for this study. Although thematic analysis has broadly been used for text-based data, including that generated through focus groups and interviews, some researchers have applied it to visual media (Walters, 2019; Walters & Carr, 2015). As Sather-Wagstaff (2011) mentioned, qualitative data analysis should ideally be flexible and customizable to a given research project rather than follow strict protocols. Therefore, every researcher should be able to modify the method to best suit their research purposes, aims and questions. Consequently, in the current example a modified version of thematic analysis, inspired by Attride-Stirling (2001), Braun and Clarke (2006), Sather-Wagstaff (2011) and (Walters, 2016) was deployed.

Phase Two: Repeated Reading to Write Preliminary Interpretations as Codes

Codes are features of data that appear interesting to the analyst (Braun & Clarke, 2006), and coding is a way to divide the data into manageable and meaningful

Table 1. 1920s Interesting Points.

• Family leisure activities (at the beach, picnicking, at the river, around the house gatherings)
• Women leisure activities (tea party, garden party, tramping, walking)
• Men leisure activities (hunting, mountaineering, camping)

Source: Developed by the authors.

segments. Creswell (2013) believes that codes developed from data should include the surprising, unusual and interesting, as well as the common. Interesting points about the albums were written down simultaneously with data collection. After looking through the albums, it was clear that individual photographs should not be the unit of data to be analyzed. Rather, the main unit of data for the research should be the whole album. The rationale for this is twofold. First, in each family album photographs are combined to tell a story, in addition to carrying a meaning of their own. Second, it was often impossible to judge whether a single photograph was taken in leisure time or not. Therefore, the best way to look at photographs was to have a holistic view of each album and let the whole album represent the information to the reader.

As the material to be analyzed for this study was, therefore, not an individual photograph, it was impossible to code each photograph. To overcome this challenge, there was a need to transform album stories into text and then continue with further steps of thematic analysis. Auerbach and Silverstein (2003) recommend that keeping a copy of your main study concerns, such as goals, questions and frameworks, in front of you while coding, helps to focus your coding decisions. The interpretation of each album was written down in the shape of narratives to give a holistic view of what was going on in each album and across all the albums in each decade (see Table 2 for an example). Saldaña (2016) also recommends that the best way to analyze visual data is through an interpretive, holistic lens guided by strategic questions rather than one word or phrase codes. In the case of this study, at first the notes were detailed and long, but codes were subsequently shaped into shorter phrases.

Phase Three: Categorizing Similar Codes

At this stage the familiarization with data was accomplished by looking through albums several times and a written document of interpretations of each decade was also prepared. Having created a long list of codes, it was time to analyze them and consider how they may be combined to form basic themes (Braun & Clarke, 2006). All codes that seemed similar were collated together to shape the candidate themes (see Table 3 for an example).

Table 2. Narratives of Albums from the 1910s.

• Women doing more separate leisure activities such as tramping, hiking and tennis
• Most of leisure activities are happening around the house- gardening, sitting on the porch or in the garden- poor transportation?

Source: Developed by the authors.

Table 3.   Collated and Combined Codes – Prior to World War II.

- Women in charge of children in picnics
- Children are appearing in garden and tea parties with their mothers
- Women in charge of food distribution and preparation
- Children are excluded from adult activities
- Children are not at the center of attention in photographs

Source: Developed by the authors.

Phase Four: Reviewing Themes

After identifying the basic themes, phase four begins with refinement of candidate themes (Braun & Clarke, 2006). At this stage, each organizing theme should be checked for coherency and consistency by reviewing codes that make up the themes (Walters, 2016). By reviewing the themes and previous codes it seemed evident that some themes needed to be collated to shape higher-level themes that share similarities (see Fig. 1 for an example).

Phase Five: Defining Themes

This phase of thematic analysis is concerned with further refining the developed themes (Braun & Clarke, 2006). Since this is a longitudinal study that illustrates changes over time, the best way to present the findings is in a linear manner that makes the findings easy to follow and illustrative. Therefore, it made sense to

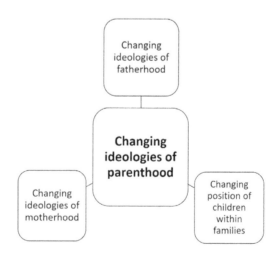

Fig. 1.   Reorganized Preliminary Themes to Shape Higher Level Themes. *Source:* Developed by the authors.

break down the data within each theme chronologically. Based on the insights gained from the preliminary readings of the data, it became apparent that in certain periods historical happenings influenced, if not determined, social norms and families. Therefore, data were organized according to historical phases (see Table 4 for an example).

Phase Six: Defining and Reporting Themes

The last phase of thematic analysis is about deriving the global theme in a way that is transparent and easy to understand (Walters, 2016). The final report should be written in a way that tells the complicated story of the data in a way that conveys the validity of the analysis to the reader (Braun & Clarke, 2006) and responds to the research question (Attride-Stirling, 2001). At this stage, everything was written in a chronological order to make sure that sufficient evidence was available from data and the final themes are capable of telling the story behind the data in a coherent and understandable way. Fig. 2 presents all of the themes identified from the full analysis of the archival photograph data set.

Conclusions and Recommendations

Despite all the challenges associated with conducting archival research, such research can be very rewarding. With specific reference to photographs, each one has a story to tell and has recorded a moment of time loaded with meaning, giving the researcher an opportunity to extract insights about that particular moment, its social construction and the individuals both in the picture and behind the camera. In particular, family snapshots are records of human life and events, through which researchers can explore how individual and family behavior constantly changes. Yet it is not only photographs that are a rich potential source of archival material. As this chapter has highlighted, archival material comes in a vast array of types and can encompass a long period of time, beginning today and heading backwards. Archival material can literally be based around all of the human senses. As such it can be verbal, visual, tactile, olfactory, and gustatory. All of this material can have a role to play in developing our understandings of leisure, in the past, the present, and into the future. Yet, as pointed out in this chapter, perhaps the best way to experience this material is not to attack it with preconceived aims

Table 4. An Example of Defining Themes.

• Changing ideologies of fatherhood
• From 1896 to 1940: Gendered Roles in Life and Leisure
• From 1940 to the mid-1960s: Rising Family Leisure Consumption
• From the 1960s to the 1970s: Visible and Involved Fathers
• From the 1980s to 2018: Purposive Fathers

Source: Developed by the authors.

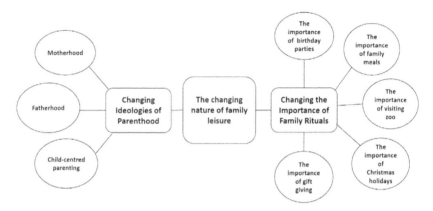

Fig. 2.   Visual Network of Final Themes Identified in the Analysis.
Source: Developed by the authors.

and objectives. Rather, given the richness of archival material and its propensity to deliver the unexpected it is better to engage with it without predetermined ideas.

If we approach archival material with an open mind there is little point in then identifying numerous ways such material could be used to answer research questions. Rather, it is best to simply say that if researchers are willing to meet the imaginative challenge that archival research at its best can be then there are myriad issues related or central to leisure that can be explored by utilizing it. What those are become limited only by the imagination of the researcher and their creative ability to unearth archival material.

Yet researchers can only unearth archival material that exists. Finding archival material in formal repositories like the national archives that many countries maintain is relatively easy, even if there are still discrepancies between the records of these archives and what is actually found in the boxes. Basically, the larger the funds associated with an archive the smaller this gap will be. However, many archives are maintained on shoestring budgets or by volunteers. Yet all of these archives are at least places where the survival of the material is assured.

Beyond these archives is a vast treasure trove of archival material that is not protected at all or whose ongoing survival is at the whim of whoever is in charge on the day. Individual companies sometimes maintain an archive of their history which may seem secure but as soon as the business goes into liquidation this certainty evaporates. An example of this relates to the insolvency of the world's oldest travel agency, Thomas Cook, in 2019. Thomas Cook had maintained a rich archive of the business stretching back to 1845. With the liquidation of Thomas Cook came the threat of the loss of the company's archive. As a result, in the immediate aftermath of the collapse of the company historians, archivists, and tourism academics from around the world have had to scramble to ensure the survival of the archive as an intact unit.

At the time of writing this chapter the outcome of this attempt is unknown. While there is still a good chance that the Thomas Cook archive will be preserved in a state that continues to enable researchers to access it the same cannot be said for other material that has already been lost. The second author, given his research interests, has periodically knocked on the doors of a variety of zoos, as leisure and tourism attractions, to enquire if they have an archive of the materials they have produced over the duration of their existence. So far, this search has found that London Zoo has a very good, if incomplete, archive. At the opposite end of the scale he has arrived at a zoo, which will remain nameless, to be told that all the marketing material (stretching back over 100 years) was placed in a landfill site a year or two before his visit. That this zoo was located only a couple of miles from a national archive center only makes this discovery more depressing.

Other zoos he has visited have presented him with rooms filled with dusty boxes filled with a pick-and-mix assortment of historical material, all of which is obviously only one step away from the bin if a "useful" purpose for the space the boxes are currently occupying ever comes up. It is these archives, unknown treasure troves all, that we need to seek out and help to preserve because once they are gone, there is no getting them back. Yet while it is easy to criticize those who throw away historical material it is equally easy to understand why they do so. Keeping this material and maintaining it so that it does not degrade to the point where it becomes useless is an expensive task and therefore we see constant questions being asked about what is "worthy" of being kept. If leisure studies academics do not engage in archival research, then they cannot help inform discussions of what should be kept and therefore cannot complain when something is not kept.

References

Almeida, J., Costa, C., & Nunes da Silva, F. (2017). A framework for conflict analysis in spatial planning for tourism. *Tourism Management Perspectives*, *24*, 94–106. doi: 10.1016/j.tmp.2017.07.021

Attride-Stirling, J. (2001). Thematic networks: An analytic tool for qualitative research. *Qualitative Research*, *1*(3), 385–405.

Auerbach, C. F., & Silverstein, L. B. (2003). *Qualitative data: An introduction to coding and analysis*. New York, NY: New York University Press.

Balomenou, N., & Garrod, B. (2019). Photographs in tourism research: Prejudice, power, performance and participant-generated images. *Tourism Management*, *70*, 201–217.

Braun, V., & Clarke, V. (2006). Using thematic analysis in psychology. *Qualitative Research in Psychology*, *3*(2), 77–101.

Brydon, L., Jenzen, O., & Nourse, N. (2019). Our pier': Leisure activities and local communities at the British seaside. *Leisure/Loisir*, *43*(2), 205–228.

Bryman, A. (2012). *Social research methods* (4th ed.). New York, NY: Oxford University Press.

Carr, N. (2011). *Children's and families' holiday experiences.* Abingdon, Oxon: Routledge.

Cave, M. (2015). What remains: Reflections on crisis oral history. In R. Perks & A. Thomson (Eds.), *The oral history reader.* London: Taylor & Francis.

Cleave, P. (2019). Food as a leisure pursuit, a United Kingdom perspective. *Annals of Leisure Research, 23*(4), 474–491.

Connolly, K., & Smale, B. J. A. (2001). Changes in the financing of local recreation and cultural services: An examination of trends in Ontario from 1988 to 1996. *Leisure/Loisir, 26*(3–4), 213–234.

Creswell, J. W. (2013). *Qualitative inquiry and research design: Choosing among five approaches* (2rd ed. ed.). Thousand Oaks, CA: SAGE.

Davidson, J. (2014). Racism against the abnormal? The twentieth century Gay games, biopower and the emergence of homonational sport. *Leisure Studies, 33*(4), 357–378.

Edwards, E. (2005). Photographs and the sound of history. *Visual Anthropology Review, 21*(1–2), 27–46.

Hodson, P. (2018). The 'Isle of vice'? Youth, class and the post-war holiday on the Isle of Man. *Cultural and Social History, 15*(3), 433–451.

Jackson, S. L. (2006). *Research methods and statistics: A critical thinking approach* (2nd ed.). Belmont, CA: Thomson Wadsworth.

Jones, L., & Denison, J. (2019). Jogging not running: A narrative approach to exploring 'exercise as leisure' after a life in elite football. *Leisure Studies, 38*(6), 831–844.

Kavanagh, E., Jones, I., & Sheppard-Marks, L. (2016). Towards typologies of virtual maltreatment: Sport, digital cultures & dark leisure. *Leisure Studies, 35*(6), 783–796.

Lashua, B. D. (2007). Making an album: Rap performance and a 'CD track listing' as performance writing in the beat of Boyle street music programme. *Leisure Studies, 26*(4), 429–445.

Lashua, B. D. (2011). An atlas of musical memories: Popular music, leisure and urban change in liverpool. *Leisure/Loisir, 35*(2), 133–152.

Margolis, E., & Zunjarwad, R. (2018). Visual research. In N. K. Denzin & Y. S. Lincoln (Eds.), *The Sage handbook of qualitative research* (5th ed.). Los Angeles, CA: Sage.

Markwell, K. (2019). Relating to reptiles: An autoethnographic account of animal-leisure relationships. *Leisure Studies, 38*(3), 341–352.

McAvoy, L., McDonald, D., & Carlson, M. (2003). American Indian/first nation place attachment to park lands: The case of the Nuu-chah-nulth of British Columbia. *Journal of Park and Recreation Administration, 21*(2), 84–104.

Navarro, R. T., Tschöke Santana, D., & Rechia, S. (2018). Public leisure space and community-based action. *Leisure Studies, 37*(6), 747–762.

Power, S. (2018). Findings from the treasure chest: Conducting archival research in tourism and hospitality. In R. Nunkoo (Ed.), *Handbook of research methods for tourism and hospitality management.* Northampton, MA: Edward Elgar Publishing.

Reilly, N., Freund, A., & Llewellyn, K. R. (2015). *The Canadian oral history reader.* Montreal, QC: Montreal McGill-Queen's University Press.

Reis, A. C., Sousa-Mast, F. R., & Vieira, M. C. (2013). Public policies and sports in marginalised communities: The case of Cidade de Deus, Rio de Janeiro, Brazil. *World Leisure Journal*, *55*(3), 229–251.

Saldaña, J. (2016). *The coding manual for qualitative researchers* (3rd ed.). Los Angeles, CA: SAGE.

Sather-Wagstaff, J. (2011). Beyond content: Thematic, discourse-centred qualitative methods for analysisng visual data. In T. Rakic & D. Chambers (Eds.), *Introduction to visual research methods in tourism* (1st ed.). New York, NY: Taylor & Francis.

Saunders, M., Lewis, P., & Thornhill, A. (2012). *Research methods for business students* (6th ed.). London: Pearson.

Snape, R. (2009). Continuity, change and performativity in leisure: English folk dance and modernity 1900–1939. *Leisure Studies*, *28*(3), 297–311.

Timothy, D. J. (2012). Archival research. In L. Dwyer, A. Gill, & N. Seetaram (Eds.), *Handbook of research methods in tourism: Quantitative and qualitative approaches*. Cheltenham: Edward Elgar Publishing.

Todorović, M., & Bakir, A. (2005). Inaudible noise: Belgrade's academy club: Legacy, old locals and new spaces. *Leisure Studies*, *24*(4), 415–434.

Walters, T. (2016). Using thematic analysis in tourism research. *Tourism Analysis*, *21*(1), 107–116.

Walters, T. (2019). Visual representations of place: The id fashion show and the "Dunedin look". *Event Management*, *23*(2), 191–206.

Walters, T., & Carr, N. (2015). Second homes as sites for the consumption of luxury. *Tourism and Hospitality Research*, *15*(2), 130–141.

Walters, T., & Duncan, T. (2015). Non-tourism magazines as sources of material in tourism research. *Anatolia*, *26*(2), 306–308.

Chapter 7

Tourism Online Reviews: Databases and Samples

Juan Pedro Mellinas and Eva Martin-Fuentes

Abstract

Millions of ratings and reviews about products are available on the Internet
for free, and they are used by academic researchers in the tourism sector.
Data from websites like TripAdvisor are replacing or complementing
traditional questionnaires and interviews. The authors are proposing a
methodology to estimate the percentage accounted for by the sample of
self-interviewed individuals over the total study population, in order to
calculate the reliability of the results obtained. Average percentages obtained
for hotels cannot be easily generalized due to the high dispersion in participation rates among hotels, even in the same city. Participation levels for
tourist attractions are substantially lower than those for hotels and are likely
biased, due to the fact that some tourists evaluate places without actually
visiting them, merely after viewing them from the outside.

Keywords: Tourism; reviews; sample; TripAdvisor; reliability; eWOM;
databases

Introduction

Web 2.0, introduced at the beginning of this century (O'reilly, 2005), opened the
doors for the contribution of content by users, so-called user-generated content
(UGC), and electronic word of mouth (eWOM). Vast databases emerged on the
Internet offering millions of ratings and reviews about products and services, free
of charge. Scholars studying consumer behavior were particularly enthusiastic
about this opportunity, and it attracted a great deal of excitement and attention
(Hidalgo, 2014).

Online reviews are a form of market research that does not require active
collection of data from primary sources. Instead, content available is to anyone
online and can be downloaded. Academic researchers in the tourism sector have

Advanced Research Methods in Hospitality and Tourism, 127–143
Copyright © 2023 Juan Pedro Mellinas and Eva Martin-Fuentes
Published under exclusive licence by Emerald Publishing Limited
doi:10.1108/978-1-80117-550-020221007

adopted this resource as it provides reviews about destinations, restaurants, hotels, theme parks, museums, airlines, etc. on websites such as TripAdvisor and HolidayCheck. Traditional questionnaires and interviews are being replaced with online reviews (Stanisic, 2016), with sophisticated software being used to download millions of reviews in a short period of time (Radojevic, Stanisic, & Stanic, 2015). Currently, TripAdvisor is the most popular source of online review data in tourism research (Li, Xu, Tang, Wang, & Li, 2018), which can be explained by the 830 million reviews stored in its database (TripAdvisor, 2019). TripAdvisor collects reviews from users that voluntarily decide to fill out a survey on its website or app, providing a sample of the visitors to a tourist spot, a restaurant, or accommodation. However, TripAdvisor does not provide basic information that is expected when conventional research is performed using surveys. There is no information on the size of the population on which the study was conducted, so it is not possible to calculate the reliability of the results obtained, such as confidence intervals and so on. Furthermore, there is no information on sample design and the possible biases that this could entail.

Frequently, hundreds or thousands of reviews are obtained about a single place, assuming without discussion or justification that the sample is representative. Some authors describe a sample of places, but there are few references to the fact that they are using a sample of individuals (those who have written reviews) in relation to the universe of users who visit the place. Applying scientific rigor, the percentage represented by the sample of self-interviewed individuals in relation to the total study population should be indicated. Surprisingly, the academic community has shown little concern toward or interest in this matter, publishing hundreds of articles without any reference to what, at least, should be noted as a limitation of their research.

To the authors' knowledge, there is only one academic article that deals with this problem. It is an initial attempt to identify the percentage of users who write reviews on websites, using a sample of 200 urban hotels in Spain in 2017 (Mellinas, 2019b). The figures obtained showed around 2% participation on TripAdvisor, but with large variations between hotels.

Using online reviews is a research methodology for hospitality and tourism which, as we will see in the subsequent sections, has gained great importance in recent years in terms of the number of articles published. However, we consider that research into this matter remains scarce, and the small sample of urban hotels studied in Spain remains unsatisfactory. It is necessary to perform a deeper study into the method itself, hence we are proposing to expand the study to a wider sample of hotels and other types of tourist attractions that are also evaluated on TripAdvisor (museums, theme parks, water parks, and observation decks).

First, we used a sample of hotels in 17 major European cities. Second, we conducted a completely new study that seeks to calculate the percentage of visitors to 100 tourist sites reviewed on TripAdvisor. The data obtained will indicate whether the typology or locations of these tourist spots determine different percentages of participation on TripAdvisor and whether the resulting percentages are similar to those shown for accommodation.

Literature Review

Internet Data Representativeness

The use of online reviews for market research in the field of consumer behavior has a number of pros and cons, as reported by Schegg and Fux (2010). The advantages are reduced costs, competitor analysis opportunities, and no interviewer biases, while the disadvantages are problems with representativeness, individualization, and lack of experience in these methodologies.

Web-based surveys have been criticized for their low Internet coverage, inflexible orders of questions, IT-related anxiety, different screen formats, technical and interface problems, reluctance of older people to respond to online surveys, perceptions of surveys as junk mail, the skewed nature of the Internet population, and privacy and security concerns (Hung & Law, 2011). It should be noted that some of these limitations were identified in the first decade of the twenty-first century, and, to a greater or lesser extent, the increasing use of the Internet and the emergence of smartphones have minimized them.

Representativeness is perhaps the most cited concern by academics analyzing the use of these methodologies via online reviews. The only people whose behavior and opinions are represented in the study are the people who decide to write reviews on a website. When millions of users are represented in a dataset, one may be inclined to think that results can be generalized due to the sheer number of observations, ignoring possible biases (Hargittai, 2015).

It is widely acknowledged that difficulties in implementing traditional offline surveys can lead to inaccuracies and biases. Discussions in this field have focused on deciding whether online surveys pose more problems than offline surveys, and whether differences are obtained in the results according to the methodology followed. While some scholars found differences between online and offline surveys (Cobanoglu, Moreo, & Warde, 2001; Cole, 2005; Dolnicar, Laesser, & Matus, 2009; Schegg & Fux, 2010), others reported no significant differences (Braunsberger, Wybenga, & Gates, 2007; Deutskens, De Ruyter, & Wetzels, 2006). One of the previously cited papers focusing on the tourism sector reported that neither online surveys nor offline surveys via traditional mail are unbiased: "Format-specific self-selection of respondents to participate leads to systematic biases in both cases" (Dolnicar et al., 2009).

Use of Databases in Tourism

There is extensive literature about the importance of UGC and its impact on consumer decisions about tourism destinations and accommodation (Dellarocas, 2003; Gretzel & Yoo, 2008; Schuckert, Liu, & Law, 2015; Vermeulen & Seegers, 2009), which address this new phenomenon from different viewpoints. The importance of the ratings and content of reviews, together with the aforementioned ease of access to online databases, has led to the proliferation of dozens of publications that use a methodology based on the collection of online reviews to conduct research on traveler behavior and satisfaction (Cantallops & Salvi, 2014;

Kwok, Xie, & Richards, 2017; Schuckert et al., 2015). Schuckert et al. (2015) identified 50 online review-related articles published in academic journals between 2004 and 2013. Kwok et al. (2017), with the most up-to-date compilation (up to July 2015), reported 67 research articles about online reviews in seven major hospitality and tourism journals.

A search on Google Scholar using the words "tripadvisor reviews" (limiting the results to 2019) shows dozens of papers whose abstracts mention that they used information from TripAdvisor reviews in their research. Similar results can be obtained when searching for "booking.com reviews" or "expedia reviews". By conducting a search in Tourism Management for 2019 using the word "tripadvisor", we identified 34 articles that mention this website. A detailed analysis of each of them shows that nine use a methodology based on the collection of TripAdvisor reviews of hotels, attractions, and museums (Bi, Liu, Fan, & Zhang, 2019; Francesco & Roberta, 2019; Gerdt, Wagner, & Schewe, 2019; Hu, Teichert, Liu, Li, & Gundyreva, 2019; Hu, Zhang, Gao, & Bose, 2019; Kirilenko, Stepchenkova, & Hernandez, 2019; Liu, Huang, Bao, & Chen, 2019; Taecharungroj & Mathayomchan, 2019; Woodman, Min-Venditti, Woosnam, & Brightsmith, 2019).

Big data is characterized by the four versus – value, volume, variety, and velocity – although the term does not have a single definition (Li et al., 2018), and understanding of the concept varies among authors (Hargittai, 2015). In this sense, some academics have taken advantage of the possibilities offered by TripAdvisor to obtain databases that undoubtedly hold a large volume of data: 17,925 hotels in 373 destinations (9,021,348 reviews) (Mellinas & Martin-Fuentes, 2019); 10,149 hotels in five Chinese cities (412,784 reviews) (Liu, Teichert, Rossi, Li, & Hu, 2017); and 69,997 hotels worldwide (8,812,826 reviews) (Martin-Fuentes, Mateu, & Fernandez, 2018). The complexity involved in handling such a vast amount of information may be lesser or greater, depending on whether only global information is collected from each hotel (number of reviews, location, star rating, global rating, rating for specific features, among others) or whether the details of each of the reviews are recorded, including the entire text written by the user.

Requested or Spontaneous Reviews

When a traveler makes a reservation through an OTA (Expedia, Booking.com, Agoda, etc.), a few days after the stay he receives an email inviting him to fill out a survey about the stay. TripAdvisor does not perform the same process, since it has no record of who has stayed at a hotel or their email address. Instead, TripAdvisor recommends owners of tourist establishments to encourage their customers to write reviews on their website through direct action at their premises or by sending emails after the customer's stay.

To encourage owners to collaborate in the task of promoting reviews, TripAdvisor argues that increasing the number of reviews increases the average score of a hotel (TripAdvisor, 2014), according to an academic article that came to this conclusion (Melián-González, Bulchand-Gidumal, & González López-Valcárcel, 2013). However, the main argument used by TripAdvisor concerns the influence of the number of reviews on hotel rankings. TripAdvisor explains that its popularity index algorithm is based on the quantity, quality and recency of reviews that a business receives on TripAdvisor (TripAdvisor, 2016). An increase in an establishment's scores is often related to an improvement in its services and facilities, which usually implies financial investment. However, increasing the number of reviews can be much easier and more affordable.

Hotels placed at the top of the rankings are considered more attractive than those in lower positions (Filieri & McLeay, 2014; Spoerri, 2008), and hotels can even be ignored when they do not appear on the first page of results. It is also widely acknowledged in the tourism sector that scores have a significant impact on prices, reservations, occupancy levels, ADR, and RevPar, etc. (Anderson, 2012; Öğüt & Onur Taş, 2012; Viglia et al., 2016; Ye, Law, Gu, & Chen, 2011).

TripAdvisor not only presents strong arguments for involving managers of tourist establishments in the collection of reviews, but it also provides tools to facilitate this task. It offers a review collection tool for sending emails called Review Express (TripAdvisor, 2017) and also a more sophisticated tool primarily available to larger hotel chains called the Review Collection Platform (RCP) (TripAdvisor, 2015).

Certain companies have adopted some of these methodologies to increase the number of reviews collected: Shangri-La Hotels (PATA, 2014), Wyndham (USA Today, 2012), Accor (TripAdvisor, 2012), and Swissôtel (PRweb, 2013). Results obtained by actively soliciting reviews have also been reported in research by private companies and scholars. Recent research on this issue shows that the ratings of requested reviews were significantly higher than those of spontaneous reviews (Litvin & Sobel, 2019).

In view of the complexity of implementing a systematic request for reviews, one might consider that these actions would be carried out primarily by large hotels. However, research collecting reviews from 17,925 hotels showed that there is an inverse relationship between the size of the hotel and its ability to collect reviews on TripAdvisor (Mellinas & Martin-Fuentes, 2019). The aforementioned authors suggested three possible explanations for this striking inverse relationship, including a more personalized treatment that enables staff to request reviews on the hotel premises with a higher level of effectiveness.

Previous Data on Participation Rates

As mentioned in the introduction, having reliable information on the percentage of travelers who write reviews about their stay is highly useful to researchers.

In the case of Booking.com, a previous article (Mellinas, 2019a) suggested that the response rate on Booking.com for urban hotels in Spain could be around 40%. After that study, which used data from 2017, Booking.com published the data on the percentage of responses to its surveys: "38% of our guests leave reviews after their stays, sharing helpful information with properties and other travelers" (Booking.com, 2019).

Expedia does not provide information on the percentage of responses, but follows a very similar process to that of Booking.com, sending customers emails after each stay. However, in this case, they may include certain incentives to increase the number of reviews, as indicated on their website: "Travelers may receive a savings voucher when they submit a review." If such incentives work effectively, Expedia may obtain even higher response rates than Booking.com.

One study adopted an interesting approach toward the matter: without trying to determine the exact response rate on TripAdvisor, it simply tried to identify the hotels that obtain more or fewer reviews per room. The results showed that hotels with fewer rooms obtained a higher rate of reviews per room than larger hotels (Mellinas & Martin-Fuentes, 2019).

Focusing on data from TripAdvisor, a study using data from 2010 to 2014 in the city of Belgrade (Mašić & Vićić, 2018) identified that the average percentage of travelers writing reviews was 0.382% during 2014 reaching 0.644% for 5-star hotels. A more recent article (Mellinas, 2019b) using data from 2017 for the main urban destinations in Spain identified participation percentages of about 2% (mean: 2.33; median: 1.95) on TripAdvisor, with more than 60% of hotels achieving percentages between 1% and 3%. The study did not find differences by category (3- or 4-star hotels), but it did find significant differences by city (from 1.88% in Valencia to 2.95% in Barcelona), which the author suggested could be due to the percentage of English speakers visiting each city.

Thus, it can be concluded that although in recent years online databases have been used intensively in the academic field, we have hardly any information on the percentage of the population represented by these samples of individuals who write reviews about their experiences. Information is only available concerning the hotel sector, but there is a total absence of data on other tourist sites that are also evaluated online.

Methodology

To calculate the percentage of visitors who write reviews on TripAdvisor for tourist spots, the number of reviews for a given period and number of visitors to the place in the same period are required. TripAdvisor includes the month and the year of every review, and some tourist spots provide information about attendance. We use the information provided by the Themed Entertainment Association and the Economics practice at AECOM (TEA, 2018) about amusement/theme parks, water parks, museums, and observation (sightseeing) experiences. Data for tourist sites is split into regional areas (North America, Latin America, and Europe).

The first 10 places of the first three categories are taken for each area, except for the case of museums in Latin America because no such data are available. In a preliminary study, we noticed that TripAdvisor is scarcely popular in Asia, so we decided to exclude places from this geographical area. In the case of observation experiences, the only data provided are those of the 20 most visited places worldwide, so we took all these data (including from Asia, for which very small figures are available). As hotels do not provide the number of customers received in a given period, this figure must be estimated. Thus, following the methodology proposed in the aforementioned study on urban hotels in Spain (Mellinas, 2019b), data of average occupancy and average length of stay in each city is required.

Average occupancy data are provided by PricewaterhouseCoopers in its annual report on the housing sector (Pwc, 2017), which includes the data considered in the 17 most important cities in Europe: Amsterdam (AMS), Barcelona (BCN), Berlin (BER), Budapest (BUD), Dublin (DUB), Frankfurt (FRA), Geneva (GEN), Lisbon (LIS), London (LON), Madrid (MAD), Milan (MIL), Paris (PAR), Oporto (OPO), Prague (PRA), Rome (ROM), Vienna (VIE), and Zürich (ZUR). The average length of stay data does not appear in any global report at the European level, although local, regional, or national authorities usually provide such data. Having obtained global data by city, the 20 hotels (3- and 4-star) closest to the city center according to TripAdvisor are selected following a criterion similar to the study carried out in Spain (Mellinas, 2019a). In this way, homogeneous criteria are followed in all cities, and more than 70% of the 3- and 4-star hotels are captured (Martin-Fuentes & Mellinas, 2018). Hotel category, number of rooms, and number of reviews on TripAdvisor in 2018 for 340 hotels, differentiating the reviews in English from other languages, are downloaded.

The number of customers per room in a city is obtained by multiplying 365 days of the year by the occupancy rate and dividing by the average length of stay. To estimate the number of customers at a hotel, the average number for the city is multiplied by the number of rooms. Although data per hotel may not be very precise, the overall figure for each city represented by the sample of 20 hotels, which includes between 800 and 3,000 rooms, could be considered very close to the reality for each destination.

Results

The results show that most of the hotels (70%) are only able to capture the reviews of less than 2% of customers; 14% of the hotels are able to get between 2 and 2.99%, while the rest (16%) can capture more than 3% of customer reviews, as can be observed in Table 1. It is important to highlight that these results are consistent with the research conducted by Mellinas (2019a) in hotels in Spain.

By city as can be seen in Table 2, the highest participation rate is in Rome, followed by Lisbon, London, Paris, Oporto, and Prague, all with rates of around 2–3%. The other cities are below 2%, with participation rates below 1% for Frankfurt, Geneva, and Berlin. Countries where German is the native language, i.e., Germany, Austria, and Switzerland, have a participation rate of 0.96% on average, while it is 2.07% for the global sample. Logically, the percentage of the total reviews written in English is higher in cities where English is the native language (London and Dublin); the lowest number of reviews in English are for Oporto, Madrid, Lisbon, and Prague. Contrary to what the previous study by Mellinas (2019a) suggested, we do not observe that the percentages of reviews in English are related to the rate of participation.

Table 1. Participation Rate on TripAdvisor by City.

Participation Rate	ROM	LIS	LON	PAR	OPO	PRA	MAD	BUD	MIL	AMS	VIE	BCN	DUB	ZUR	GEN	BER	FRA	Total
0–0.99%	3	1	1	5	8	8	7	4	6	8	9	5	11	11	11	12	18	128
1–1.99%	6	5	7	7	7	3	5	9	7	6	6	11	6	7	8	8	2	110
2–2.99%	2	7	4	4	1	6	5	3	4	1	3	3	2	2	1	0	0	48
3–3.99%	3	5	4	1	1	0	1	2	1	4	2	1	1	0	0	0	0	26
>4%	6	2	4	3	3	3	2	2	2	1	0	0	0	0	0	0	0	28

Table 2. Descriptive Hotel Data by City.

City	Reviews Mean (SD)	Rooms Mean (SD)	Reviews in English %	Participation Rate Mean (SD) %
ROM	1098.75 (809.81)	46.40 (49.25)	58.46	3.01 (2.03)
LIS	903.30 (528.85)	42.50 (14.87)	47.17	2.76 (1.11)
LON	2153.95 (1784.56)	162.05 (110.08)	84.65	2.64 (1.33)
PAR	998.40 (1116.42)	52.80 (66.08)	64.95	2.19 (2.02)
OPO	631.80 (466.45)	52.70 (39.97)	31.83	2.09 (2.38)
PRA	1042.60 (829.01)	62.85 (52.54)	45.63	2.04 (2.26)
MAD	975.25 (900.34)	51.50 (51.09)	38.15	1.97 (1.56)
BUD	1787.50 (2087.34)	91.85 (64.62)	53.83	1.91 (1.25)
MIL	1054.60 (716.91)	86.10 (97.87)	53.17	1.81 (1.38)
AMS	1797.45 (1234.25)	90.20 (63.14)	68.29	1.74 (1.27)
VIE	1446.50 (897.37)	112.80 (61.76)	49.47	1.41 (1.05)
BCN	1705.80 (1066.57)	112.20 (70.01)	62.42	1.39 (0.77)
DUB	1913.95 (1205.39)	137.05 (92.63)	83.73	1.24 (0.74)
ZUR	654.70 (429.16)	52.20 (31.44)	68.11	1.10 (0.59)
GEN	510.25 (328.14)	68.75 (32.24)	61.17	0.86 (0.52)
BER	2273.55 (2609.34)	230.00 (216.90)	49.27	0.90 (0.31)
FRA	629.00 (554.98)	95.85 (65.70)	49.47	0.51 (0.30)

The size of the hotels also varies depending on the city, with Berlin's hotels having the highest number of rooms on average, followed by those of London and Dublin; these three cities also capture the highest number of reviews on average, which can be explained by the fact that more rooms can accommodate more customers who in turn write more reviews (Martin-Fuentes, 2016).

A mean comparison of participation rates has been conducted by hotel size, hotel category, and city following the same technique as other studies (Hernández-Méndez, Muñoz-Leiva, & Sánchez-Fernández, 2015; Martin-Fuentes & Mellinas, 2018; Martin-Fuentes, Mellinas, & Parra-Lopez, 2020). In this sample, hotel category is divided into 3- and 4-star. Levene's test to assess the equality of variances and Student's t-test distribution for independent samples are conducted. The assumption of homogeneity is met ($p > 0.05$), and Student's t-test shows that there are no mean differences between participation rates ($t = -0.513$; $p = 0.608$); therefore, hotel category (3- or 4-star) does not play a role in capturing a higher or a lower number of reviewers in relation to the number of customers at a hotel.

For hotel size, dividing the hotel into small (from 1 to 20 rooms), medium (from 21 to 80 rooms), and large (more than 80 rooms), an ANOVA pairwise comparison test is performed. To check the equality of variances, Levene's test is performed, and the assumption of homogeneity is not met ($p < 0.001$). Then, a one-way ANOVA post hoc Games-Howell test (as there are different variances) is performed, and the results confirm that there is a significant effect of mean participation rate for all hotel sizes ($p < 0.05$). Smaller hotels have the capacity to attract on average 2.85% of reviews, medium hotels 1.81%, and the largest ones 1.35%. This is very similar to what was discovered in the previous study that analyzed the "reviews per room" parameter (Mellinas & Martin-Fuentes, 2019).

In the case of attractions, the results show a lower participation rate, of 0.078% on average, and the observation decks, at 0.25%, are the tourist spots with the highest participation rate. By regions, Europe has the highest participation with 0.097%, as can be observed in Tables 3 and 4. In the top 20 in terms of partici-pation rate (>0.20%) are observation decks not in Asia (14), four water parks, one theme park (Xcaret Park, Mexico), and one museum (the British Museum).

By tourist spot typology, an ANOVA pairwise comparisons test is performed. Levene's test confirms there is no equality of variances ($p < 0.001$). Then, the one-way ANOVA post hoc Games-Howell test confirms that there is a significant effect of mean participation rate for observatories ahead of the other categories ($p < 0.05$), while among the other three typologies there are no statistically significant differences. By region, the ANOVA test confirms that there are no statistically significant differences in participation rates between regions. Asia had only six spots, and due to its low participation, this region is excluded from the test.

Table 3. Participation Rates by Tourist Spot.

Typology	N	Participation Rate Mean (SD) %	Reviews in English (%)
Museum	20	0.0590 (0.0373)	64.25
Observation	14	0.2445 (0.0924)	59.50
Theme park	30	0.0434 (0.0529)	39.07
Water park	30	0.0476 (0.0749)	47.94
Total	94	0.0780 (0.0950)	50.05

Table 4. Participation Rates by Geographical Region.

Zone	N	Participation Rate Mean (SD) %	Reviews in English (%)
Europe	35	0.0972 (0.1062)	45.86
Latin America	22	0.0654 (0.0943)	13.13
North America	37	0.0673 (0.0833)	76.61
Total	94	0.7799 (0.0951)	50.30

Discussion

Regarding the data obtained on the participation rate at hotels, we observed important variations in figures. On the one hand, the cities in countries in which German is the main language present lower rates, which may be due to the significant presence of HolidayCheck (Schegg & Fux, 2010), which is as popular as TripAdvisor in these countries and probably captures a major portion of traveler reviews. On the other hand, we observe significant variations among other cities, even within the same country (ROM-MIL; MAD-BCN), for which there is not such a clear explanation.

The substantial differences we find between hotels at the same destination are also noteworthy. We see how among the 20 hotels at each destination (excluding German-speaking), there are hotels whose participation rate is less than 1% and others with a rate of more than 3%. Therefore, although we can say that the participation rate in TripAdvisor is close to 2% for European capitals (close to 1% for German-speaking countries), it is difficult to generalize these figures due to the significant variations observed, measured by the high standard deviations. There are cities such as Oporto and Prague with even higher standard deviations than the mean, showing a high level of dispersion in participation rates among hotels in the same city.

These data suggest that the level of involvement of each hotel in collaborating with TripAdvisor to capture reviews is decisive. Hotels that do not participate in this task at all can barely reach 1%, while those that are more active can exceed 3%. For the former, we obtain totally spontaneous reviews, while in the most active we obtain a significant percentage of requested reviews.

The fact that most tourism spots have thousands of reviews can give an initial impression of high participation in TripAdvisor, although this does not correspond to the reality This observation is aligned with Hargittai's (2015) suggestion that it may appear that results with millions of users represented in a dataset can be generalized, ignoring possible biases. We have observed that participation levels are substantially lower than those of hotels, approximately 20 times less than the participation rate (0.075%). TripAdvisor is known and promoted as a hotel review platform, which may result in many potential users ignoring the possibility of reviewing tourist spots.

The results by geographical area reveal substantially higher levels of participation in Europe than in America. When the analysis is performed focusing on typology, we observe very similar figures for museums, theme parks, and water parks, but substantially higher participation rates for observation decks. These places achieve rates three times higher than the other three typologies, which could be up to five times higher if we eliminate the six observation decks in Asia to calculate the average (0.24% in this case).

We believe that these differences may be due to the fact that many of those who write a review about an observation deck have not actually entered the structure but have merely gone to the observation point. Places like the Eiffel Tower and the Empire State Building can be admired from the outside and thus generate reviews on TripAdvisor. However, the data we have about attendance at these places only includes people who purchased a ticket to access the attraction. Conversely, we consider that there will be very few travelers who write a review about a museum, theme park, or water park without having actually visited them.

Conclusions

From the point of view of hotel management implications, review participation on TripAdvisor indicates that hotels that have higher participation rates probably use different techniques to encourage their customers to give their opinions. Thus, if a hotel doubles or triples its percentage of reviews with respect to another, it is because the former encourages customers to write reviews, while the latter does nothing to favor such a practice. Proof of this is that small hotels have a higher participation rate than large hotels, much along the same lines as the research conducted on reviews per room by Mellinas and Martin-Fuentes (2019). In this sense, a closer relationship and greater involvement with customers contributes to a higher percentage of responses.

Methodologies based on the massive collection of data from websites such as TripAdvisor can be very useful in the investigation of different aspects of the tourism field. However, the use of an appropriate methodology must involve quantifying relevant aspects such as sample size in relation to the universe of individuals under study. It is true that the TripAdvisor platform provides researchers with millions of reviews with which their analyses may be performed more easily, quickly and economically, but it should still be taken into account that most people either do not review their experiences or use other review platforms. TripAdvisor only represents around 2% of visitors in the case of most hotels and amounts to under 0.1% in tourist spots. The 830 million reviews are impressive, but TripAdvisor does not generate response rates over 30%, as Booking.com and Expedia can achieve by asking all their customers to write a review.

Regarding the theoretical contribution of this research, we can conclude that studies using large amounts of data from websites and opinion platforms on the Internet can also display biases, as well as the use of other methodologies using online and offline surveys, which are not exempt from such bias (Dolnicar et al., 2009).

The data obtained suggest that in the case of hotels we have "requested" and "spontaneous" (organic) reviews. Furthermore, in the case of observation decks, we have reviews from people who have accessed the place and people who have simply admired it from the outside. In both cases, reviewers may assign different opinions and scores depending on their profiles, which could lead to possible statistical biases. In the case of hotels, these differences have already been tested in an initial study detecting higher scores for requested reviews (Litvin & Sobel, 2019). It would be interesting to perform similar tests regarding observation decks, since the data suggests that most travelers write reviews without actually having entered the place they review. It seems reasonable to suspect that there could be differences in evaluations between those who bought a ticket and entered a place and those who merely saw it from the outside.

We suspect that this situation could be repeated at other types of tourism spots not analyzed in this study. Buildings such as cathedrals or palaces are interesting both from the outside (for free) and from the inside. Some emblematic examples are the Colosseum in Rome, La Sagrada Familia in Barcelona, and the Tower of London. This issue can have important implications for the managers of these monuments who try to measure the satisfaction of their visitors through the reviews on TripAdvisor. If the reviews come mainly from people who have not accessed the site, the conclusions obtained may be erroneous.

The information outlined in this paper could serve as an excuse for many tourism professionals to ignore online reviews in their business management. However, the fact that we may not be dealing with a source of information as reliable as one might initially think, it would be inappropriate for any business to ignore the hundreds or thousands of reviews that are made available to them quickly, explicitly and free of charge. It is no longer an option to return to the days when decisions were based on reports from departmental heads or expensive ad-hoc market research. Online reviews should be taken into consideration by any tourism business, trying to better understand the nature, origin and level of reliability of these valuable data.

Limitations and Future Research

Although this study significantly expands the sample size and the variety of locations analyzed in comparison to previous research, using larger sample sizes would provide more detailed data and enable the development of more sophisticated statistical models. Moreover, having accurate data on the number of guests in hotels in a given period of time would provide highly accurate data on TripAdvisor review participation rates.

Other websites also collect scores and reviews, such as Yelp, HolidayCheck, Facebook, and Google Places, although they have been used less in academia. Although the resources and the hotels analyzed in our study are from all over the world and the data used are taken from TripAdvisor, which is the largest platform of online travel reviews, this website may create cultural bias because it is used by some nationalities more than others. Empirical replications using other platforms to determine whether there are behavioral differences according to nationality may provide further insight for this discussion. It would be highly useful to be able to access specific data on the percentage of people who review an attraction having only seen it from the outside, and ascertain the difference in scores between this group and those who purchase a ticket and actually visit it.

Acknowledgments

This study was partially funded by the Spanish Ministry of the Economy and Competitiveness: research project TURCOLAB ECO2017-88984-R.

References

Anderson, C. K. (2012). The impact of social media on lodging performance. *Cornell Hospitality Report*, *12*(15), 4–11.

Bi, J.-W., Liu, Y., Fan, Z.-P., & Zhang, J. (2019). Wisdom of crowds: Conducting importance-performance analysis (IPA) through online reviews. *Tourism Management*, *70*, 460–478. doi:10.1016/j.tourman.2018.09.010

Booking.com. (2019). List your apartment, hotel, holiday home or B&B on Booking. com. Booking.com. Retrieved from https://join.booking.com/

Braunsberger, K., Wybenga, H., & Gates, R. (2007). A comparison of reliability between telephone and web-based surveys. *Journal of Business Research*, *60*(7), 758–764.

Cantallops, A. S., & Salvi, F. (2014). New consumer behavior: A review of research on eWOM and hotels. *International Journal of Hospitality Management*, *36*, 41–51.

Cobanoglu, C., Moreo, P. J., & Warde, B. (2001). A comparison of mail, fax and web-based survey methods. *International Journal of Market Research*, *43*(4), 1–15.

Cole, S. T. (2005). Comparing mail and web-based survey distribution methods: Results of surveys to leisure travel retailers. *Journal of Travel Research*, *43*(4), 422–430.

Dellarocas, C. (2003). The digitization of word of mouth: Promise and challenges of online feedback mechanisms. *Management Science*, *49*(10), 1407–1424.

Deutskens, E., De Ruyter, K., & Wetzels, M. (2006). An assessment of equivalence between online and mail surveys in service research. *Journal of Service Research*, *8*(4), 346–355.

Dolnicar, S., Laesser, C., & Matus, K. (2009). Online versus paper: Format effects in tourism surveys. *Journal of Travel Research*, *47*(3), 295–316.

Filieri, R., & McLeay, F. (2014). E-WOM and accommodation: An analysis of the factors that influence travelers' adoption of information from online reviews. *Journal of Travel Research*, *53*(1), 44–57.

Francesco, G., & Roberta, G. (2019). Cross-country analysis of perception and emphasis of hotel attributes. *Tourism Management*, *74*, 24–42. doi:10.1016/j.tourman.2019.02.011

Gerdt, S.-O., Wagner, E., & Schewe, G. (2019). The relationship between sustainability and customer satisfaction in hospitality: An explorative investigation using eWOM as a data source. *Tourism Management*, *74*, 155–172. doi:10.1016/j.tourman.2019.02.010

Gretzel, U., & Yoo, K. H. (2008). Use and impact of online travel reviews. In P. O'Connor, W. Höpken, & U. Gretzel (Eds.), *Information and communication technologies in tourism* (pp. 35–46). Vienna: Springer. doi:10.1007/978-3-211-77280-5_4

Hargittai, E. (2015). Is bigger always better? Potential biases of big data derived from social network sites. *The Annals of the American Academy of Political and Social Science*, *659*(1), 63–76.

Hernández-Méndez, J., Muñoz-Leiva, F., & Sánchez-Fernández, J. (2015). The influence of e-word-of-mouth on travel decision-making: Consumer profiles. *Current Issues in Tourism*, *18*(11), 1001–1021. doi:10.1080/13683500.2013.802764

Hidalgo, C. (2014). Saving big data from big mouths. *Scientific American*. Retrieved from https://www.scientificamerican.com/article/saving-big-data-from-big-mouths/

Hung, K., & Law, R. (2011). An overview of Internet-based surveys in hospitality and tourism journals. *Tourism Management*, *32*(4), 717–724. doi:10.1016/j.tourman. 2010.05.027

Hu, F., Teichert, T., Liu, Y., Li, H., & Gundyreva, E. (2019). Evolving customer expectations of hospitality services: Differences in attribute effects on satisfaction and Re-Patronage. *Tourism Management*, *74*, 345–357. doi:10.1016/j.tourman. 2019.04.010

Hu, N., Zhang, T., Gao, B., & Bose, I. (2019). What do hotel customers complain about? Text analysis using structural topic model. *Tourism Management*, *72*, 417–426. doi:10.1016/j.tourman.2019.01.002

Kirilenko, A. P., Stepchenkova, S. O., & Hernandez, J. M. (2019). Comparative clustering of destination attractions for different origin markets with network and spatial analyses of online reviews. *Tourism Management*, *72*, 400–410. doi:10.1016/ j.tourman.2019.01.001

Kwok, L., Xie, K. L., & Richards, T. (2017). Thematic framework of online review research: A systematic analysis of contemporary literature on seven major hospitality and tourism journals. *International Journal of Contemporary Hospitality Management*, *29*(1), 307–354.

Litvin, S. W., & Sobel, R. N. (2019). Organic versus solicited hotel TripAdvisor reviews: Measuring their respective characteristics. *Cornell Hospitality Quarterly*, *60*(4), 370–377. doi:10.1177/1938965518811287

Liu, Yi, Huang, K., Bao, J., & Chen, K. (2019). Listen to the voices from home: An analysis of Chinese tourists' sentiments regarding Australian destinations. *Tourism Management*, *71*, 337–347. doi:10.1016/j.tourman.2018.10.004

Liu, Y., Teichert, T., Rossi, M., Li, H., & Hu, F. (2017). Big data for big insights: Investigating language-specific drivers of hotel satisfaction with 412,784 user-generated reviews. *Tourism Management*, *59*, 554–563. doi:10.1016/j.tourman. 2016.08.012

Li, J., Xu, L., Tang, L., Wang, S., & Li, L. (2018). Big data in tourism research: A literature review. *Tourism Management*, *68*, 301–323. doi:10.1016/j.tourman.2018. 03.009

Martin-Fuentes, E. (2016). Are guests of the same opinion as the hotel star-rate classification system? *Journal of Hospitality and Tourism Management*, *29*, 126–134. doi:10.1016/j.jhtm.2016.06.006

Martin-Fuentes, E., Mateu, C., & Fernandez, C. (2018). Does verifying uses influence rankings? Analyzing Booking.com and tripadvisor. *Tourism Analysis*, *23*(1), 1–15.

Martin-Fuentes, E., & Mellinas, J. P. (2018). Hotels that most rely on Booking. com–online travel agencies (OTAs) and hotel distribution channels. *Tourism Review*, *73*(4), 465–479.

Martin-Fuentes, E., Mellinas, J. P., & Parra-Lopez, E. (2020). Online travel review rating scales and effects on hotel scoring and competitiveness. *Tourism Review*. *ahead-of-print*(ahead-of-print). doi:10.1108/TR-01-2019-0024

Mašić, S., & Vićić, S. (2018). An analysis of belgrade hotel guest? Incilination for posting reviews on the TripAdvisor. *Quaestus*, *12*, 108–119.

Melián-González, S., Bulchand-Gidumal, J., & González López-Valcárcel, B. (2013). Online customer reviews of hotels: As participation increases, better evaluation is obtained. *Cornell Hospitality Quarterly*, *54*(3), 274–283.

Mellinas, J. P. (2019a). Dependency of Spanish urban hotels on Booking.Com. *Tourism Analysis, 24*(1), 3–12. Retrieved from https://doi.org/info:doi/10.3727/108354219X15458295631909

Mellinas, J. P. (2019b). What percentage of travelers are writing hotel reviews? In A. Artal-Tur, M. Kozak, & N. Kozak (Eds.), *Trends in tourist behavior: New products and experiences from Europe* (pp. 161–174). Cham: Springer International Publishing. doi:10.1007/978-3-030-11160-1_10

Mellinas, J. P., & Martin-Fuentes, E. (2019). Does hotel size matter to get more reviews per room? *Information Technology & Tourism, 21*(2), 165–180. doi:10.1007/s40558-018-0126-7

Öğüt, H., & Onur Taş, B. K. (2012). The influence of internet customer reviews on the online sales and prices in hotel industry. *Service Industries Journal, 32*(2), 197–214. doi:10.1080/02642069.2010.529436

O'reilly, T. (2005). *What is Web 2.0: Design patterns and business models for the next generation of software*. O'Reilly Media.

PATA. (2014). Shangri-La hotels and resorts study shows review collection partnership with TripAdvisor leads to more reviews and higher ratings. PATA. Retrieved from https://www.pata.org/shangri-la-hotels-and-resorts-study-shows-review-collection-partnership-with-tripadvisor-leads-to-more-reviews-and-higher-ratings/

Pwc. (2017). Best placed to grow? European cities hotel forecast for 2018 and 2019. Retrieved from https://www.pwc.com/gx/en/hospitality-leisure/assets/european-cities-hotel-forecast-2018-2019.pdf

PRweb. (2013). Market metrix and TripAdvisor team up to help hospitality companies improve their online reputation. PRWeb. Retrieved from https://www.prweb.com/releases/2013/4/prweb10622793.htm

Radojevic, T., Stanisic, N., & Stanic, N. (2015). Solo travellers assign higher ratings than families: Examining customer satisfaction by demographic group. *Tourism Management Perspectives, 16*, 247–258. doi:10.1016/j.tmp.2015.08.004

Schegg, R., & Fux, M. (2010). A comparative analysis of content in traditional survey versus hotel review websites. In U. Gretzel, R. Law, & M. Fuchs (Eds.), *Information and communication technologies in tourism 2010* (pp. 429–440). Vienna: Springer.

Schuckert, M., Liu, X., & Law, R. (2015). Hospitality and tourism online reviews: Recent trends and future directions. *Journal of Travel & Tourism Marketing, 32*(5), 608–621. doi:10.1080/10548408.2014.933154

Spoerri, A. (2008). Authority and ranking effects in data fusion. *Journal of the American Society for Information Science and Technology, 59*(3), 450–460. doi:10.1002/asi.20760

Stanisic, N. (2016). *Recent trends in quantitative research in the field of tourism and hospitality*. (SSRN Scholarly Paper ID 2875849). Social Science Research Network. Retrieved from https://papers.ssrn.com/abstract=2875849

Taecharungroj, V., & Mathayomchan, B. (2019). Analysing TripAdvisor reviews of tourist attractions in Phuket, Thailand. *Tourism Management, 75*, 550–568. doi:10.1016/j.tourman.2019.06.020

TEA. (2018). Theme index, museum index 2018. Themed Entertainment Association. Retrieved from https://www.aecom.com/theme-index/

TripAdvisor. (2012). 300 million people view TripAdvisor content on sites other than TripAdvisor each month. MediaRoom. Retrieved from https://tripadvisor. mediaroom.com/2012-12-01-300-Million-People-View-TripAdvisor-Content-on-Sites-Other-than-TripAdvisor-Each-Month

TripAdvisor. (2014). More reviews, higher rating. TripAdvisor Insights.

TripAdvisor. (2015). Key insights from "using guest reviews to pave the path to greater engagement". *TripAdvisor Insights*. Retrieved from https://www. tripadvisor.com/TripAdvisorInsights/w842

TripAdvisor. (2016). Everything you need to know about the TripAdvisor popularity ranking algorithm. TripAdvisor Insights.

TripAdvisor. (2017). The complete review express guide. TripAdvisor Insights. Retrieved from https://www.tripadvisor.com/TripAdvisorInsights/n2159/complete-review-express-guide

TripAdvisor. (2019). About TripAdvisor. TripAdvisor. Retrieved from https:// tripadvisor.mediaroom.com/UK-about-us

USA Today. (2012). Wyndham to invite guests to review its hotels on TripAdvisor. *USA Today*. Retrieved from https://www.usatoday.com/story/hotelcheckin/2012/ 10/09/wyndham-tripadvisor-consumer-reviews/1622111/

Vermeulen, I. E., & Seegers, D. (2009). Tried and tested: The impact of online hotel reviews on consumer consideration. *Tourism Management, 30*(1), 123–127. doi:10. 1016/j.tourman.2008.04.008

Viglia, G., Viglia, G., Minazzi, R., Minazzi, R., Buhalis, D., & Buhalis, D. (2016). The influence of e-word-of-mouth on hotel occupancy rate. *International Journal of Contemporary Hospitality Management, 28*(9), 2035–2051.

Woodman, C. J., Min-Venditti, A. A., Woosnam, K. M., & Brightsmith, D. J. (2019). Water quality for guest health at remote Amazon ecotourism lodges. *Tourism Management, 72*, 202–208. doi:10.1016/j.tourman.2018.11.014

Ye, Q., Law, R., Gu, B., & Chen, W. (2011). The influence of user-generated content on traveler behavior: An empirical investigation on the effects of e-word-of-mouth to hotel online bookings. *Computers in Human Behavior, 27*(2), 634–639.

Chapter 8

Application of Text Mining Approaches in Hospitality and Tourism

Gözde Öztürk and Abdullah Tanrisevdi

Abstract

The purpose of this chapter is to shed light on researchers and practitioners about sentiment analysis in hospitality and tourism. The technical details described throughout the chapter with a case study to provide clarifying insights. The proposed chapter adds significantly to the body of text mining knowledge by combining a technical explanation with a relevant case study. The case study used supervised machine learning to predict overall star ratings based on 20,247 comments related to Royal Caribbean International services for determining the impact of cruise travel experiences on the evaluation company process. The results indicate that travelers evaluate their travel experiences according to the most intense negative or positive feelings they have about the company.

Keywords: Data mining; text mining; sentiment analysis; machine learning; supervised learning; review rating prediction

Introduction

In recent years, rapid developments in information and communication tech-nologies accelerated the growth of digital data and led to the formation of large data repositories. It can be argued that these data repositories, stored in digital media and of which more than 80% are unstructured or semi-structured (Ramanathan & Meyyappan, 2013), are worthless unless they are operational-ized for a specific purpose. Data repositories gain value only if they become more meaningful and contribute to the production of information. In this sense, data mining, which enables mass data to become meaningful and functional, includes the processes of obtaining previously unknown, hidden, meaningful, and useful patterns in the data by means of database systems, machine learning, artificial intelligence, and statistical methods. Data mining studies in which text is treated

Advanced Research Methods in Hospitality and Tourism, 145–162
Copyright © 2023 Gözde Öztürk and Abdullah Tanrisevdi
Published under exclusive licence by Emerald Publishing Limited
doi:10.1108/978-1-80117-550-020221008

as data constitute a process called text mining. Text mining is the process of extracting relevant information and meaning from unstructured texts (Hotho, Nürnberger, & Paaß, 2005).

Information obtained from tourists' online comments, have a significant impact on destination choice (Jalilvand & Samiei, 2012), travel planning (Gretzel & Yoo, 2008; Litvin, Goldsmith, & Pan, 2008), purchasing decision process (Sparks & Browning, 2011), and purchase intention. Online comments can provide businesses opportunities to understand the buying behavior of tourists, for helping businesses provide tailored products and services to the customer (Boateng, 2016). In addition, developing customer management (Choi, Lehto, & Morrison, 2007; Kuttainen, Lexhagen, Fuchs, & Höpken, 2012; Ye, Zhang, & Law, 2009), creating customer loyalty, avoiding potential customer dissatisfaction by interacting more with customers, and implementation of specific marketing strategies are among the other important benefits and contributions of customer comments to business processes (Tao & Kim, 2019). Thus, service providers need to pay more attention to consumer comments so that they can fully meet and survive the needs of consumers in increasing competition. It is nearly impossible to obtain meaningful information by manually analyzing individuals' feelings and thoughts from textual data consisting of online comments. The necessity of studies that automatically reveal meaningful information is obvious. In that context, sentiment analysis is a field of study that supports the implementation of natural language processing techniques to automatically extract, identify and analyze subjective opinions in source materials (Bross, 2013). The purpose of sentiment analysis is to determine the contextual polarity of a given text, which can be positive or negative, and then classify the sentiments expressed by individuals.

In the field of hospitality and tourism, sentiment analysis provides useful information related to tourist's feelings and opinions that makes it possible to direct administrative activities toward contributing to the development of the enterprise for tourism authorities. This chapter presents a review rating prediction approach which is a main task of sentiment analysis by using a case study for hospitality and tourism practitioners. The chapter is beneficial for businesses providing operability to managerial activities and will help the improvement of marketing strategies for businesses.

Literature Review

Data Mining and Text Mining

Data mining is the process of extracting information from data with the help of artificial intelligence, machine learning, statistics, and database systems (Hand, 1998). Text mining, which specifically accepts texts as viable data sources, refers to the process of extracting information and meaning from texts. Nearly all of the database repositories containing company information are available in text documents (Ur-Rahman & Harding, 2012). However, keeping text documents containing information that is useful to many organizations or individuals is still unstructured and, without processing, is a major obstacle to the rapid processing of information and its exploitation. Therefore, text mining algorithms have been created as an automated approach to the analysis of various text documents. Text mining algorithms generally refer to the process of converting text-based unstructured data into meaningful information.

Text mining is the process of discovering interesting and important patterns from a large amount of textual data (Weiss, Indurkhya, Zhang, & Damerau, 2010). Text mining process consists of collecting unstructured data, converting unstructured data into structured data, identifying patterns from structured data, implementing pattern analysis, and ultimately extracting valuable and relevant information. In general, many text-based data such as SMS, newspaper articles, voice recordings, patient records, and official documents can be converted into meaningful data with the help of text mining. Text mining is being used in many fields such as cybercrime (Kontostathis, Edwards, & Leatherman, 2010), biomedicine (Gong, 2018), and education (Agrawal & Batra, 2013). Text mining is also widely used in fields of tourism and hospitality. Studies carried out in the latter fields tend to emphasize customer feedback (Ordenes, Theodoulidis, Burton, Gruber, & Zaki, 2014), service recovery (Lee, Singh, & Chan, 2011), destination management (Kim, Lee, Shin, & Yang, 2017), and customer (dis)satisfaction (Sezgen, Mason, & Mayer, 2019).

Sentiment Analysis

Sentiment analysis, also called opinion mining, is a field of study that addresses the application of natural language processing, computational linguistics, and text analytics to automatically identify and classify subjective information in natural language texts (Luo, Chen, Xu, & Zhou, 2013). It can determine subjectivity and polarity strength of given textual content (Nasukawa & Yi, 2003), thus making it possible to reveal the attitudes, opinions, sentiments, evaluations, appraisals, and emotions of an individual about services, issues, or even events through relevant textual content (Liu & Zhang, 2012).

Sentiment analysis is conducted at three levels: document, sentence, and aspect. The document level analysis aims to classify whether a whole opinion document expresses a positive or negative sentiment or opinion (Turney, 2002). The sentence level identifies whether the sentence is subjective or objective. If the sentence is subjective, then it determines whether each sentence expresses a positive or negative opinion. The aspect level aims to classify the sentiment with respect to the specific aspects of entities (Liu, 2012).

There are essentially three approaches to sentiment analysis: lexicon-based, machine learning, and hybrid approaches. Lexicon-based sentiment analysis utilizes an emotional lexicon for determining the polarity of textual content (Turney, 2002). Machine learning is a branch of artificial intelligence that gives computers the ability to learn without being explicitly programmed (Samuel, 1959). Machine learning itself can be divided into two sub-categories: supervised and unsupervised learning methods. In supervised learning, labeled input and output datasets are used for classification to provide a learning algorithm for future data processing (Jatana, 2018). These labeled data guide the learning process and are used to interpret the incoming data. On the other hand, in unsupervised learning, the structure or distribution underlying the data is used to obtain more information about the data (Safavian & Landgrebe, 1991). Unlike supervised learning, this learning method uses unlabeled data sets to discover the hidden structure and find similar patterns within input data. The hybrid approach uses a combination of machine learning and lexicon-base approaches. This combination improves the classification performance (Ahmad, Aftab, Ali, & Hameed, 2017).

In the field of hospitality and tourism, sentiment analysis approaches have been variously used. Misopoulos, Mitic, Kapoulas, and Karapiperis (2014) used lexicon-based sentiment analysis to determine the aspects of airline customer service that make customers satisfied, unsatisfied, and even delighted. Markopoulos, Mikros, Iliadi, and Liontos (2015) applied supervised learning to examine hotel reviews written in modern Greek. Bucur (2015) proposed a system that extracted hotel reviews and classified them using unsupervised learning to facilitate hotel customers' decision-making processes. Kim et al. (2017) examined visitors' perceptions of destination services through a hybrid analysis of travelers' online review data.

Review Rating Prediction

The positive or negative intensity of a review's sentiment is shown by the overall rating (Wang, Xiong, Huang, & Li, 2018). Due to this relationship between sentiment and rating sentiment analysis, sentiment analysis is suitable for review rating prediction. As indicated in Tang, Qin, Liu, and Yang (2015), review rating prediction is a fundamental task of sentiment analysis. Review rating prediction helps determine the author's evaluation of reviews with a numerical representation. Some comment systems provide an overall rating field for users. These rating fields are subjective and therefore different for each individual (Gojali & Khodra, 2016). For example, different users providing similar reviews might still rate the product itself differently, or they might give it the same rating while having very different reasons for doing so. In that context, an objective automatic rating generator based on sentiment and aspect of the comment is needed.

Songpan (2017) proposed a method for proving the inconsistency between customer ratings and review content in the hotel industry. In this study, their proposed method is based on Naive Bayes and Decision Tree algorithms for predicting the sentiment probability of each review. They tried to estimate the overall rating of each review with the help of the resulting sentiment probabilities. However, they neglected the effects of certain aspects on review ratings.

Yang, Zhang, Yu, and Wang (2013) proposed a Point of Interest recommendation algorithm called Location Based Social Matrix Factorization (LBSMF). LBSMF applies SentiWordNet for predicting the overall rating of tips – a tip being a short text that describes users' comments about venues. LBSMF first splits each tip into sentences and calculates scores of each sentence before summing all sentiment scores of each sentence. The sum of the sentiment scores is then converted into a rating. The LBSMF calculates the rating of tips with unsupervised prediction methodology. The features are selected as a noun phrase and a weight is assigned to each feature with the help of SentiWordNet. As indicated in Ganu, Elhadad, and Marian (2009) and Gojali and Khodra (2016), negative and positive sentences have a direct effect on the overall rating score. Ganu et al. (2009) calculate a rating score with the help of sentiments of the sentences in a given comment. First they count the number of negative and positive sentences, then they put these numbers into the equation that they propose to find out the rating on a scale of 1–5.

Case Study: Evaluation of Cruise Passengers' Comments Using Text Mining

Research Background

Customer experience is a multidimensional structure that involves emotional, cognitive, sensorial, behavioral, and social components (Schmitt, 1999). It is important to examine different perspectives of experiences containing sensory perceptions, feelings and emotions, creativity and reasoning, and social relationships to better understand customers' experiences (Pinker, 1997). In the present study, we investigate the impact of cruise traveler experiences on the cruise company evaluation process based on affective (sentiment analysis) and cognitive attributes, the latter across 11 aspects. As in Ganu et al. (2009), we split the given comment into sentences and take into account the aspect sentiments of each sentence. We then calculate the weighted average of aspect probability of the whole comment while considering the positive or negative aspect sentiments. Unlike the method proposed in Ganu et al. (2009), which merely counts the negative and positive sentences, we also take into account the probability of aspect sentiment of each sentence. The probability of aspect sentiment indicates how likely a given sentence fits an estimated aspect sentiment. We tried to answer two research questions to determine which aspects cruise travelers focus on or ignore and how their positive or negative feelings affect this process.

- Research Question 1 (*RQ1*): Do cruise travelers make an overall star rating based on the most dominant aspect?
- Research Question 2 (*RQ2*): Do cruise travelers make an overall star rating that reveals the average sentiment?

To answer these research questions, we proposed two different rating prediction methods based on polarity and aspect probabilities of comments. In order to answer *RQ1*, we used two methods for assigning sentiment polarity of the comment. In the first method, polarity and aspect probabilities of comment sentences are determined. 0 a result of this comparison, the sentiment polarity with the highest classification probability value is assigned as the sentiment polarity of the comment. In the second method, polarity and aspect probabilities of comment sentences are determined. Positive and negative sentences of a comment are determined and positive and negative sentences in a comment are counted. The polarity type having maximum appearance is assigned as the polarity of the comment. For these two methods, the probability value of the class with the dominant aspect in the sentiment polarity indicates the rating value expected to be obtained from the comment. According to the rating value of comment, an overall star rating of comment is assigned with the help of our proposed overall rating scale for *RQ1*.

In order to answer *RQ2*, polarity of comments and aspect probabilities of comment sentences are determined with the help of the classification algorithm. Considering comments' sentiment type and aspects' probability values, the overall rating is determined with the help of the strong influencing polarity (SIP). A given comment most probably will have multiple aspects with positive and negative polarities. To uncover the strong influencing polarity, we found out average aspect probabilities of both negative and positive comments. Next, we extracted the average aspect probability of negative sentences from average aspect probability of positive sentences for finding out the SIP value. The equation of SIP is shown below.

$$\text{SIP} = \text{AVG (positive comments)} - \text{AVG(negative comments)} \qquad (1)$$

where AVG (positive comments) is the average aspect probability of positive comments and AVG (negative comments) is the average aspect probability of negative comments. According to SIP value, overall star rating of comment is assigned with the help of our proposed overall rating scale for *RQ2*. In addition, we compare these prediction methods for determining whether cruise travelers give an overall star rating value according to the most intense negative or positive feeling about their cruise experience or give an average overall rating value according to positive or negative overall cruise experiences.

Data Source

Data is composed of user reviews posted on cruisecritic.com (https://www.cruisecritic.co.uk/) (Cruisecritic.com, 2020). The comments were written by passengers who traveled with Royal Caribbean International. The data includes 20,247 customer reviews of 24 cruise ships.

Data Collection

A Chrome plugin called Web Scraper was used to collect user-generated content (UGC) data. An algorithm suitable for Web Scraper is first defined. Then, a 1.2 GB sample of 39,203 customer reviews was taken between 11 and 30 April 2018 over a 480-hour period. Among these data, some comments were removed in accordance with various criteria (e.g., comments with no emotion, no sense of integrity, no rating value, only rating value, no comment sentences), and the data was reduced to 20,247 cruise customer reviews.

Proposed Method

The proposed method consists of three parts; Prediction of Comment's Sentiment Polarity, Prediction of Comment's Aspect, and Prediction of Comment's Overall Rating Value. In the Prediction of Comment's Sentiment Polarity part, the pre-processed comment is fed to the polarity classifier as input for predicting whether it is a positive or negative comment. After the sentiment of the comment is pre-dicted, the Prediction of Comment's Aspect part begins by putting the comment in to the aspect classifier as input. If the predicted sentiment polarity of the comment is positive, the aspect of the comment is predicted from a total of 11 different aspects indicating positive feelings about "embarkation," "shore excursions," "public rooms," "enrichment activities," "onboard experiences," "price-value," "dining," "entertainment," "fitness and recreation," "service," and "cabin." In contrast, if polarity is negative, the comment is given as input to the aspect classifier, which is generated by training negative and labeling 11 different features which are same as the positive aspects. Thus, the aspect classifier deter-mines the aspects to which the positive and negative comment data belong. In the Prediction of Comment's Overall Rating Value part, the overall rating value of the comment is calculated by taking into consideration the polarity and aspect probabilities of the comment.

Creating Corpus

Corpus simply refers to the regular and structural cohesion of a large number of texts. Commenting a sentence might contain multiple polarities and aspects. In this study, the corpus was created by treating each sentence as a document. The corpus contains a total of 5,600 comment sentences.

Data Pre-Processing

First, data labeling was performed to create a training set for the classification algorithm and to determine to which class the data belongs. Among 20,247 comments, 5,600 comment sentences were labeled with:

- "Positive" and "negative" for polarity prediction.
- "Embarkation," "shore excursions," "public rooms," "enrichment activities," "onboard experiences," "price-value," "dining," "entertainment," "fitness and recreation," "service," and "cabin" for predicting the aspect of the comments.
- Comments' overall rating values given by cruise passengers for comparing star rating values.

The process by which researchers read and assign class labels to each training data is called manual labeling (Liu, Li, Lee, & Yu, 2004). However, to minimize bias in the labeling process, the coding process needs to be performed by different encoders. In this study, apart from the author of the study, assistance was received from two doctoral students. The students labeled training sets in two categories: polarity and aspect. The similarity rate of the data set encoded by different encoders is important to consider (Fidan & Öztürk, 2015) and indicates the reliability of the research. In this study, the internal consistency formula of Miles and Huberman (1994) was used.

$$\Delta = C \div (C + \partial) \times 100 \tag{2}$$

Where;

Δ: Reliability coefficient
C: Number of agreed codes
∂: Number of disagreed codes

As a rule of thumb, anything above 80% internal consistency means the research has enough reliability (Miles & Huberman, 1994). In the present study, polarity labeling consistency was 83% and aspect labeling consistency was 81% among encoders. Therefore, we can say that the coding has passed the threshold. In the text preprocessing for transforming textual data into a more useful format, we employed tokenization; removed punctuation, stop words, and numbers; converted words in the text to uppercase or lowercase; and applied Porter stemming.

Classification Algorithm

The purpose of the classification algorithm is to learn how to distribute the training data and then classify correctly the non-class test data. For measuring efficiency performance of the classification algorithm, we used a confusion matrix to evaluate the algorithmic results. It contains the actual class label and estimated class label numbers in the sample class. Accuracy, precision, recall, and F-measure are indicators in the confusion matrix and are used to describe the performance of the classification model.

In this study, an algorithm was selected from the machine learning algorithms in the scikit-learn, a Python library designed for certain functions such as classification algorithm, image processing, and machine learning facilitation. A total of 4,600 comments were used as a training set and 1,000 as a test set. The training set was assigned as an input to the seven classification algorithms in the scikit-learn library: namely, Decision Tree, K Nearest Neighbor (KNN), LinearSVC, Logistic Regression, Multinominal Naive Bayes, SGDC Classifier and Random Forest. Then, classification accuracy values and F-score values were examined. The LinearSVC algorithm had the highest classification accuracy and F-score value over the given training set. Therefore, the LinearSVC algorithm was used as the classification algorithm of this study. Tables 1 and 2 depict classification accuracies and F-score values of the seven algorithms.

Table 1. Polarity Classifier Accuracy and F-Score Values.

Model Name	Average F-Score	Accuracy
DecisionTreeClassifier	0.81	0.7854
KNeighborsClassifier	0.68	0.6402
LinearSVC	**0.85**	**0.8184**
LogisticRegression	0.79	0.7921
MultinomialNB	0.80	0.7827
RandomForestClassifier	0.83	0.6674
SGDClassifier	0.84	0.8043

Table 2. Aspect Classifier Accuracy and F-Score Values.

Model Name	Average F-Score	Accuracy
DecisionTreeClassifier	0.68	0.6636
KNeighborsClassifier	0.29	0.3713
LinearSVC	**0.74**	**0.7199**
LogisticRegression	0.73	0.7141
MultinomialNB	0.69	0.6868
RandomForestClassifier	0.71	0.3655
SGDClassifier	0.73	0.7202

Findings

Predicting Sentiment Polarity of the Comment

We created training and testing sets. The training set was composed of 80% of the corpus (4,600 comment sentences) and the testing set of 20% of the corpus (1,000 comment sentences). The training set was assigned as an input to LinearSVC because, as can be seen Table 1, it has the highest accuracy and F-score value. In Table 1, the polarity classification accuracy value of the LinearSVC algorithm is 81% and the F-score value is 85%.

Predicting Aspect of the Comment

At this phase, positive polarity comments are given as input to the classification algorithm, which is trained with positive comment data and manually labeled with 11 different aspects. The same process is employed for comments with negative polarity. As explained earlier, the classification algorithm helps determine the aspect class to which the positive and negative comments belong. As can be seen in Table 2, the aspect classification accuracy value of the LinearSVC algorithm is 71% and the F-score value is 74%.

Predicting Overall Rating Value of the Comment

At this phase, the overall rating value of the comment is predicted with the help probabilities of comments' sentiments and aspects. We proposed two different rating prediction methods and overall star rating scales according to *RQ1* and *RQ2*, as explained in the research background section. In *RQ1*, we tried to reveal whether cruise travelers give an overall star rating value according to the most intense negative or positive feeling about their cruise experience. In order to answer *RQ1*, we proposed two different methods based on assigning the sentiment polarity of comment. In first rating prediction method, polarity and aspect probabilities of comment sentences are determined by using the classification algorithm. Comment sentences are grouped and compared with each other according to their polarity type.

- *Method 1.* The sentiment polarity with the highest classification probability value is assigned as the sentiment polarity of the comment.
- *Method 2.* Comment sentences are counted to determine comment sentences with maximum polarity type. Maximum polarity type is assigned as the polarity of the comment.

According to the two methods, we revealed the aspect with the highest probability value in determined sentiment polarity. The highest probability value of aspect in specified polarity is assigned as the overall rating value of comment. Table 3 shows overall star rating scale for *RQ1*. Overall star rating values of the comments are made according to this scale.

In *RQ2*, we tried to reveal whether cruise travelers give an average overall rating value according to their cruise experiences. In order to answer *RQ2*, we tried to determine the weighted average probability value in effective polarity with the help of the strong influencing polarity (SIP). Table 4 shows the star rating scale for *RQ2*.

Table 3. Overall Star Rating Scale for *RQ1*.

Range	Type of Emotion	Overall Rating
100–51	Negative	★☆☆☆☆
50–0		★★☆☆☆
0	Neutral	★★★☆☆
0–50	Positive	★★★★☆
51–100		★★★★★

Table 4. Overall Star Rating Scale for *RQ2*.

Range	Type of Emotion	Overall Rating
−1 – (−0.51)	Negative	★☆☆☆☆
−0.5–0		★★☆☆☆
0	Neutral	★★★☆☆
0–0.5	Positive	★★★★☆
0.51–1		★★★★★

Results

Using three different methods, the predicted overall star rating values and overall star rating values given by the traveler are compared based on the polarity and aspect values of the comments. Table 5 depicts consistency percentages of the three methods. For *RQ1*, the consistency percentages between predicted overall star rating values and traveler overall star rating values are 78% and 80%, respectively. For *RQ2*, the percentage of consistency between predicted star ratings and traveler star ratings is 9%.

Based on the research findings, it can be argued that the passengers made evaluations according to the most intense negative or positive sentiments they obtained after their Royal Caribbean International experience (Fig. 1). It is understood that these evaluations are made by bringing together the positive or negative services they received at an average value. All 11 aspects were examined in the context of the comment sentences. Fig. 2 shows the distribution of the comments of the 11 aspects according to whether they were positive and negative. As a result, it is understood that 11 aspects are seen more in positive comment sentences, which, in turn, indicates that positive comments about the business outweigh the negative comments.

Regarding aspects in the comments, it is understood that aspects "shore excursions," "onboard experience," "service," "dining," and "entertainment" are

Table 5. Consistency Percentages of Overall Star Rating Values by Three Methods.

	Method 1	Method 2	Method 3
The number of true predicted star rating value	15,987	16,246	2,009
The number of false predicted star rating value	4,260	4,001	18,238
Percentage of consistency	78%	80%	9%

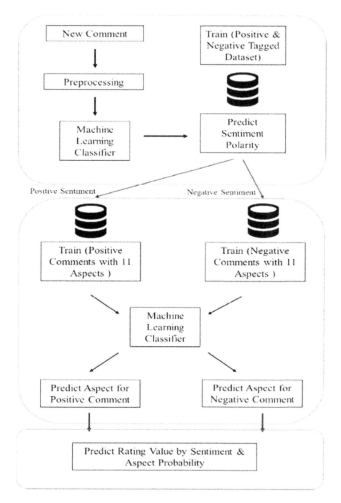

Fig. 1.   Overview of Proposed Method. *Source:* Developed by the authors.

involved mostly in the positive comments (Fig. 3). On the other hand, it is seen that aspects "onboard experience," "shore excursions," "service," "public rooms," and "dining" are involved mostly in the negative comments (Fig. 4).

After determining the positive and negative weight, it is examined which of the 11 characteristics were dominant for the passengers, taking into account 20,247 comments. The method applied is able to predict the overall star rating values of the comments with a probability of 80%. However, the feature values of 2,595 comments out of 20,247 cannot be predicted since the sentences in the comment

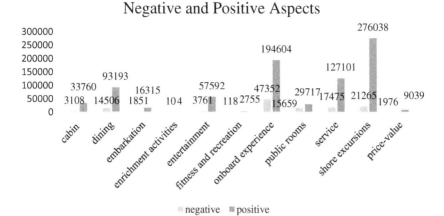

Fig. 2.   The Number of Aspects in Positive and Negative Comment
Sentences.

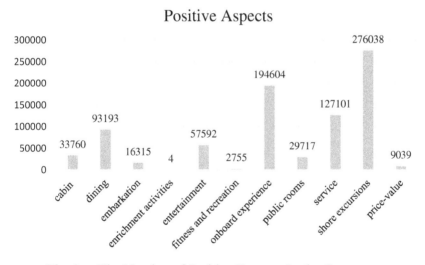

Fig. 3.   The Number of Positive Features in the Comments.

have an equal number of dominant aspects. Fig. 5 shows the aspects that customers consider with a probability of 80% when making overall star ratings. As
can be seen in Fig. 5, when evaluating the business with a general star rating,
passengers rated 11 features with a probability of 80%. They took account of
"shore excursions," "onboard experience," "service," "dining," "entertainment,"
"public rooms", "cabin," "embarkation" and "price-value" while "enrichment
activities" and "fitness and recreation" seemed to be the least important features.

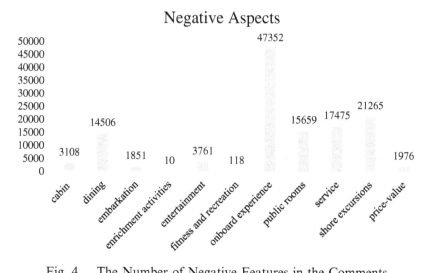

Fig. 4.   The Number of Negative Features in the Comments.

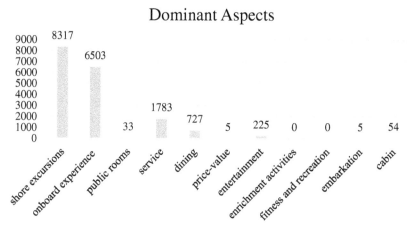

Fig. 5.   Passengers' Overall Star Rating Aspects, Ranked by
Importance.

Conclusions

This chapter focused on sentimental analysis in hospitality and tourism. With the rapid development in internet technologies and online tourism web sites, there is a huge amount of textual data waiting for analysis. Analyzing these textual data undoubtedly provides a unique opportunity for the business to understand its shortcomings. In this context, this chapter presents how to organize and analyze textual data for extracting customer sentiments from a large collection of documents to improve business operations and performance. In this chapter, review rating prediction approach, which seeks to predict and identify ratings corresponding to the customer reviews, is undertaken via a case study. In the case study, the cruise passenger comments about Royal Caribbean International on cruisecritic.com were examined to determine the impact of cruise travel experiences on the cruise company evaluation process based on affective and cognitive attributes.

We proposed two different rating prediction methods for determining important and unimportant aspects for cruise travelers about their cruise experience and the effects of their positive or negative feelings on the evaluation process. We discovered that cruise travelers evaluate the company with their most intense positive or negative feelings. In addition, travelers pay more attention to the "shore excursions" than any other aspects. This is consistent with previous research. Shore excursions refer to mainland-based activities of cruise passengers (Buzova, Sanz-Blas, & Cervera-Taulet, 2018). Petrick, Tonner, and Quinn (2006) and Teye and Leclerc (1998) argue that shore excursions are of vital importance to the cruise experience. Papathanassis (2017) emphasizes that shore routes continue to be an important part of cruise vacations, although cruise ships themselves are known as floating holiday resorts. It can be further argued that "enrichment activities" and "fitness and recreation" are unimportant aspects for cruise travelers in their evaluation process. Customer feedback is an important source of data for customer satisfaction in light of growing competition in the cruise industry. Cruise companies will have the opportunity to give quicker feedback to customers by considering these overall ratings. A swift feedback system will prevent customer complaints and customer dissatisfaction due to service errors, negative word of mouth, and so on.

In our proposed approach, the overall rating value is calculated according to sentiment and aspect probabilities of a given comment. In this way, it is possible determine how much the aspects of comments effect the overall rating. The company can provide the traveler with special services in line with the aspects that the traveler considers to be very important, important, or insignificant. Thus, it will be possible to eliminate problems within the company. By examining customer comments, it will also be possible for the company to determine its priority needs and perform budgeting according to said needs. Ultimately, the company will increase customer satisfaction by responding to customer requests and will ensure efficient use of business resources along the way.

References

Agrawal, R., & Batra, M. (2013). A detailed study on text mining techniques. *IJSCE*, *2*(6), 118–121.

Ahmad, M., Aftab, S., Ali, I., & Hameed, N. (2017). Hybrid tools and techniques for sentiment analysis: A review. *International Journal of Multidisciplinary Sciences and Engineering*, *8*(3), 29–33.

Boateng, H. (2016). Customer knowledge management practices on a social media platform:A case study of MTN Ghana and Vodafone Ghana. *Information Development, 32*(3), 440–451.

Bross, J. (2013). *Aspect-oriented sentiment analysis of customer reviews using distant supervision techniques.* Ph.D. thesis, Freie Universität Berlin.

Bucur, C. (2015). Using opinion mining techniques in tourism. *Procedia Economics and Finance, 23,* 1666–1673.

Buzova, D., Sanz-Blas, S., & Cervera-Taulet, A. (2018). 'Tour me onshore': Understanding cruise tourists' evaluation of shore excursions through text mining. *Journal of Tourism and Cultural Change, 17*(3), 1–18.

Choi, S., Lehto, X. Y., & Morrison, A. M. (2007). Destination image representation on the web: Content analysis of Macao travel related websites. *Tourism Management, 28*(1), 118–129.

Cruisecritic.com. (2020). Retrieved from https://www.cruisecritic.co.uk/

Fidan, T., & Oztürk, I. (2015). The relationship of the creativity of public and private school teachers to their intrinsic motivation and the school climate for innovation. *Procedia-Social and Behavioral Sciences, 195,* 905–914.

Ganu, G., Elhadad, N., & Marian, A. (2009). Beyond the stars: Improving rating predictions using review text content. *WebDB, 9,* 1–6.

Gojali, S., & Khodra, M. L. (2016). Aspect based sentiment analysis for review rating prediction. In 2016 international conference on advanced informatics: Concepts, theory and application (ICAICTA) (pp. 1–6).

Gong, L. (2018). Application of biomedical text mining. *Artificial Intelligence: Emerging Trends and Applications, 417.*

Gretzel, U., & Yoo, K. H. (2008). Use and impact of online travel reviews. In *Information and communication technologies in tourism* (pp. 35–46).

Hand, D. J. (1998). Data mining: Statistics and more? *The American Statistician, 52*(2), 112–118.

Hotho, A., Nürnberger, A., & Paaß, G. (2005). A brief survey of text mining. *Ldv Forum, 20*(1), 19–62.

Jalilvand, M. R., & Samiei, N. (2012). The impact of electronic word of mouth on a tourism destination choice: Testing the theory of planned behavior (TBP). *Internet Research, 22*(5), 591–612.

Jatana, V. (2018). Dive into machine learning. Retrieved from https://www.researchgate.net/publication/328614973_Dive_Into_Machine_Learning

Kim, S., Lee, K. Y., Shin, S., & Yang, S. B. (2017). The effects of tourism information quality in social media on destination image formation: The case of Weibo. *Information & Management, 54*(6), 687–702.

Kontostathis, A., Edwards, L., & Leatherman, A. (2010). Text mining and cybercrime. In M. W. Berry & J. Kogan (Eds.), *Text mining: Applications and theory.* New York, NY: John Wiley & Sons.

Kuttainen, C., Lexhagen, M., Fuchs, M., & Höpken, W. (2012). Social media monitoring and analysis of a Swedish tourism destination. In Proceedings of the 2nd conference on advances in hospitality and tourism marketing and management (AHTMM).

Lee, M. J., Singh, N., & Chan, E. S. W. (2011). Service failures and recovery actions in the hotel industry: A text-mining approach. *Journal of Vacation Marketing, 17*(3), 197–207.

Litvin, S. W., Goldsmith, R. E., & Pan, B. (2008). Electronic word-of-mouth in hospitality and tourism management. *Tourism Management, 29*(3), 458–468.

Liu, B. (2012). Sentiment analysis and opinion mining. *Synthesis Lectures on Human Language Technologies, 5*(1), 1–167.

Liu, B., Li, X., Lee, W. S., & Yu, P. S. (2004). Text classification by labeling words. *AAAI, 4*, 425–430.

Liu, B., & Zhang, L. (2012). A Survey of opinion mining and sentiment analysis. In *Mining text data* (pp. 415–463). Boston, MA: Springer.

Luo, T., Chen, S., Xu, G., & Zhou, J. (2013). *Trust-based collective view prediction*. New York, NY: Springer.

Markopoulos, G., Mikros, G., Iliadi, A., & Liontos, M. (2015). Sentiment analysis of hotel reviews in Greek: A comparison of unigram features, *Cultural tourism in a digital era*. Cham: Springer.

Miles, M., & Huberman, A. (1994). *Qualitative data analysis: An expanded sourcebook*. Thousand Oaks, CA: Sage.

Misopoulos, F., Mitic, M., Kapoulas, A., & Karapiperis, C. (2014). Uncovering customer service experiences with Twitter: The case of airline industry. *Management Decision, 52*(4), 705–723.

Nasukawa, T., & Yi, J. (2003). Sentiment analysis: Capturing favorability using natural language processing. In Proceedings of the 2nd international conference on knowledge capture, USA, Oct. 23–25. Sanibel Island, FL.

Ordenes, F. V., Theodoulidis, B., Burton, J., Gruber, T., & Zaki, M. (2014). Analyzing customer experience feedback using text mining: A linguistics-based approach. *Journal of Service Research, 17*(3), 278–295.

Papathanassis, A. (2017). Cruise tourism management: State of the art. *Tourist Review, 72*, 104–119.

Petrick, J. F., Tonner, C., & Quinn, C. (2006). The utilization of critical incident technique to examine cruise passengers' repurchase intentions. *Journal of Travel Research, 44*(3), 273–280.

Pinker, S. (1997). *How the mind works*. New York, NY: Norton.

Ramanathan, V., & Meyyappan, T. (2013). Survey of text mining. In *International conference on technology and business management* (pp. 508–514).

Safavian, S. R., & Landgrebe, D. A. (1991). Survey of decision tree classifier methodology. IEEE Transactions on Systems. *Man and Cybernetics, 21*, 660–674.

Samuel, A. L. (1959). Some studies in machine learning using the game of checkers. *IBM Journal of Research and Development, 3*(3), 210–229.

Schmitt, B. H. (1999). *Experiential marketing*. New York, NY: Free Press.

Sezgen, E., Mason, K. J., & Mayer, R. (2019). Voice of airline passenger: A text mining approach to understand customer satisfaction. *Journal of Air Transport Management, 77*, 65–74.

Songpan, W. (2017). The analysis and prediction of customer review rating using opinion mining. In IEEE 15th international conference on software engineering research, management and applications.

Sparks, B. A., & Browning, V. (2011). The impact of online reviews on hotel booking intentions and perception of trust. *Tourism Management, 32*(6), 1310–1323.

Tang, D., Qin, B., Liu, T., & Yang, Y. (2015). User modeling with neural network for review rating prediction. In *Twenty-fourth international joint conference on artificial intelligence*.

Tao, S., & Kim, H. (2019). Cruising in Asia: What can we dig from online cruiser reviews to understand their experience and satisfaction. *Asia Pacific Journal of Tourism Research*, *24*(6), 514–528.

Teye, V. B., & Leclerc, D. (1998). Product and service delivery satisfaction among North American cruise passengers. *Tourism Management*, *19*(2), 153–160.

Turney, P. D. (2002). Thumbs up or thumbs down? Semantic orientation applied to unsupervised classification of reviews. In Proceedings of the 40th Annual Meeting of the Association for Computational Linguistics, Philadelphia.

Ur-Rahman, N., & Harding, J. A. (2012). Textual data mining for industrial knowledge management and text classification: A business oriented approach. *Expert Systems with Applications*, *39*, 4729–4739.

Wang, B., Xiong, S., Huang, Y., & Li, X. (2018). Review rating prediction based on user context and product context. *Applied Sciences*, *8*(10), 1849.

Weiss, S. M., Indurkhya, N., Zhang, T., & Damerau, F. (2010). *Text mining: Predictive methods for analyzing unstructured information*. New York, NY: Springer.

Yang, D., Zhang, D., Yu, Z., & Wang, Z. (2013). A sentiment-enhanced personalized location recommendation system. In Proceedings of the 24th ACM conference on hypertext and social media (pp. 119–128).

Ye, Q., Zhang, Z., & Law, R. (2009). Sentiment classification of online reviews to travel destinations by supervised machine learning approaches. *Expert Systems with Applications*, *36*(3), 6527–6535.

Chapter 9

Qualitative Analysis of Social Media Historical Data: A Case Study of Twitter and Tourism Boycotts

Ismail Shaheer, Neil Carr and Andrea Insch

Abstract

Social media is noted for its usefulness and contribution to destination marketing and management. Social media data is particularly valued as a source to understand issues such as tourist behavior and destination marketing strategies. Among the social media platforms, Twitter is one of the most utilized in research. Its use raises two issues: the challenge of obtaining historical data and the importance of qualitative data analysis. Regarding these issues, the chapter argues that retrieving tweets using hashtags and keywords on the Twitter website provides a corpus of tweets that is valuable for research, especially for qualitative inquiries. In addition, the value of qualitative analysis of Twitter data is presented, demonstrating, among other things, how such an approach captures in-depth information, enables appreciation and inclusion of the nonconventional language used on social media, distinguishes between "noise" and useful information, and recognizes information as the sum of all parts in the data.

Keywords: Social media; qualitative inquiry; qualitative analysis; tourism boycotts; Twitter; hashtags

Introduction

The growing prominence of the links between social media and tourism has been increasingly recognized (Sigala, Christou, & Gretzel, 2012). This has contributed to social media being identified as an essential element of destination marketing and management (Hays, Page, & Buhalis, 2013). As a result, data from social media (often referred to as big data) has been viewed as a valuable source for

Advanced Research Methods in Hospitality and Tourism, 163–178
Copyright © 2023 Ismail Shaheer, Neil Carr and Andrea Insch
Published under exclusive licence by Emerald Publishing Limited
doi:10.1108/978-1-80117-550-020221009

research, particularly to help understand issues related to tourist behavior and destination marketing strategies (Li, Xu, Tang, Wang, & Li, 2018). As social media platforms become older they are also an increasingly valuable source of longitudinal data, rather than just being able to provide information about current events and views.

Among the numerous existing social media platforms, Twitter is one of the most utilized for research. Academics, consultancy firms, tourism providers, and DMOs utilize Twitter data to make informed decisions and offer suggestions for the tourism industry (Park, Ok, & Chae, 2016). Despite the increasing usage of Twitter data for research, two important points are raised: challenges in obtaining historical data (Bruns & Liang, 2012) and the importance of analyzing Twitter data qualitatively to gain deeper insights than are provided by quantitative analysis (Burns, Blumenthal, & Sitter, 2020). These points relate to the dearth of attention given to obtaining and using historical social media data in tourism, and the qualitative analysis of such material within tourism studies.

Researchers face challenges to collect data from social media platforms, especially longitudinal data. The main obstacles faced by researchers are high cost, and limitations on the amount and period of data. As part of their business model, some social media companies have monetized their data. The data can be purchased primarily from third parties, which is expensive, making it a significant constraint for researchers to obtain the data (Zimmer, 2015). Social media providers restrict the amount and period of data that can be retrieved (Weller & Kinder-Kurlanda, 2015). These restrictions on accessing the data can often dictate the choices researchers have to make (Debreceny, Wang, & Zhou, 2019), sometimes forcing them to quit the research or search for alternative options.

This chapter presents a hands-on approach to acquiring historical data from the Twitter platform using a case study of tourism boycotts which employed Twitter data, focusing on tweets and the profile of Twitter users. In addition, the chapter contributes to the discussion of the relative importance of the qualitative analysis of social media data that enables a more in-depth understanding of the phenomenon studied (Bermingham & Smeaton, 2011).

The utilization of tourism boycotts as a case study is related to the influence social media has on social movements (Masip, Ruiz-Caballero, Suau, & Puertas, 2020). Social media has helped increase the number of social movements, including tourism boycotts, in the last decade (Shaheer, Carr, & Insch, 2018). Tourism boycotts are seen as a global movement involving a large number of people happening in the online space, which can generate a significant and varied amount of data on Twitter. These factors make tourism boycotts an ideal case study to explore social media data. It is important to recognize that the focus of this chapter is not tourism boycotts, although they are used as a case to provide examples for the discussion. Rather, tourism boycott calls in social media are utilized as a lens through which to explore the qualitative analysis of social media historical data in relation to tourism.

Social Media Data in Research

The global use of social media has increased exponentially in the last decade (Chaffey, 2019). There are many social media platforms (e.g., Facebook, Twitter), which provide numerous advantages and opportunities, such as instant communication and global access. Consequently, social media has been adopted by individuals, organizations, and governments as an important communication platform.

The adoption of social media by individuals and organizations was closely followed by researchers who identified the significant potential of the data social media users generate. Social media has become an important source for researchers to understand various phenomena, especially studies that require the opinions and perceptions of the global community (Pak & Paroubek, 2010). Social media data is analyzed by researchers to propose suggestions for various groups, such as businesses and governments. For instance, Burnap, Gibson, Sloan, Southern, and Williams (2016) used data from Twitter to predict the 2015 general election in the United Kingdom. Song and Liu (2017) used big data to estimate tourist demand. Among the various social media platforms, Twitter is one of the most popular social media platforms amongst the general population and researchers utilizing social media (Jungherr, 2015).

Twitter

Twitter is a social network site that was founded in 2006. Today, it boasts more than 314 million active users worldwide (Statista, 2021). The service allows users to post micro-blogs limited to 280 characters, each called a tweet (Jürgens & Jungherr, 2016). Twitter users generate a significant amount of data, which can take many forms, including sharing news, expressing opinions, and promoting products. The topics discussed can revolve around elections in a particular country, coverage of protests, holiday experiences and desires, or just mundane tweets, such as "I am at the gym," among other things. Effectively, what is placed on social media is only restricted by the imagination of the users. The light touch approach taken by many social media providers in terms of policing content means that both socially acceptable and controversial material is present on social media. This is a controversial reality but it clearly adds to the richness of the potential data for researchers.

The utilization of tweets to better understand complex social issues has been growing among researchers. For example, Chang (2010) demonstrated that the use of hashtags on Twitter resembles the Diffusion of Innovation theory, whereby people's online behavior largely mirrors their offline behavior. Within a tourism context, Kang and Schuett (2013) used peoples' behavior of sharing travel experiences on social media to explain social influence theory.

Research Context

The cases used in this chapter to demonstrate the collection and qualitative analysis of Twitter data are based on research undertaken by Shaheer (2019) that explores participation in tourism boycott calls. The underlying reason for the boycott calls was concern for the welfare of animals. Tweets posted calling for a tourism boycott of China (dog meat festival), Kerala, India (stray dog culling), Spain (bullfighting), and South Africa (hunting) were used in the study. The following sections describe how historical data were retrieved and analyzed.

Data Collection

At the time (in 2016) the data collection exercise was undertaken there were four access points to Twitter data, as summarized in Table 1. The table provides information about how data can be accessed and the limitations of the tweets' access points that informed the data access point selected by the researcher. Most of the existing studies (e.g., Bigné, Oltra, & Andreu, 2019; Pak & Paroubek, 2010) employ data collection methods using the Twitter API or access a third party database (refer to Table 1). Collecting data through Twitter API requires extensive technical knowledge (e.g., programming). Even with technical

Table 1. Twitter Data Access Points (Shaheer, 2019).

Data Access Points	Details
Twitter website	• The website is free to access • Historical data can be browsed manually • User-friendly and no technical knowledge required
Twitter API – Streaming API	• Allows researchers to extract tweets as they happen with a query (real time) • Requires researchers to go through an authentication procedure to provide a key and access token, which enables them to connect to the server to retrieve the tweets • Retrieves only 1% of the tweets, based on any given query (Guo & McCombs, 2016)
Twitter API – Search API	• Tweets retrieved from the last seven days (Twitter, 2017) • Tweets retrieved, based on relevance rather than completeness. Hence, an unknown percentage of data is omitted from the collection process, making it challenging for accurate sampling procedures (Borra & Rieder, 2014)
Twitter data through third parties	• Sells access to the full firehose (all tweets) on a given query (e.g., specific hashtag) • The price of a corpus of data is high (Zimmer, 2015)

knowledge (or help from experts), the earliest Tweets researchers can capture goes back seven days (Twitter, 2017). Besides collecting data through the Twitter API, data can also be accessed through the Twitter website or purchased via a third party database. The option of purchasing data from a third party was not viable because it is expensive (Zimmer, 2015).

Not having a viable and feasible method to collect historical tweets (past tweets, from across the duration of the existence of the social media platform or the phenomenon being studied) is problematic as the necessary data for the study included past tweets (beyond the seven days cut-off point imposed by Twitter) and the profiles of the Twitter users who posted these tweets. For example, researchers who want to explore the changes in a discussion (e.g., themes) of an event (e.g., Christchurch earthquake in relation to tourism) may need to look at Tweets prior to the earthquake, from the point of the earthquake, and across the months/years following it to fully understand the phenomenon.

Gaining a complete historical dataset from Twitter, or any other social media platform, is not realistic. However, as the study highlighted in this chapter takes a qualitative approach, it did not require such a dataset (Makarem & Jae, 2016). For the purpose of this chapter, qualitative inquiry is defined as exploring the phenomenon (i.e., tourism boycotts) to reach an in-depth understanding (of what was happening on Twitter in relation to tourism boycott calls). In contrast, quantitative inquiries focus on generalizing aspects of the phenomenon using a large number of individuals (i.e., Twitter users). A more detailed discussion of qualitative and quantitative research approaches is provided by Choy (2014).

Consequently, tweets were collected using the Twitter website, as the study did not require a large sample, at least not in relation to the scale of a sample demanded for a quantitative study. Fig. 1 shows a summary of the data collection and analysis process from the point of identifying data needs to analyzing the data. More detail information about each step is provided in the following sections.

A preliminary search of Twitter was undertaken to identify the search terms to be used to identify the tweets for the study (Woo et al., 2018). The preliminary search helped identify the most commonly used hashtags and keywords on Twitter associated with the boycotts studied. It is important to note that even though research using Twitter data relies heavily on tweets organized by hashtags (Weber, Garimella, & Teka, 2013), users may post without hashtags. Thus, both keywords and hashtags were employed to search for the tweets. In addition to the destination boycott search terms (e.g., Spain + boycott), specific search terms related to the reason for the boycott trigger, such as "bullfighting Spain," were employed. Fig. 2 presents the search terms and hashtags used to identify the tweets associated with Spain's tourism boycott from the Twitter platform. For every search term used, a hashtag search was also undertaken by including the hashtag (#) as a prefix to the word and omitting the space between words. A similar process was followed to collect data for the other destination boycotts included in the study.

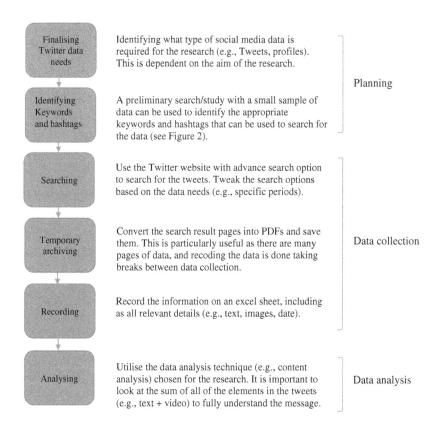

Fig. 1.   Process of Planning, Data Collection, and Analysis. *Source:* Adapted from Shaheer (2019).

The data were collected between 1st August and September 5, 2016 using the advance search option on the Twitter website (available at https://twitter.com/search-advanced?lang=en). A manual scrolling method was employed, where the researcher typed the keyword or hashtag and pressed "search" and kept the mouse on auto-scrolling until the end of the available tweets. With the initial click of the search button, only tweets that can be displayed on the computer screen are visible. Hence, scrolling is required for the tweets to appear that are below the web page perimeter. After the scrolling had stopped, the page(s) were saved as PDF files.

A total of 52,644 tweets were collected, with the earliest tweets going as far back as the year 2009. Relevant tweets for the study were individually searched on the Twitter website to retrieve information about the Twitter users who posted the tweets. The information that was collected also included profiles of Twitter users who supported the original tweets (e.g., retweeting). It is difficult to manage Twitter data due to the format and the amount of data (Jürgens & Jungherr, 2016). Hence, care was taken to ensure they were stored in a way that was readily

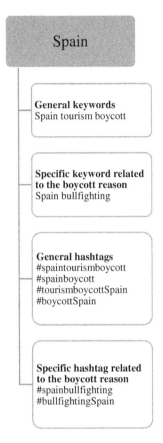

Fig. 2.   Search Hashtags (#) and Keywords – Spain.

available and practical for use in the analysis, without much complication and further processing. The information in Table 2 was entered onto an Excel sheet.

Data Analysis

Content analysis was employed to analyze the data. Content analysis is commonly used in social media studies, particularly with Twitter data (e.g., Makarem & Jae, 2016). Content analysis is described as "a research method for the subjective interpretation of the content of data through the systematic classification process of coding and identifying themes or patterns" (Hsieh & Shannon, 2005, p. 1278). The content analysis was conducted on two levels: a basic level (manifest level) that is a descriptive account of the data, and a higher level (latent level) of analysis, which is a more interpretive analysis. A combination of emojis in a tweet or a profile description needs to be understood from a latent level because as a combination it can provide a message similar to the

Table 2. Information Recorded.

Information Recorded	Details
Tweet	Includes the text and the hashtags
Twitter handle of the Twitter user	The unique username assigned to a Twitter user
Location of the Twitter user	If identified or mentioned in the profile description
Hashtags used	A word or phrase preceded by a hash sign (#)
Date of the tweet posted	
Number of retweets	A reposting/sharing of an original tweet
Number of *like* (including a list of Twitter users who *liked*)	Likes are represented by a small heart at the bottom of the tweet and are used to show appreciation for a tweet.
Listed Twitter users who were *mentioned*	A mention is when someone uses the @ sign immediately followed by the Twitter handle of a user.
Profile description of the Twitter users	Profile description is the short bio of the Twitter user which appears under the name and the Twitter handle
Identification if an image was included	The image was described and archived, using the name of the destination, Twitter handle and date posted.
Identification if a video was included	A description was provided, including a link to the video. The downloaded video was saved using the name of the destination, Twitter handle and date posted.
Identification if a hyperlink was included	A description of the information provided at the linked site was recorded with the link to the site.

hieroglyphics used in ancient Egypt. For example, a text such as "ban bull-fighting" is self-explanatory and can be understood from a manifest level. However, the combination of text "Someone hoping to make a difference #NeverGiveUp" followed by emojis of animals (Fig. 3) should be analyzed at a higher level (latent level). The combination of these elements (text and emojis) in the tweet can be understood as a Twitter user trying to make a difference for the welfare of animals by calling for the boycott of destinations perceived to neglect the welfare of animals. The analysis of the message enabled the researcher to understand why people were participating in the boycott calls of tourism destinations.

Someone hoping to make a difference #NeverGiveUp 🐼🐨🐼🐱🐾🐍🐘

Fig. 3.   A Tweet That Requires Latent Analysis.

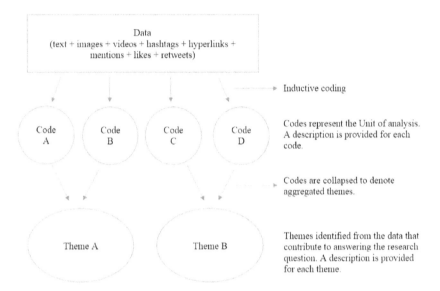

Fig. 4.   Content Analysis.

The tweets were coded thematically to explore common themes based on the aim of the research (i.e., strategies used in the tweets to mobilize support for the boycotts) (see Fig. 4). An inductive coding technique was utilized so that new information that emerged was not overlooked by relying on pre-existing themes identified from previous studies (Azungah, 2018). An inductive approach is a data-driven approach (Samarasekara, Fukahori, & Kubota, 2011), and was particularly useful given that Twitter data can be so varied.

In the initial phase, a coding template was utilized in which codes were recorded along with the supporting information from the tweets. The codes denote the unit of analysis. All the codes were given a description to ensure the code represented the data it was associated with. In the second phase, the codes that were generated were compared with existing literature to identify themes that contributed to the aim of the study. Similar to codes, the themes were also provided with descriptions for clarity.

Implications and Observations

The following sections discuss the implications and observations from the case studies, focusing on the sufficiency and applicability of the data collected, and the advantages of a qualitative analysis of social media data.

Data Sample

The data collected from the Twitter platform were sufficient to answer the research questions (Shaheer, 2019). The number of Twitter profiles collected (i.e., 4,559) and the 2,152 tweets were suitable for a qualitative inquiry to address the aim of the study: to explore participation in tourism boycott calls as a result of animal welfare concerns on the Twittersphere. However, it is important to be mindful that research that uses a sample dataset from social media may be criticised for making inferences without having a complete dataset (Barratt, Ferris, & Lenton, 2015). This is despite the fact that studies that utilise data from samples of populations (e.g., surveys) do not receive the same criticism. To develop an understanding of a phenomenon, a qualitative analysis of a sample of tweets or Twitter users is more than adequate (Theocharis, Lowe, Van Deth, & García-Albacete, 2015).

Missing Important Information

The most popular social media platforms, such as Twitter, Instagram, and Facebook, allow users to geotag their posts (Tuarob, Tucker, Salathe, & Ram, 2014). Thus, in studies where the location of the Twitter user is essential, it is common for researchers to collect and utilize geotagged tweets (Padilla, Kavak, Lynch, Gore, & Diallo, 2018). However, this is only possible if the user enabled the location identification. Twitter users who indicated the location information on their profile description (which many do) without enabling the location will not be included in the analysis. Therefore, in studies that use a particular group of users (i.e., those who use specific hashtags), some of them may be excluded in the analysis. This can be remedied by a qualitative analysis (i.e., what the current study employed), by reading the profile descriptions of Twitter users who have not enabled the location, but have provided the information in the profile descriptions (Vieweg, Hughes, Starbird, & Palen, 2010). In the current study, 34% of the cases the locations of the Twitter users was only observed in the profile description (for example, see below).

I am from God's Own Country, Incredible India.

Non-Conventional Language

The language used in social media does not conform to standard languages (Tuarob et al., 2014). In addition, it is rapidly evolving and changing with time and events. A simple "#MeToo" hashtag in a post can be powerful and meaningful. The language used in social media is a result of the online space being used by a melting pot of cultures. Partly due to the informal nature of the interactions and the limitations of the characters allowed, users of social media have created a language of their own. Using abbreviations such as LOL (laughing out loud), or the use of multiple emojis can be as meaningful as writing a full paragraph (Walther & D'addario, 2001). The task of evaluating the multiple variations and combinations of elements (texts, hashtags, and emojis) used in tweets can be daunting, especially when the different combinations of the components can have different meanings. However, it is vital to understand the meaning of the post in order to thoroughly analyze the dataset. This can be particularly important in exploratory studies (Lyles, López, Pasick, & Sarkar, 2013) because the domain or the issue is largely undefined.

The importance of qualitative analysis was noted in the current study in many instances. For example, a tweet included a link to a petition (https://www.the-petitionsite.com/819/229/714/st%E2%80%A6%20%E2%80%A6%20/#Boycott-Spain%20#BoycottFrance%20untilthey%20#EndBullfighting%204Ever) calling for the end of bullfighting, hashtags of the boycott target and reasons for the boycott call (i.e., #BoycottSpain, #BoycottFrance, #EndBullfighting). Such tweets require the researcher to analyze the data with a qualitative approach to fully understand the message. As cumbersome as it is, qualitative inquiry equips the researcher with suitable analytical tools to understand such messages.

Supplementary Information to Make Sense of the Data

Often in tweets users include a combination of elements that may need supplementary information to understand the whole message (Gokulakrishnan, Priyanthan, Ragavan, Prasath, & Perera, 2012). For example, Gokulakrishnan et al. (2012) state that some tweets may include hyperlinks that provide supplementary information about the emotion of the poster associated with the subject being discussed. In the current study, there were several instances where it was essential to get some background information about the elements included in the tweets to understand the whole tweet. For example, in response to the boycott calls of Kerala, the following tweet was posted.

> Message to Boycott Kerala Campaign https://youtu.be/ljoMQFWOsC8

It was essential to visit the YouTube video and analyze what the message conveys in relation to the tweet posted. This tweet was in retaliation to the boycott campaign and posted in defense of the initiative to cull street dogs. Such posts may be omitted in an automated aggregating quantitative analysis and could change the outcome of the findings. For example, only 1% of the tweets included defensive tweets, while the rest were in favor of the boycott. Thus, including and analyzing such tweets becomes vital for a comprehensive understanding of the issues associated with the research. In a quantitative analysis, minor or even no importance may be given to further understanding the supplementary information included in the tweets that assisted the researcher to fully appreciate the nature of the data.

Extracting Information from 'Noise'

Social media data can be high in noise (i.e., spam, and irrelevant information for the research) due to the heterogeneity of postings, such as the writing styles and inclusion of different elements (Tuarob et al., 2014). However, this seemingly useless noise may provide useful information if observed critically, which is a fundamental aspect of qualitative analysis. It may be a tiresome process to analyze each element included in a post, but as noted in the current research, such careful analysis revealed critical information.

In the boycott calls of Spanish tourism, some Twitter users mentioned "#cataloniaisnotSpain." This may seem irrelevant, just an example of Twitter users taking advantage (i.e., hashtag hijacking) of the tourism boycott of Spain to air their political grievances (see Castells, 2014 for the political conflicts between Catalonia and Spain's administration). However, information behind the hashtag tells a different story. Bullfighting in Catalonia (a semi-autonomous region in Spain) was banned in 2010. The ban was declared unconstitutional by Spain in 2016. However, Catalonia has never held a bullfight since 2010. There is a broader issue of political dynamics within Spain that sees bullfighting used as a backdrop to wider internal conflicts. One of the possible implications of the hashtag is that Catalans are trying to avoid a tourism boycott and they are informing the audience they do not have bullfighting practices in their region.

Holistic Understanding

A qualitative analysis of the tweets enables researchers to understand the full meaning of a tweet. A qualitative approach is particularly important due to the heterogeneity of tweets, as well as the multiple elements that can be included in a single tweet, such as images, text, and videos. Each element in a tweet should be analyzed to understand the overall intended meaning of the tweet. In discussing qualitative analysis, Dey (2003, p. 249) notes how "the whole is greater than the sum of its parts," using the analogy of how individual bricks can be fitted together to become a wall.

In the current study, during the analysis process, it was observed that individual elements in a tweet (e.g., images and hashtags) needed to be combined to understand the complete meaning of the tweet. This recognizes how an image, video, or hashtag can complement the text in the tweet, and vice versa, to provide meaningful insights into the twitter users intentions (Braun & Clarke, 2006). For instance, a tweet included the text "I'd never go on holiday to Spain #*boycott-Spaintourism*," and an image of a bull in a bullfighting arena with multiple *banderillas* (decorated spiked sticks, not unlike harpoons) stabbed into its body. The text alone in the tweet does not provide information for the reader to understand the reason for the boycott call. Instead, the text, hashtag and the image together present a meaningful message that bullfighting was the reason for the Twitter user's intention not to visit Spain. In comparison, a quantitative analysis may take the individual elements in the tweet out of context and provide contradictory conclusions.

Conclusion and Recommendations

This purpose of this chapter is to presents a hands-on approach to acquiring historical data from the Twitter platform and contributes to the discussion of the relative importance of the qualitative analysis of social media data. Social media will continue to be employed by researchers given the numerous advantages and opportunities it offers as a source of information. The use of social media in research is particularly applicable to the tourism discipline as tourism providers increasingly utilize social media in the marketing and the delivery of services they provide. In addition, a large percentage of people around the world have adopted social media as a part of their lives, providing researchers with a window into their behavior, views, and desires. Although many new social media platforms continue to be introduced, Twitter remains a highly popular platform among researchers. Often researchers have a need to collect historical social media data in relation to a past event or ongoing events. It is possible to obtain sufficient longitudinal data from Twitter without having to rely on highly technical methods or incurring a significant financial cost. The data collection method outlined in this chapter is particularly suitable and applicable for qualitative analysis of Twitter data.

The intention of the chapter is not to reject the quantitative analysis of social media data, as such analyses can have their advantages and are more suitable for particular research objectives. Instead, this chapter highlights the importance of studying social media through a qualitative approach due to the many benefits and opportunities it can offer for a more insightful understanding of the phenomenon studied. At the same time caution is urged. Evidence is beginning to appear of researchers utilizing social media as an easy route to collecting data where more traditional methods could have been more appropriate. Social media based research is valid and important but done correctly it is no easier than any other data collection process. Furthermore, while useful, social media data cannot answer all our research questions. In short, social media data should not be used as a short cut to undertaking rigorous research.

References

Azungah, T. (2018). Qualitative research: Deductive and inductive approaches to data analysis. *Qualitative Research Journal, 18*(4), 383–400.

Barratt, M. J., Ferris, J. A., & Lenton, S. (2015). Hidden populations, online purposive sampling, and external validity: Taking off the blindfold. *Field Methods, 27*(1), 3–21.

Bermingham, A., & Smeaton, A. (2011). On using Twitter to monitor political sentiment and predict election results. In Paper presented at the proceedings of the workshop on sentiment analysis where AI meets psychology, Chiang Mai, Thailand.

Bigné, E., Oltra, E., & Andreu, L. (2019). Harnessing stakeholder input on Twitter: A case study of short breaks in Spanish tourist cities. *Tourism Management, 71*, 490–503.

Borra, E., & Rieder, B. (2014). Programmed method: Developing a toolset for capturing and analyzing tweets. *Aslib Journal of Information Management, 66*(3), 262–278.

Braun, V., & Clarke, V. (2006). Using thematic analysis in psychology. *Qualitative Research in Psychology, 3*, 77–101.

Bruns, A., & Liang, Y. E. (2012). Tools and methods for capturing Twitter data during natural disasters. *First Monday, 17*(4). doi:10.5210/fm.v17i4.3937

Burnap, P., Gibson, R., Sloan, L., Southern, R., & Williams, M. (2016). 140 characters to victory?: Using Twitter to predict the UK 2015 general election. *Electoral Studies, 41*, 230–233.

Burns, V. F., Blumenthal, A., & Sitter, K. C. (2020). How Twitter is changing the meaning of scholarly impact and engagement: Implications for qualitative social work research. *Qualitative Social Work, 19*(2), 178 191.

Castells, A. (2014). Catalonia and Spain: Political and fiscal conflict. *Pole Sud, 40*(1), 59–80.

Chaffey, D. (2019). *Global social media research summary 2019*. Retrieved from https://www.smartinsights.com/social-media-marketing/social-media-strategy/new-global-social-media-research/

Chang, H. C. (2010). A new perspective on Twitter hashtag use: Diffusion of innovation theory. *Proceedings of the American Society for Information Science and Technology, 47*(1), 1–4. doi:10.1002/meet.14504701295

Choy, L. T. (2014). The strengths and weaknesses of research methodology: Comparison and complimentary between qualitative and quantitative approaches. *IOSR Journal of Humanities and Social Science, 19*(4), 99–104.

Debreceny, R. S., Wang, T., & (Jamie), Z., M. (2019). Research in social media: Data sources and methodologies. *Journal of Information Systems, 33*(1), 1–28.

Dey, I. (2003). *Qualitative data analysis: A user friendly guide for social scientists.* New York, NY: Routledge.

Gokulakrishnan, B., Priyanthan, P., Ragavan, T., Prasath, N., & Perera, A. (2012). Opinion mining and sentiment analysis on a Twitter data stream. In Paper presented at the international conference on advances in ICT for emerging regions (ICTer2012), Colombo, Sri Lanka.

Guo, L., & McCombs, M. (2016). *The power of information networks: New directions for agenda setting.* New York, NY: Routledge.

Hays, S., Page, S. J., & Buhalis, D. (2013). Social media as a destination marketing tool: Its use by national tourism organisations. *Current Issues in Tourism, 16*(3), 211–239.

Hsieh, H.-F., & Shannon, S. E. (2005). Three approaches to qualitative content analysis. *Qualitative Health Research, 15*(9), 1277–1288.

Jungherr, A. (2015). *Analyzing political communication with digital trace data: The role of Twitter messages in social science research.* Heidelberg: Springer.

Jürgens, P., & Jungherr, A. (2016). A tutorial for using Twitter data in the social sciences: Data collection, preparation, and analysis. Retrieved from http://ssrn.com/abstract=2710146

Kang, M., & Schuett, M. A. (2013). Determinants of sharing travel experiences in social media. *Journal of Travel & Tourism Marketing, 30*(1–2), 93–107.

Li, J., Xu, L., Tang, L., Wang, S., & Li, L. (2018). Big data in tourism research: A literature review. *Tourism Management, 68*, 301–323.

Lyles, C. R., López, A., Pasick, R., & Sarkar, U. (2013). "5 mins of uncomfyness is better than dealing with cancer 4 a lifetime": An exploratory qualitative analysis of cervical and breast cancer screening dialogue on Twitter. *Journal of Cancer Education, 28*, 127–133.

Makarem, S. C., & Jae, H. (2016). Consumer boycott behavior: An exploratory analysis of Twitter feeds. *Journal of Consumer Affairs, 50*(1), 193–223.

Masip, P., Ruiz-Caballero, C., Suau, J., & Puertas, D. (2020). Media and Twitter agendas for social mobilizations: The case of the protests in defense of the public healthcare system in Spain. *International Journal of Communication, 14*, 3355–3376.

Padilla, J. J., Kavak, H., Lynch, C. J., Gore, R. J., & Diallo, S. Y. (2018). Temporal and spatiotemporal investigation of tourist attraction visit sentiment on Twitter. *PLoS One, 13*(6). doi:10.1371/journal.pone.0198857

Pak, A., & Paroubek, P. (2010). Twitter as a corpus for sentiment analysis and opinion mining. In Proceedings of the seventh conference on international language resources and evaluation (LREC'10), European language resources association (ELRA), Valletta, Malta.

Park, S. B., Ok, C. M., & Chae, B. K. (2016). Using Twitter data for cruise tourism marketing and research. *Journal of Travel & Tourism Marketing, 33*(6), 885–898.

Samarasekara, G. N., Fukahori, K., & Kubota, Y. (2011). Environmental correlates that provide walkability cues for tourists: An analysis based on walking decision narrations. *Environment and Behavior, 43*(4), 501–524.

Shaheer, I. (2019). *Tourism boycott calls by Twitter users due to concerns for the welfare of animals.* (Thesis, Doctor of Philosophy). University of Otago. Retrieved from http://hdl.handle.net/10523/9715

Shaheer, I., Insch, A., & Carr, N. (2018). Tourism destination boycotts–are they becoming a standard practise? *Tourism Recreation Research, 43*(1), 129–132.

Sigala, M., Christou, E., & Gretzel, U. (2012). *Social media in travel, tourism and hospitality: Theory, practice and cases.* Surrey: Ashgate Publishing, Ltd.

Song, H., & Liu, H. (2017). Predicting tourist demand using big data. In Z. Xiang & D. R. Fesenmaier (Eds.), *Analytics in smart tourism design (pp.* 13–29). Cham: Springer.

Statista. (2021). Number of Twitter users worldwide from 2019 to 2024 (in millions). Retrieved from www.statista.com

Theocharis, Y., Lowe, W., Van Deth, J. W., & García-Albacete, G. (2015). Using Twitter to mobilize protest action: Online mobilization patterns and action repertoires in the occupy wall street, indignados, and Aganaktismenoi movements. *Information, Communication & Society, 18*(2), 202–220.

Tuarob, S., Tucker, C. S., Salathe, M., & Ram, N. (2014). An ensemble heterogeneous classification methodology for discovering health-related knowledge in social media messages. *Journal of Biomedical Informatics, 49*, 255–268.

Twitter. (2017). Twitter developer documentation. Retrieved from https://dev.twitter.com/rest/public/search

Vieweg, S., Hughes, A. L., Starbird, K., & Palen, L. (2010). Microblogging during two natural Hazards events: What Twitter may contribute to situational awareness. In Paper presented at the proceedings of the CHI 2010: Crisis informatics, Atlanta, GA.

Walther, J. B., & D'addario, K. P. (2001). The impacts of emoticons on message interpretation in computer-mediated communication. *Social Science Computer Review, 19*(3), 324–347.

Weber, I., Garimella, V. R. K., & Teka, A. (2013). Political hashtag trends. In P. Serdyukov, P. Braslavski, S. O. Kuznetsov, J. Kamps, S. Rüger, E. Agichtein, … E. Yilmaz (Eds.), *Advances in information retrieval 35th European conference on IR research (ECIR 2013)* (pp. 857–860). Heidelberg: Springer.

Weller, K., & Kinder-Kurlanda, K. E. (2015). Uncovering the challenges in collection, sharing and documentation: The hidden data of social media research? In Proceedings of international AAAI conference on web and social media, Oxford: United Kingdom.

Woo, H., Cho, H. S., Shim, E., Lee, J. K., Lee, K., Song, G., & Cho, Y. (2018). Identification of keywords from Twitter and web blog posts to detect influenza epidemics in Korea. *Disaster Medicine and Public Health Preparedness, 12*(3), 352–359.

Zimmer, M. (2015). The Twitter archive at the library of congress: Challenges for information practice and information policy. *First Monday, 20*(7). doi:10.5210/fm.v20i7.5619

Chapter 10

Photo-Elicitation Using Q-Method to Extract Group Sense of Place for a Marine Park in Borneo

Paulin Poh Lin Wong and Balvinder Kaur Kler

Abstract

This study identifies and interprets the experiences and relationships of a host community to a marine national park in Sabah, Malaysian Borneo, as it transformed from a local recreation site into an international tourist destination. This chapter elaborates on an original and innovative amalgamation of qualitative methods used to collect data consisting of verbal and pictorial techniques, including focus group interviews, visitor employed photography, and an adapted Q-methodology incorporating photo-elicitation. The research design for data collection is provided as a guideline to illustrate how the study progressed through two essential parts. This study contributes to a gap in method on how to extract pictorial measures on a collective basis to systematically to produce group place meanings. Recommendations are suggested based on the challenges faced in this study. This innovative qualitative method was successful in deriving sense of place for a marine park.

Keywords: Sense of place; host community; focus groups; visitor employed photography; photo-elicitation; Q-methodology

Introduction

Over and above the stigma of qualitative methods as "soft science" (Phillimore & Goodson, 2004), the critical turn in tourism continues to shift support toward using this approach to study social life. The means of designing a robust qualitative study with due attention to trustworthiness issues is expressed in the literature (Denzin & Lincoln, 1998; Lincoln & Guba, 1985). Qualitative research has to be designed with due thought to producing knowledge and not merely alluding

Advanced Research Methods in Hospitality and Tourism, 179–197
Copyright © 2023 Paulin Poh Lin Wong and Balvinder Kaur Kler
Published under exclusive licence by Emerald Publishing Limited
doi:10.1108/978-1-80117-550-020221010

to "anything goes" (Silverman, 2017). This chapter highlights an innovative amalgamation of qualitative methods designed to collect data to understand host community place meanings for a marine national park: focus group interviews and visitor employed photography (VEP) with an adapted Q-methodology. Data collection was divided into two parts. First, a focus group interview to understand host community experiences and relationships with the marine park. Part two employed VEP with a subsequent photo-elicitation session using Q-sort and a second focus group interview with the same participants to discuss results from the Q-sort process. The purpose of this sequential combination is to gain an understanding of collective meanings and reasonings based on the pattern and ranking-results of the photographs.

Besides strengthening the trustworthiness of this study through method triangulation and the added benefits of visual images to evoke memories, this combination of methods solved the problem of using visual or pictorial measures for a group. In qualitative studies, pictorial measures are unlikely to standalone but are usually combined with verbal measures (Stedman, Beckley, Wallace, & Ambard, 2004) and applied to individual experiences or interviews. In fact, the reason why there is a dearth of studies carrying out pictorial measures on a collective basis is that there is simply no way to justify these photographs collectively. This concern was addressed by including an adapted Q-method, namely the Q-sort into the equation of photo-elicitation and focus groups resulting in the sorted set of photographs' capacity to represent the focus groups. This method enabled group place meanings to be extracted systematically, addressing a gap in method that uses pictorial and verbal measures. Therefore, VEP played an important role in producing data for the Q-sort. Fig. 1 illustrates the combination of qualitative methods used in this exploratory study on place meanings for groups.

The key objective of this study was to identify meaningful experiences at a marine park for the host community through their participation in recreation. This chapter is structured to provide a brief review of the literature which clarifies the need for the innovative methods used in the study. Each method is presented

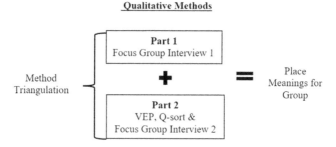

Fig. 1.   Method Triangulation to Understand Place Meanings for Groups.

briefly before the research design followed by guidelines for combining focus group interviews, VEP and the adapted Q-methodology with examples and data from this study.

Place Meanings for a National Park

Essentially, national parks are public spaces shared by visitors composed of both residents ("hosts") and tourists ("guests") (Kaltenborn & Williams, 2002). Hosts, or the host community are residents who live in and around the vicinity of high amenity areas and are directly or indirectly involved with and/or affected by tourism development (Stedman, Amsden, & Kruger, 2006). One perspective suggests tourism developers should assess the values assigned by a host community to places and preserve what is meaningful to ensure quality experiences continue for all visitors (Bricker & Kerstetter, 2006). National parks as tourism destinations were initially established to provide the local community with places to experience nature (Saarinen, 2007). This initial goal should not be forgotten as tourism continues to take center stage turning national parks into highly visited tourism destinations (Puhakka, 2008).

People form attachments to places because of meaningful human experiences expressed as the cognitive, emotional, and functional bonds that produce a sense of place (SoP) (Halpenny, 2010). SoP can be understood by recognizing place meanings or the intangible experiences mirroring the value of the place (Wynveen, Kyle, Absher, & Theodori, 2011). In the recent decade, place attachment studies have examined people-place relationships due to relevance to important processes (Lewicka, 2011; Manzo & Devine-Wright, 2013; Scannell & Gifford, 2010). Positive past experiences in a spatial setting have demonstrated people form attachments to national parks influencing their satisfaction and pro-environmental behavior (Ramkissoon, Smith, & Weiler, 2013). Attachment to place is linked to positive health and community participation outcomes, including a better quality of life, enhanced physical and psychological health, satisfying social relationships, and greater satisfaction with the physical environment (Anton & Lawrence, 2014). Access to recreation places for the community is a facet of social sustainability with a relationship to "identity creation, social, political and cultural capital, and even happiness and sense of place" (McClinchey, 2017, p. 5). However, tourism development may impede access to recreation place for the host community. In the case of national parks, incorporating host community SoP into the planning and development process has received greater attention in the leisure and recreation literature than tourism (Amsden, Stedman, & Kruger, 2011; Halpenny, 2010; Ramkissoon et al., 2013; Ramkissoon, Weiler, & Smith, 2012; Wynveen, Kyle, & Sutton, 2010).

This study focuses on Tunku Abdul Rahman Marine Park (TARP) in Sabah, Malaysian Borneo. TARP is the first marine national park in Sabah and a popular tourism destination that attracts both local recreationists and tourists due to its strategic proximity to the capital city, Kota Kinabalu, a mere 20 minutes on a speedboat ride. Gazetted in 1974, it covers an area of 50 square kilometers and consists of five islands: Gaya, Sapi, Manukan, Mamutik, and Sulug, which continue to generate high tourism receipts for marine tourism in Sabah. TARP offers a range of activities, accommodation, and services for visitors. The activities are scuba diving, windsurfing, sea walking, picnicking, parasailing, kayaking, and snorkeling, among others. Accommodation caters to different markets, from camping sites to luxury resorts located on the islands. TARP is governed by the Board of Trustees of Sabah Parks under the Ministry of Tourism, Culture, and Environment (Sabah). This study explored how tourism development affected host community relationships to TARP. This objective was achieved by conducting an empirical investigation into place meanings to understand host community experiences, relationships, and implications for continued tourism development on TARP.

The Method: Combining Focus Group Interviews, VEP, and Q-Methodology to Derive SoP for a Tourism Destination

In line with the research questions and objectives, this exploratory study was designed within an interpretive inquiry paradigm to understand a host community's experiences and relationships to the marine park. The interpretative philosophy refers to reality that is formed by the intangible, mental construction of human experiences (Guba & Lincoln, 1994) that share the meanings and understanding of knowledge. This study focused on *Erlebnis* (lived experiences) and sought *Verstehen* (understanding) of the multi-faceted reality of the complicated world through the eyes of those experiencing these experiences; the understanding of this phenomenon displayed through the interpretation of the researchers (Henn, Weinstein, & Foard, 2006). Therefore, the value-laden nature of this study meant researchers were immersed in the experiences of the study participants in the role of the researcher as instrument (Goodson & Phillimore, 2004). The general research question asked, *what sense of place does the host community have for TARP?* In order to understand SoP, the concept of space, place, and place meanings form the foundations of this study. Subsequently, the host community was the choice of subject as an understudied stakeholder in tourism development. Following the main question of this study, three sub-research questions were presented:

(1) What experiences in TARP are meaningful for the host community?
(2) What types of relationships do host community have with TARP?
(3) How do host community relationships transform due to tourism development?

The research design is novel and combines data from focus group interviews, VEP, and Q-Sort, which enhances the credibility of findings and provides a systematic way to understand "host" place meanings for TARP. In doing so, the triangulation of methods was built into the research design. It was assumed that this combination of qualitative methods would offer the potential of providing an

555555

in-depth understanding of place-related emotions and meanings to illuminate the value of the place.

   This approach was further divided into two categories: verbal and pictorial. The verbal approach or focus group interviews had the exploratory capacity to access group thoughts, experiences, and meaning beyond individual interviews (Gillham, 2005). Meanwhile, the pictorial approach – VEP method and subsequently, photo-elicitation technique evoked a deeper human consciousness element by using visual images during interviews that allow a different way of retrieving information and response (Harper, 2002). In addition to that, Q-methodology assisted in providing a systematic way to study subjective views and beliefs that are important to understand the reasoning behind people's behavior (Brown, 1993) and describe a group or population viewpoint (Exel & Graaf, 2005). The adapted Q-method used here to add a Q-sort into the equation of photo-elicitation and focus group interviews, was able to assess collective thoughts, meanings, sentiments, and experiences of the participants in a systematic way to identify their relationships with TARP. A brief review of each method is presented next.

Focus Group Interviews

The core purpose of focus group interviews is for researchers to induce participants' feelings, beliefs, and attitudes by manipulating group processes without taking a central role (Gladman & Freeman, 2012). The focus group interview provides access to not only understanding group meanings but also the processes and normative understanding of the topic of discussion (Bloor, Frankland, Thomas, & Robson, 2001). One of the main features of interviews is evoking memories of experiences for participants. When these interviews are done in a group setting, rich data will be provided on the group meanings associated with the issue (Bloor et al., 2001) and stronger feelings can usually be evoked (Gillham, 2005). In tourism, focus groups are used when there is a need to find out about experiences, viewpoints and attitudes toward tourism-related concepts; host-guest interactions and the values and attitudes of residents toward local tourism developments (Jennings, 2010). Therefore, it is rationalized that focus group interviews are a suitable tool to understand host community place meanings. However, interviews alone might not evoke deep memories, which photographs can do, more so, when participants in a study take those images which led us to VEP.

Visitor Employed Photography

This study utilized the VEP method to gather photos from participants and the photo-elicitation technique and Q-sort to draw meanings from photos taken by participants during the study. VEP is a photo-based approach popular among leisure researchers and requires participants to capture photographs during the study (Stedman et al., 2004). The key purpose of VEP is to use images for photo-elicitation which Harper (2002) refers to as the idea of inserting visual images into the interview process. Photo-elicitation technique has been associated with the ability to evoke memories that are related to place attachment and understanding of place meanings (Beckley, Wallace, Stedman, & Ambard, 2007; Harper, 2002; Jennings, 2010; Stedman et al., 2004; Tonge, Moore, Ryan, & Beckley, 2013). In this study, the act of sorting images during the Q-sort created a form of photo elicitation.

With reference to Jennings (2010), visual methods are more appreciated than ever for their contribution to tourism studies. Among some of the reasons that induce the acceptance of photo-elicitation as a valid method is that images can conjure deeper into the consciousness of participants (Prosser, 2013). Scientific proof indicates that image processing takes up more brain capacity as compared to word processing, thus not only can photo-elicitation stimulate more but also a different type of information (Harper, 2002; Jennings, 2010). As Stedman et al. (2004) noted, photography is usually a familiar and pleasant activity; participants' willingness to be involved in the exercise will be heightened as will their engagement with the study. In fact, taking photographs helps sharpen observational skills, inducing participants to analyze their surroundings through the camera's limited view, allowing them to consider what to include or exclude in a photograph (Garrod, 2007).

In one study, Tonge et al. (2013) used photo-elicitation technique to explore place attachment in Ningaloo Marine Park, north-western Australia. Participants were provided with a camera to capture photographs of the park, which revealed a special moment for them and subsequently interviewed using this photograph as a prompt. Photos taken are viewed as enablers that help participants reflect on their views, experiences, and biases and assist in evoking memories by freezing the special moment in a photograph. Besides that, Beckley, Stedman, Wallace, and Ambard (2007) used a similar approach, but instead of having visitors as participants, their study population was based on the community members. The criterion for photography supersedes not just the place but also people and things that can evoke strong meanings. As suggested by Beckley et al. (2007), to study place meanings, it is logical to use tools such as photo-taking that illustrate important places and allow participants to refresh their minds about places that evoke memories. What was needed was a method to understand these photographs (data) in an organized manner which led to incorporation of Q-Methodology.

Q-Methodology

Q-methodology (QM) is originally a quantitative method that aimed to make sense of qualitative data and the common subsequent step after a Q-sort is to subject the rankings to factor analysis (Brown, 1993). Exel and Graaf (2005) provide a clear and extensive introduction on using QM to learn about subjective measures such as a person's views, beliefs and opinions in a systematic way. In tourism, a paper by Stergiou and Airey (2011) encouraged the use of QM for critical tourism research which focuses on exploration and subjectivity. The nuances of this method include specific terms such as the concourse (collection of all possible materials on the topic of discussion), Q-set (sample of the concourse), P-set (participants), and Q-sort (P-Set sorting the Q-Set). The QM was adapted for this study by incorporating data from VEP in the following manner: (1) the Q-set selection was derived by researchers from the database of meaningful photos taken by participants; (2) during the Q-sort participants picked various meaningful photographs collectively which informed the photo-elicitation in the second focus group interview; (3) factor analysis was unnecessary as the purpose of the Q-sort was to arrange the Q-set. Hence, we refer to it as the adapted Q-method for visual data (Wong, 2019; Wong & Kler, 2016). Essentially, the researcher produced a Q-set from the concourse and participants (P-set) conducted produced a Q-sort to categorize the photographs as illustrated in Fig. 2.

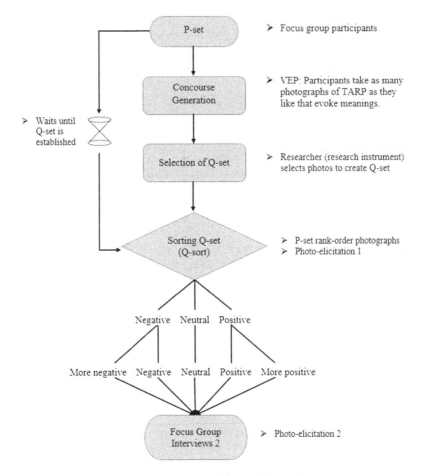

Fig. 2.   Illustration of an Adapted Q-Method Process.

This step is justified based on the value-laden nature of this study, where the researcher is the instrument and an integral part of the data collection process.

The application of QM in combination with other techniques is available in more recent tourism literature. Dewar, Li, and Davis (2007) found cultural background determined what was considered novel in their QM study on differences in group-specific perceptions of photographic images of travel destinations between university students in Canada and China. A study by Hunter (2013) focused on understanding resident subjectivities as tourism stakeholders in Orchid Island, Taiwan used QM with 42 statements on tourism discourse sorted by 34 respondents. Four key subjectivities were identified which contribute to how residents perceive tourism development and their role in small islands. QM has been applied in combination with ethnography particularly as it has shown to do justice to the complexities and nuances of lived experiences and adds value to researcher reflexivity (Wijngaarden, 2017). In a study on place meanings for outdoor recreation professionals, Huang, Qu, and Montgomery (2017) asked 30 participants to complete a theoretically grounded Q-sort of statements to uncover "how do you find meaning in the outdoors." Quantitative analysis was used to extract the factors that make a tourism destination meaningful. In comparison, the combination in this study of focus group interviews, VEP and QM through photo-elicitation to understand host community SoP is novel. Moreover, photo elicitation occurred naturally during the Q-sort by the P-set collectively and contributed to further elicitation during the second focus group interview.

Research Design

Fig. 3 illustrates the research design for this study. Data collection has two sections, and each clarifies which techniques were incorporated at each stage to ensure trustworthiness. For part one, the study aimed for and achieved a purposive sample of the host community who visit TARP for leisure and recreation purposes. The "host community" of TARP was defined as residents of Kota Kinabalu city as they lived in the marine parks' vicinity. The sampling choice was for a purposive, homogenous sample of a composition-focused (the topic of discussion is relevant to experiences) and strangers-constructed (have not met before) focus group (Parker & Tritter, 2012). An important factor was the voluntary and dedicated participation in response to the recruitment drive which took place via flyers posted in public noticeboards and shared online between February 2015 and August 2016. Participants were pre-screened to meet the purposive sampling criteria (Jennings, 2010) and were recruited on a first-come-first-served basis.

Purposive sampling criteria were created to ensure focus group members encompassed city residents that are most likely to visit TARP. The criteria included having direct experiences and have visited at least two islands in TARP. Following Breen (2006), the study recruited participants with similar experiences (homogenous) divided into different focus groups (Patton, 1990). Under this strategy, the study selected a small sample of participants that were similar in background and experiences in each group. This scope was then funneled into

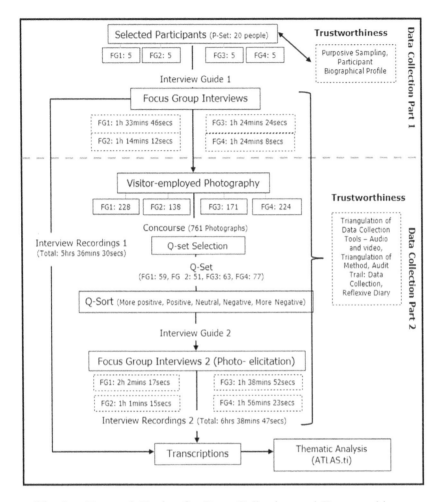

Fig. 3. Research Design for Data Collection and Trustworthiness.

different categories of city residents to include those from different generations and different employment backgrounds as a broad scope. This scope was used to create the recruitment criteria for the focus groups. Both purposive sampling and the creation of a biographical profile for each participant support transferability. Following the rationale of sampling (Patton, 2002), the four groups, when amalgamated, represent a purposive sample of the Kota Kinabalu host community who visit TARP for leisure and recreation:

(1) Working Adults (local, non-tourism related):

- Generation- X (born in between year 1961–1981)
- Generation- Y (born in between year 1982–2000)

(2) Tourism Industry Employees (Governmental and travel trade)
(3) Expatriates (Minimum stay of five years in Kota Kinabalu)

The literature on sample size selection for focus group method suggests a range of participant count per group, but the exact number of participants is yet to be conclusive (Patton, 2002). Nevertheless, the key factor is to achieve a functional focus group interview that produces richness of data. Based on Fern (2001), five participants were recruited for each focus group in this study. As the participants were required to participate in both part one and two of the study as a group, this required a higher commitment than the usual one-off focus group interview. Two interview guides were created for the focus group interviews. Fig. 2 provides details of the length of focus group interviews and the number of photographs contributed by each focus group through VEP. Data was analyzed through a thematic analysis (Braun & Clarke, 2013) using ATLAS.ti version 7, a qualitative data analysis software. Finally, data was interpreted based on themes and sub-themes to answer research questions. This chapter elaborates on the novel combination of methods used in this qualitative study and does not cover the data analysis or findings of host community meanings for TARP.

Guidelines for Combining Focus Group Interviews, VEP and Q-Sort

This section presents the guidelines for data collection for any study which chooses to combine focus group interviews, VEP and Q-sort with photo elicitation. The focus here is on data collection and the provision of an audit trail to support the transferability and dependability of this study.

Data Collection

Data collection was split into two components: part one consisted of focus group interviews, and part two involved VEP, photo-elicitation using Q-sort, and the second focus group interview. As part of the incentive, participants received a free day trip to all four accessible islands (Sapi, Gaya, Manukan, & Mamutik) in TARP (including jetty and conservation fees), as well as a packed lunch. For this purpose and convenience, a speedboat was chartered for each park visit (four in total), providing a more relaxing timespan for the VEP segment. In total, there were four groups of five participants, which meant the data collection circuit repeated four times. However, this depended on when a purposive, homogenous sample of a composition-focused and strangers-constructed focus group of five participants was available and prepared to meet. The recruitment drive faced the obstacle of willing participants dropping out completely or unable to meet at the eleventh-hour, forcing a postponement of the entire process to a new date. An online pre-screening was conducted with potential participants to ask if they owned a phone with a camera or a digital camera with at least five megapixels in resolution and their willingness to use their gadgets during the VEP phase. This pre-screening clearly stated the activities, potential dates, and the need to participate in both parts one and two of data collection.

Part One: Focus Group Interviews I

On the chosen date, participants met in a meeting room on Manukan island courtesy of park authorities or in the Royal Malaysian Custom office at the Jesselton Point jetty with a conducive environment for group discussions. The purpose of the study was reiterated, and the participants signed a consent form. Before the interviews, participants were asked to pick a pseudonym for themselves and explain why they chose it as an ice-breaking activity, which ensured a smoother interview session. An interview guide (Table 1) was used to initiate a discussion about their experiences and relationships with TARP. The interview guide was based on the three main components of Place: Activities, Resource, and Conceptions (Pearce, 2005) and adapted from Schroeder (1996) who developed a set of questions to identify place meanings.

The principal researcher took a marginal position and only steered the conversation to the right track when it went off-topic with the occasional prompt to gain more depth (Parker & Tritter, 2012). All focus groups interviews were recorded on both audio-enabled video recording and a separate audio recording. Audio recordings were transcribed and compared to the video for comparison focusing on expressions and emotions. On the same morning, once the FG interviews ended, participants were ferried across to the islands.

Part Two: VEP, Q-Sort, and Focus Group Interviews II

Part Two of data collection involved an innovative combination of VEP and an adapted Q-method for visual data followed by a second focus group interview

Table 1. Interview Guide.

Interview Guide Focus Group I (Summary)
A. Background of Participants ("How frequently do you visit TARP?")
B. Activities and Conceptions (Interview questions include "Please describe your favorite activities in TARP and what participation in these activities means to you"? "What thoughts, feelings, memories or people related to these activities makes it special for you"?)
C. Resource and Conceptions (What is meaningful to you here on the island? What changes do you notice in TARP from your past visits? How do you feel about these changes?)
D. Overall TARP experience (How would you describe TARP to others who have not been here?)

based on the Q-sort results. The VEP segment required participants to visit two of their favorite islands and take photographs (no limit given) of what was meaningful to them about the islands. Each participant was given a photo-taking instruction sheet (Table 2) and photo-taking tags. Participants were asked to snap a photo-taking tag before commencing to indicate where the photographs were taken, specifically which island.

Each group spent approximately between 45 minutes to an hour on each island. At the end of the trip, at the jetty, each participant transferred photographs to a portable computer using card readers and phone cables prepared in advance. In total, 761 photographs were derived from the four field trips. Participants were thanked and reminded to attend the next segment of part two in the next few days.

Photo Elicitation Using Q-Sort and Focus Group Two

Concourse in this study refers to all the photographs taken by participants, which numbered 761. In this adapted Q-method, the integral role of the researcher as the instrument was assumed by the principal researcher who drew samples of photographs (digital) to represent the concourse or the Q-set. This task included omitting unclear, repetitive, and unrelated images to the instructions given, based on familiarization with the focus group interview transcripts and TARP as a fellow host community resident. A total of 250 photographs were developed (hard-copy) and numbered for the Q-sort segment (as depicted in Table 3).

Next, the participants (P-set) gathered at meeting rooms in a local university to engage in photo-elicitation to sort the Q-set into categories. Each P-set consisted of the same focus group members from part one; as such there were four P-sets who collectively conducted the Q-sort process with the same Q-set (250

Table 2. Photo-Taking Instructions.

Photo-Taking Instructions
i.   *Photo-taking tags supplied* Please take a photo of the tag before you begin at each island.
ii.   Take as many photos as you want.
iii.   Photos can include anything: the environment, people, facilities or activities you have thoughts/feelings/experience with.
iv.   If there is any personal experience or memories that you would like to highlight, please take *two identical photos, one with your finger*
v.   Do not be bound by time (e.g., If there is a hut or tree you used to hang out at but it is not there anymore, just take a photo of that spot with your fingers)

Table 3. Photo Data Based on Focus Groups.

Focus Group (P-Set)	Concourse (# of Photos Taken)	Q-SET (Representative Set of Photos)
FG1 – Gen X	228	59
FG2 – Gen Y	138	51
FG3 – Tourism	171	63
FG4 – Expat	224	77
TOTAL	**761**	**250**
	Average **38** photos per person	

Table 4. Q-Sort Instructions.

Q-Sort Instructions

Concourse: 250 Photographs Representing Meaningful Images Taken by 20 Participants During Island Visits (in Random Order)

i.	You are required to separate these photos into three categories – positive, negative, and neutral.
ii.	Please keep your discussion to a minimal level in this process.
iii.	As there are five people in this group, please vote if there is any disagreement.
iv.	If a photo did not go into the category that you think it should, please note down the photo number and which category it should be in. You may use these notes during the discussion later.

After the first level of sorting

v.	Now please sort again from the positive and negative categories.
vi.	From this positive pile, sort them into positive and more positive.
vii.	And from the negative pile, sort them into negative and more negative.

photographs) on different dates. The Q-sort instructions were printed out and read to participants (Table 4).

With minimal discussion and through a voting system (using pen and paper), participants sorted the photos first into categories of positive, *neutral*, and negative feelings. Then, a further sorting of *positive, more positive, negative*, and *more negative* was conducted from the positive and negative pile. The outcome of the Q-sort for each category was noted and is depicted in Table 5.

As Q-methodology is originally a quantitative method making sense of qualitative data, the usual subsequent step is to subject the rankings of Q-sort to a factor analysis, which was deemed unnecessary for the purpose of this study. As

Table 5. Photo Data After Q-Sort.

	After Q-Sort				
Focus Group (P-Set)	More Positive	Positive	Neutral	Negative	More Negative
FG1 – Gen X	22	9	12	3	13
FG2 – Gen Y	10	6	16	12	7
FG3 Tourism	26	9	14	4	9
FG4 – Expat	20	19	21	7	10
TOTAL	**78**	**43**	**63**	**26**	**39**

Table 6. Interview Guide Focus Group 2 (Summary).

Interview Guide Focus Group 2 (Summary)
i.   For the more positive, positive, negative, and more negative group of photographs, what are the elements that stood out for you in this photo? What does the image in this photo mean to you?)
ii. Neutral photographs (Is there any photo that you wish to discuss? Why?)
iii. What thoughts, feelings, experiences, and people connected with photo #___ stood out for you?

such, the final segment moved to a second focus group interview (Table 6) to discuss the results from the Q-sort process (Fig. 4).

By combining photo-elicitation and Q-sort with focus group interviews, this study was able to gain an understanding of collective meanings and reasonings behind the pattern of the type and ranking-results of the photographs in a systematic way. In sum, the method identifies the importance of VEP and a combination of verbal and pictorial attributes that contributes to participants' SoP.

For the purpose of a clear audit trail for data collection, various additional documents are available, including dates of focus groups, length of interviews, length of transcripts, as well as full verbatim transcripts for parts one and two of the focus group interviews. Both functional and personal reflexivity were addressed with a one-page expression of the principal researcher's experiences of the marine park in the past decade.

Conclusion and Recommendations

A qualitative study consumes the researcher in that rich, thick description is a necessary part of the process at every stage. The research design though systematic, is open to human intervention, that of the participants. Theoretically

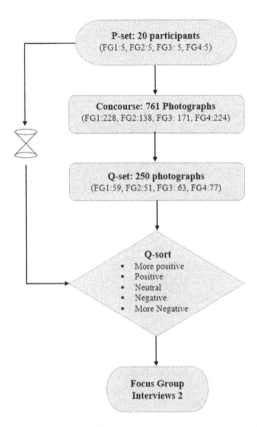

Fig. 4.   Part Two – Photo Elicitation Using Q-Sort and Focus Group
Two.

rationale, the purposive sample of five participants per homogenous, composition focused, strangers constructed focus group participants were hard to organize. The overall recruitment process took a longer time than expected as it was a challenge to assemble all five participants on the same day. Often time went by between the recruitment drive and reaching this number, and at that point, someone would drop out due to other commitments. Perhaps this combination of the purposive sample, is better suited to groups in the same line of work, who could meet sooner with ease. Additionally, the two-part data collection process, which essentially dictates participation from the same members of all four focus groups twice, is also fallible. Delays took place when the second focus group interview had to be postponed due to one or two members becoming unavailable. Due to the purpose of the study, which is to amalgamate group place meanings, it was imperative to have everyone present. These are logistical issues that need to be considered in detail to avoid delays. Future work should continue to push the boundaries of applying this adapted QM in tourism research seeking to understand group experiences. The incorporation of technology has great potential in reducing these data collection setbacks while ensuring authentic data, for example, the use of crowdsource through review websites or social media.

Regardless, tourism researchers seeking to uncover the voice of the voiceless in understudied areas or communities should attempt the use of these methods. Participants feel respected when the research design incorporates activities within focus groups and clarifies their contributions. By the end of data collection, these strangers-constructed focus group participants forged a sense of camaraderie due to the various data collection stages and the segments which needed their participation. All participants enjoyed the VEP segment as well as the photo-elicitation with Q-sort. The second focus group interview based on the Q-set provided an avenue for thought-provoking discussions. Ultimately, the key question to ask is did this combination of focus group interviews, VEP and photo-elicitation with Q-sort ensure valid conclusions and answer the research questions? Indeed, this combination of methods was systematic and illuminative in deriving host community place meanings to a marine park.

References

Amsden, B. L., Stedman, R. C., & Kruger, L. E. (2011). The creation and maintenance of sense of place in a tourism-dependent community. *Leisure Sciences, 33*(1), 32–51.

Anton, C. E., & Lawrence, C. (2014). Home is where the heart is: The effect of place of residence on place attachment and community participation. *Journal of Environmental Psychology, 40*, 451–461.

Beckley, D., Stedman, R., Wallace, S., & Ambard, M. (2007). Snapshots of what matters most: Using resident-employed photography to articulate attachment to place. *Society & Natural Resources: An International Journal, 20*(10), 913–929.

Bloor, M., Frankland, J., Thomas, M., & Robson, K. (2001). *Focus groups in social research.* London: SAGE Publications Ltd.

Braun, V., & Clarke, V. (2013). *Successful qualitative research: A practical guide for beginners.* London: SAGE Publications Ltd.

Breen, R. L. (2006). A practical guide to focus-group research. *Journal of Geography in Higher Education, 30*(3), 463–475.

Bricker, K. S., & Kerstetter, D. (2006). Saravanua ni vanua: Exploring sense of place in the rural highlands of Fiji. In G. Jennings & N. Nickerson (Eds.), *Quality tourism experiences* (pp. 99–109). New York, NY: Routledge.

Brown, S. R. (1993). A primer on Q methodology. *Operant Subjectivity, 16*, 91–138. Retrieved from http://facstaff.uww.edu/cottlec/QArchive/Primer1.html

Denzin, N. K., & Lincoln, Y. S. (1998). *Strategies of qualitative inquiry.* Thousand Oaks, CA: SAGE Publications Inc.

Dewar, K., Li, W. M., & Davis, C. H. (2007). Photographic images, culture, and perception in tourism advertising: A Q methodology study of Canadian and Chinese university students. *Journal of Travel & Tourism Marketing, 22*(2), 35–44.

Exel, J. & Graaf, G. D. (2005). Q methodology: A sneak preview. Retrieved from http://qmethod.org/articles/vanExel.pdf. Accessed on January 17, 2016.

Fern, E. F. (2001). *Advanced focus group research*. Thousand Oaks, CA: Sage Publications.

Garrod, B. (2007). A snapshot into the past: The utility of volunteer-employed photography techniques in planning and managing heritage tourism. *Journal of Heritage Tourism, 2*, 14–35.

Gillham, B. (2005). *Research interviewing: The range of techniques*. Berkshire: Open University Press.

Gladman, A., & Freeman, D. (2012). Focus groups. In R. Barnard & A. Ryan (Eds.), *Researching language teacher cognition and practice: International case studies to illuminate methodological issues* (pp. 68–89). Bristol: Multilingual Matters.

Goodson, L., & Phillimore, J. (2004). The inquiry paradigm in qualitative tourism research. In J. Phillimore & L. Goodson (Eds.), *Qualitative research in tourism: Ontologies, epistemologies and methodologies* (pp. 30–45). London: Routledge.

Guba, E. G., & Lincoln, Y. S. (1994). Competing paradigms in qualitative research. In N. K. Denzin & Y. S. Lincoln (Eds.), *Handbook of qualitative research* (pp. 105–117). Thousand Oaks, CA: SAGE.

Halpenny, E. (2010). Pro-environmental behaviors and park visitors: The effect of place attachment. *Journal of Environmental Psychology, 30*(4), 409–421.

Harper, D. (2002). Talking about pictures: A case for photo elicitation. *Visual Studies, 17*(1), 13–26.

Henn, M., Weinstein, M., & Ford, N. (2006). *A short introduction to social research*. London: SAGE Publications Ltd.

Huang, Y., Qu, H., & Montgomery, D. (2017). The meanings of destination: A Q method approach. *Journal of Travel Research, 56*(6), 793–807.

Hunter, W. C. (2013). Understanding resident subjectivities toward tourism using Q method: Orchid Island, Taiwan. *Journal of Sustainable Tourism, 21*(2), 331–354.

Jennings, G. (2010). *Tourism research*. Milton, QLD: John Wiley & Sons Australia Ltd.

Kaltenborn, B. P., & Williams, D. R. (2002). The meaning of place: Attachments to Femundsmarka National park, Norway, among tourists and locals. Norsk Geografisk Tidsskrift. *Norwegian Journal of Geography, 56*, 189–198.

Lewicka, M. (2011). Place Attachment: How far have we come in the last 40 years? *Journal of Environmental Psychology, 31*(3), 207–230.

Lincoln, Y. S., & Guba, E. G. (1985). *Naturalistic inquiry*. Newbury Park, CA: Sage Publications.

Manzo, L., & Devine-Wright, P. (Eds.), (2013). *Place attachment: Advances in theory, methods and research* (pp. 23–36). New York, NY: Routledge.

McClinchey, K. A. (2017). Social sustainability and a sense of place: Harnessing the emotional and sensuous experiences of urban multicultural leisure festivals. *Leisure/Loisir, 41*(3), 391–421.

Parker, A., & Tritter, J. (2012). Focus group method and methodology: Current practice and recent debate. In G. R. Walden (Ed.), *Focus Group Research* (Vol. 2, pp. 97–112). London: SAGE Publications.

Patton, M. Q. (1990). Designing qualitative studies. In M. Q. Patton (Ed.), *Qualitative evaluation and research methods* (pp. 169–186). Beverly Hills, CA: Sage.

Patton, M. Q. (2002). *Qualitative research & evaluation methods*. Thousand Oaks, CA: Sage Publications Inc.

Pearce, P. L. (2005). *Tourist behaviour: Themes and conceptual schemes.* Clevedon: Channel View Publications.

Phillimore, J., & Goodson, L. (2004). Progress in qualitative research in tourism. Epistemology, ontology and methodology. In J. Phillimore & L. Goodson (Eds.), *Qualitative research in tourism: Ontologies, epistemologies and methodologies* (pp. 3–29). London: Routledge.

Prosser, J. D. (2013). Visual methodology: Toward a more seeing research. In N. K. Denzin & Y. S. Lincoln (Eds.), *Collecting and interpreting qualitative materials* (pp. 177–211). Thousand Oaks, CA: Sage Publications.

Puhakka, R. (2008). Increasing role of tourism in Finnish National Parks. *Fennia, 186*(1), 47–58.

Ramkissoon, H., Smith, L. D. G., & Weiler, B. (2013). Relationships between place attachment, place satisfaction and pro-environmental behaviour in an Australian National Park. *Journal of Sustainable Tourism, 21*(3), 434–457.

Ramkissoon, H., Weiler, B., & Smith, L. D. G. (2012). Place attachment and pro-environmental behaviour in National Parks: The development of a conceptual framework. *Journal of Sustainable Tourism, 20*(2), 257–276.

Saarinen, J. (2007). Protected areas and regional development issues in northern peripheries: Nature protection, traditional economies and tourism in the Urho Kekkonen National Park, Finland. In I. Mose (Ed.), *Protected areas and regional development in Europe: Towards a new model for the 21st century* (pp. 199–211). Aldershot: Ashgate.

Scannell, L., & Gifford, R. (2010). Defining place attachment: A tripartite organizing framework. *Journal of Environmental Psychology, 30,* 1–10.

Schroeder, H. (1996). *Voices from Michigan's Black River: Obtaining information on special places for natural resource planning.* (General Technical Report NC-184). US Department of Agriculture, Forest Services, North Central Forest Experiment Station, St. Paul, MN.

Silverman, D. (2017). *Doing qualitative research: A practical handbook* (5th ed.). London: SAGE publications limited.

Stedman, R., Amsden, B. L., & Kruger, L. (2006). Sense of place and community: Points of intersection with implications for leisure research. *Leisure/Loisir, 30*(2), 393–404.

Stedman, R., Beckley, D., Wallace, S., & Ambard, M. (2004). A picture and 1000 words: Using resident-employed photography to understand attachment to high amenity places. *Journal of Leisure Research, 36*(4), 580–606.

Stergiou, D., & Airey, D. (2011). Q-methodology and tourism research. *Current Issues in Tourism, 14*(4), 311–322.

Tonge, J., Moore, S., Ryan, M., & Beckley, L. (2013). Using photo-elicitation to explore place attachment in a remote setting. *Electronic Journal of Business Research Methods, 11*(1), 41–50.

Wijngaarden, V. (2017). Q method and ethnography in tourism research: Enhancing insights, comparability and reflexivity. *Current Issues in Tourism, 20*(8), 869–882.

Wong, P. P. L. (2019). Sense of place of host community in tourism development: The case of Tunku Abdul Rahman Park, Sabah. [Doctoral dissertation summary] *European Journal of Tourism Research, 23,* 212–216.

Wong, P. P. L., & Kler, B. K. (2016). Photo-elicitation using Q-method in focus groups: An innovative method in recognising sense of place for a Marine Park in

Borneo, Malaysia. In *Proceedings of HONG KONG 2016: 2nd Global tourism & Hospitality Conference and 15th Asia Pacific Forum for Graduate students research in tourism* (Vol. 2, pp. 131–146). School of Hotel & Tourism Management, Hong Kong Polytechnic University. 16–18 May 2016.

Wynveen, C. J., Kyle, G. T., Absher, J. D., & Theodori, G. L. (2011). The meanings associated with varying degrees of attachment to a natural landscape. *Journal of Leisure Research*, *43*(2), 290–311.

Wynveen, C. J., Kyle, G. T., & Sutton, S. G. (2010). Place meanings ascribed to marine settings: The case of the great barrier reef Marine Park. *Leisure Sciences*, *32*, 270–287.

Chapter 11

Including the 'Voices' of Animals in Tourism, Hospitality, and Leisure Research

Giovanna Bertella

Abstract

In recent decades, our knowledge and perceptions of animals have changed considerably. An increasing number of scholars are interested in exploring animals and their roles in the context of tourism, hospitality and leisure. Recent studies have covered both practical and theoretical aspects of this topic, sometimes including considerations of animal ethics. This chapter argues that it is time to reflect on the research ethics and methodological implications of such emerging perspectives. The chapter presents a literature review addressing the shift in tourism, hospitality and leisure studies from a human/animal dualism and anthropocentrism focus to a recognition and inclusion of animals' perspectives. It develops a set of guidelines for a methodology intended to underpin research about and involving animals, inspired by the ecofeminist care tradition and elaborated on in light of the reviewed literature and the author's personal experience. Three main approaches are identified: fictional, multispecies ethnography, and multispecies technology-based approaches.

Keywords: Research ethics; animals in tourism/hospitality/leisure; animal ethics; multispecies ethnography; fiction; technology-based research methods

Introduction

The way we – humans – view nonhuman animals (hereafter referred to as animals) and the roles they play in our lives differ greatly according to the animal species and the specific historical and cultural context (Dhont & Hodson, 2019; Herzog, 2010; Joy, 2011; Serpell, 1996). An increasing number of scholars are engaging in debate about animals in tourism, hospitality and leisure (e.g., Carr, 2009; Fennell, 2011; Markwell, 2015), discussing issues from various perspectives and with different approaches, such as animal ethics and actor network theory

Advanced Research Methods in Hospitality and Tourism, 199–211
Copyright © 2023 Giovanna Bertella
Published under exclusive licence by Emerald Publishing Limited
doi:10.1108/978-1-80117-550-020221011

(Danby, Dashper, & Finkel, 2019). These studies all share the position that human–animal relations are central to our experience of the world and, some scholars argue, to our self-perceptions and views and treatment of others (Bertella, 2018; Yudina & Grimwood, 2016).

As the debate about animals in tourism, hospitality and leisure is developing relatively rapidly, this chapter argues that the time has come to consider the methodological implications of such a debate. To date, some studies have focused on practical issues relating to animals in tourism, hospitality and leisure, such as the case of traveling pets (Carr & Cohen, 2009; Taillon, MacLaurin, & Yun, 2015). Other scholars have noted that it is scientifically correct – and ethically important – to recognize animals as sentient beings with an intrinsic value (e.g., Burns, 2015; Fennell, 2011; Kline, 2018). In line with this position and the consequent view of animals as subjects, some recent studies have attempted to address animals' perspectives by, for instance, investigating swim-with-dolphins tourism from the dolphins' perspectives (Bertella, Fumagalli, & Williams-Grey, 2019).

The understanding of animals as subjects with an intrinsic value, who are entitled to views and opinions about the activities they are involved in (e.g. travel and wildlife tours), has clear implications for how research about such activities should be conducted. Ethically speaking, conducting research about animals as subjects should align with principles and values similar to those required for scientists investigating social phenomena. This position implies going beyond respecting the five animal welfare freedoms, which include freedom from hunger/ thirst, discomfort, pain/injury/disease and fear/distress, as well as freedom to express normal behavior (Fennell, 2011). Rather, the principles that Israel and Hay (2006) outlined for researching humans can be advanced to apply to research practices that help protect individual animals, groups of animals and their environments, as well as minimize possible harm and increase the good in the animals' world. To date, only a few studies have reflected on these methodological considerations (Dashper & Brymer, 2019).

This chapter focuses on the following question: how can animals' "voices" be included in research practice? Animals' voices refer to the animals' perceptions and points of view about the tourism-related activities they are involved in, such as staying in hotels, living in zoos and participating in outdoor activities. This chapter aims to explore how animals might experience such activities and to provide the reader with a set of guidelines for conducting research about and with animals.

Researchers' conceptualization of animals and consideration of the ways we can and should interact with them is the premise for reflection on methodological aspects of research about animals in tourism, hospitality and leisure. Therefore, I begin this chapter by describing my own philosophical position with regard to animals and human–animal relations. The reason for including this section is the importance of openness when dealing with potentially controversial issues. The chapter then goes on to review the literature concerning the inclusion of the animals' perspectives in tourism, hospitality and leisure studies, focusing in particular on the studies' methodological choices. The next section presents the guidelines developed by the author regarding the inclusion of animals' perspectives in tourism, hospitality and leisure research. These guidelines are exemplified by the studies presented in the literature review and my first-hand experience, with the latter being viewed as a possible source of valuable suggestions. The conclusion briefly summarizes the main contributions of the chapter and offers some reflections on the future of research about and with animals.

An Ecofeminist Perspective on Animals

The position presented here regarding the conceptualization of animals was inspired by the philosophical perspective of ecofeminism, which acknowledges the sentience of animals and their complex cognitive and emotional lives, rejecting human/animal dualisms (Adams & Gruen, 2014; Gaard, 1993; Gruen, 2011). Ecofeminists following the care tradition have highlighted humans' moral obligation to care for and act responsibly and compassionately toward animals (Donovan & Adams, 2007). The attentiveness that humans should extend to animals refers not only to animals at the species level but also to individual animals, each of whom is viewed as a unique member of a network of individuals (Gruen, 2015). In this network, humans can be included as potential "friends" in the case of domesticated animals and "stewards" in the case of wildlife. Ecofeminists have noted that animal–human interactions can vary according to context and the type of animals involved and should be based on respect for such differences, including the peculiarities of individual animals. In this way, relationships that are meaningful to both parties – humans and animals – can be developed (Gruen, 2015).

In contrast to other animal ethics traditions (utilitarianism, animal rights), ecofeminism has been critical of the exclusive use of rationality in our reflections about ethical issues (Adams & Gruen, 2014). Ecofeminism encourages the adoption of relational and affective, as well as intellectual, reasoning. Such a multifaceted form of intelligence should be applied to the consideration of any human activity, including those involving one or more animals, which aligns with the ecofeminist notion that values and actions are inseparable (Birkeland, 1993). Respect and care for animals can be declared verbally, but, more importantly, it should also be demonstrated in the way we choose to perform ordinary and extraordinary activities. This approach is relevant to tourism, hospitality and leisure activities, as briefly outlined in the introduction, as well as to research practices about such activities, as explained in the following pages.

Researching Animals in Tourism, Hospitality, and Leisure

From Human/Animal Dualism and Anthropocentrism Toward Multispeciesism and the Emergence of Animals' Voices

Studies investigating animals in tourism and leisure contexts have long used traditional research methods and adopted an anthropocentric standpoint (Haanpää, Salmela, García-Rosell, & Äijälä, 2019). Quite often, research about interactions between humans and animals has focused on the effects of the former on the latter or vice versa. Typically, these studies have adopted methods such as surveys and interviews for humans and observations of animals, as is the case in a study by Curtin (2006) on the effects of close encounters with dolphins on humans and another by Parsons (2012) on the effects of whale-watching tourism on the animals. The choice to focus on either humans or animals tends to confirm, and perhaps reinforce, human/animal dualisms. The prevalence of an anthropocentric approach is exemplified by Campos, Mendes, do Valle, and Scott (2016), who, while discussing co-creation, exclusively explored tourists' perspectives through in-depth interviews and in no way problematized animals as co-creators.

However, a shift is currently occurring from such human/animal dualistic and anthropocentric perspectives toward a recognition of the relational aspect of human–animal encounters and, in some cases, animal agency. A 2019 special issue of *Leisure Studies*, entitled "Multispecies Leisure," was dedicated to leisure activities involving humans and other animal species. This special issue provided an excellent source for learning about recent advances in methodologies applied to investigating experiences involving animals. These experiences were often explored by applying autoethnography – more precisely, by relying on multi-species research teams consisting of researchers and some animals. This approach was referred to as *multispecies ethnography* or *ethnography after humanism* (Hamilton & Taylor, 2017; Kirksey & Helmreich, 2010).

Regarding the animals involved in the relevant articles from the special issue of *Leisure Studies,* it is important to note that the researchers had a close relationship with them and/or possessed good theoretical and practical knowledge of the species to which they belonged. This was also the case with the reflections of Carr (2014) concerning dogs in leisure activities. Dashper and Brymer (2019) stated that the researcher "needs to have knowledge and experience of the individual(s) involved, and preferably be intimately connected to the experience under consideration" (p. 404). Dashper and Brymer (2019) further noted that phenomenological approaches are preferred for gaining a deep and holistic understanding of the contexts and nuances of human and animal experiences.

A phenomenological approach was employed effectively by Nottle and Young (2019), who used *autoethnography* to explore the leisure activities of their respective dogs. The data for this study derived mainly from six years of conversations, photo sharing and social media postings. In this case, it was evident how the selection of the multispecies team members and methods of data collection were influenced by, and influenced, the philosophy underpinning the research in terms of ontology (animals as the subjects, not the objects, of research) and epistemology (animals as co-creators of knowledge about shared experiences). With regard to the study's methodological contributions, Nottle and Young (2019) noted how their approach gave them the opportunity to highlight the risk of generalizing and overlooking important individual differences and peculiarities of animals when investigating experiences involving humans and animals.

Autoethnography was also adopted by Wilkinson (2018) in combination with *egomorphism*. Egomorphism perceives others' inner worlds through the adoption of a "like me" approach, which differs from the "human-like" approach of anthropomorphism by focusing on the selfhood of sentient beings, regardless of which species they belong to, and departing from the view of animals as objects. Wilkinson (2018) described a captive chameleon's experience of everyday activities at a vivarium and concluded by suggesting a reconsideration of leisure spaces in more empathetic terms.

With regard to animals as knowledge co-creators, Harmon (2019) used a methodological approach in which the data emerged from a person's story as told to the researcher's dog. Harmon (2019) defined his study's methodology as a derivative of narrative ethnography as it involved meetings between a person and a dog facilitated and witnessed by the researcher. In this approach, the animal acted not only as a facilitator but also as a co-creator of the data. Importantly, the researcher observed how the connection between the dog and the person was not a "given" but emerged from the unique traits of the dog and the human in the specific context.

Narratives, this time fictional, were also used by Dashper and Brymer (2019) in the *Leisure Studies* special issue, as well as by Äijälä, Jylkäs, Rajab, and Vuorikari (2021). Dashper and Brymer (2019) elaborated on their reflections about multi-species leisure based on a fictional horse-riding event, while Äijälä et al. (2021) were inspired by technological changes and imagined a futuristic scenario in which it was possible to experience a dog sledding tour from the perspective of a dog.

In a similar way to Äijälä et al. (2021), technology played an important role in the study by Haanpää et al. (2019) concerning Arctic animal-based experiences. However, rather than a futuristic type of technology, Haanpää et al. (2019) drew on a well-developed, relatively accessible one, using videography to interpret and theorize animal-based tourism as a context for multispecies relationships. The authors discussed the methodological challenges of capturing the non-linguistic, sensuous and embodied qualities of such relationships, emphasizing that their approach could contribute to the development of more inclusive tourism and future.

Animals' Voices: Challenges and Possibilities

A few scholars have attempted to report on animals' perspectives in the tourism, hospitality and leisure literature: the study about swim-with-dolphins tourism mentioned above, a study on the thoughts of a pig rescued from slaughter at a rural event, and a study in which orcas tell the scientific and tourism community what they think about whale-watching (Bertella et al., 2019; Bertella, 2020, 2021). The approaches used in these studies rely on fiction and, in one case, on developing potential future scenarios (Banks & Banks, 1998; Reinhold, 2018; Yeoman & Postma, 2014). The authors of these works attempted to convey the animals' voices and highlight the considerable challenges stemming from our circumscribed view of the animal world. These challenges can be addressed through an interdisciplinary approach to research, as suggested by Dashper and Brymer

(2019). Accordingly, Bertella et al. (2019) combined their theoretical and practical knowledge from academia and the non-profit sector to develop a fictional dolphin–tourist dialogue. Another means of approaching these challenges is to gain knowledge about animals by consulting the available literature; for example, Bertella (2020) used various sources to learn about pigs and their cognitive and emotional capacities.

Another challenge in investigating animals' perspectives concerns the imbalance of power when writing in someone else's name, as discussed by Bertella et al. (2019) and Bertella (2020) with reference to the 2013 book *Speaking for animals: Animal autobiographical writing* by animal studies scholar Margo DeMello. The complexities of a situation in which a human "holds the pen" and claims to represent the voice of an animal echo some arguments about the need to overcome traditional methods of qualitative research that may reinforce power mechanisms (Denzin & Lincoln, 2011; Höckert & Grimwood, 2019; Hollinshead, 2013). In particular, the risk of "epistemic violence" when research is conducted "on or about" instead of "with or by" is highly relevant to studies about animals. Bertella et al. (2019) and Bertella (2020) have argued that instead of claiming to speak *for* animals, scholars writing fictional narratives in which animals express their views should aim to develop plausible stories based on explicitly described sources of information and inspiration.

Bertella et al. (2019) and Bertella (2020) related this latter aspect to creative writing criteria – namely, to creative analytic practice (CAP) (Parry & Johnson, 2007; Richardson & St. Pierre, 2005). One criterion concerns the development of plausible stories, as mentioned above. The CAP approach invites researchers not to underestimate the aesthetic aspects of narratives, highlighting the engagement and curiosity that fictional narratives should provoke in readers. In particular, the narratives should aim to trigger new ideas and perspectives.

Guidelines for Researching Animals' Perspectives

Table 1 presents a set of guidelines developed to assist students and scholars interested in exploring the perspectives of animals involved in tourism, hospitality and leisure.

The first guideline concerns the ontological and epistemological dimensions of researching animals' perspectives on tourism and leisure activities. Guidelines 3a, 3b and 3c present three main approaches that can be adopted to investigate such perspectives and are exemplified in the following text by my personal experience. The final guideline derives from my belief, inspired by ecofeminist thinking, about the moral obligation to encourage practices that contribute to the respectful and caring inclusion of animals in our lives.

Reflexivity and philosophical and practical clarifications: Reflect on your conceptualization of animals and the type of researcher–animal interactions that will occur during the research.

Before engaging in research that aims to investigate animals' perspectives, it is important for the researcher to reflect on and clarify how they view the animals

Table 1. Methodological Guidelines for Researching Animals' Perspectives.

1. Reflexivity and philosophical and practical clarifications
Reflect on your cconceptualization of animals and the type of
researcher–animal interactions that will occur during the research.

2. Theoretical and practical knowledge
Evaluate whether you have the knowledge, competence, skills and
experience to understand the perspectives of the investigated animal(s).

3a. Fictional approach
Use creativity and develop thought-provoking narratives.

3b. Multispecies ethnographic approach
Consider whether it is possible and opportune to directly involve one or
more animals in the research.

3c. Multispecies mixed method
Combine traditional methods with the use of technology to collect
relevant animal and human data.

4. Research practical implications and impact on animals
Reflect on the possible effects of your research on the animals and how
to make the research valuable for the animals themselves.

involved. As noted in the introduction, openness in this regard is crucial due to potentially conflicting views about the conceptualization of animals. If working within a research team, these views should be clarified when the team is first established. As various individuals involved in the research might perceive animals differently, this is an opportune time to consider whether and how these differences might influence the research. The conceptualization of animals underlying the research should also be presented to other subjects potentially involved in some phases of the research (e.g. practitioners from the tourism and hospitality industry) and the final recipients (e.g. readers of scientific journals, undergraduate students and the general public).

Practical considerations regarding the animals should also be in focus at an early stage of any research concerning one or more animals, especially with regard to empirical data collection; for example, the researcher(s) should reflect on what types of interactions with the animal(s) will occur during the research. Reflections and discussions about the ethical rules to follow and what will/will not be acceptable should occur before a collaborative research project begins.

My own experience of reflecting on my personal thoughts and values regarding the differences and similarities between animals and humans, as well as among various animal species, may be helpful to researchers considering this part of the research process. During this process, I read some literature about animal ethics (in particular, the care tradition within eco-feminism), and although I found this reading interesting and useful, feelings of frustration and powerlessness were quite common. These feelings occurred particularly when I attempted to deeply understand and communicate animals' perspectives on activities that could be potentially or undoubtedly harmful (e.g., close encounters with wild animals or the use of animals as food). It is important that researchers aiming to explore animals' voices are aware of and prepared for this potential outcome. When I worked with other investigators on a study about the animals' perspectives on specific leisure and tourism experiences, I found my collaborators through my personal network, after having read some of their work; hence, my selection was based on their concern, interest, and sensibility regarding animal issues, among other factors.

Theoretical and practical knowledge: Evaluate whether you have the knowledge, competence, skills and experience to understand the perspectives of the investigated animal(s).

Scholars aiming to investigate the perspectives of one or more animals should have relatively good theoretical and practical knowledge of that specific animal species and, when relevant and possible, the individual animal(s) that the research focuses on. Possible limitations might be overcome by the involvement of other people in the research (e.g., the recruitment of co-researchers or assistants or assistance from experienced people and practitioners, such as pet owners, veterinarians and animal keepers) and through a literature review (e.g., scientific and grey literature).

I have adopted both strategies to overcome limits in my knowledge about certain animal species involved in the tourism and leisure experiences that I have investigated. For one study, I relied on the input and assistance of two co-authors: a biologist and a representative of a non-governmental animal protection and conservation organization. The co-authorship resulted in a fruitful collaboration from which I gained new knowledge and inspiration for future projects. For another study, unable to identify appropriate co-researchers, I consulted the literature about the animal species I intended to research. My passion for the animal world was a good starting point for identifying relevant authors and publications to further investigate the scientific literature and reports about the specific animal species.

Fictional approach: Use creativity and develop thought-provoking narratives.

As presented in the previous section about the CAP approach, fictional narratives should be engaging and generate curiosity and new questions. Narratives developed for scientific inquiry should be able to provide material for discussions about theoretical advances and practical implications. It is important to be aware that fictional stories presenting animals' thoughts and emotions may be criticized and accused of, for example, anthropomorphism. The researcher should, therefore, make sure to properly reflect on Guidelines 1 and 2 and act accordingly.

In the fictional narratives that I developed, I adopted several writing techniques to engage readers and provoke curiosity and reflection. These techniques include first-person narrative, the use of terms intended to reflect sounds and concepts in animal language, reverse chronology, visual techniques, irony and the use of citations from popular works (novels and films). Creative writing blogs have been important sources for learning about these techniques, while novels and poetry have also served as major sources of inspiration. While developing these narratives, I clearly found that the main messages emerging from them conflicted with the dominant view of the investigated activities; consequently, I paid particular attention to developing stories that suggested alternative views without directly criticising the dominant one and people holding different views from mine.

Multispecies ethnographic approach: Consider whether it is possible and opportune to directly involve one or more animals in the research.

As presented in the literature review, multispecies research teams comprising the researchers and their pets are a possibility for conducting research about and with animals. Multispecies research teams in which the animal members belong to a wild species are almost impossible, excluding cases of domesticated wild animals. An example of such cases acceptable from an ecofeminist perspective might involve rescued wild animals cared for in human settings that are open to visitors (e.g. sanctuaries). These cases might be relevant to the exploration of human–animal encounters and the inclusion of the animals' perspectives. Another example might be an investigation of the potential mutual value of such encounters. The possibility of involving one or more animals as knowledge "co-creators" depends on whether and to what extent the specific animals are suitable for this task. It is important that the researcher is aware that the animal(s) may be unwilling to be involved in the research activities.

My personal experience of this aspect derived from two studies, one of which concerned dog walking. The methodology for this study was similar to that used by the multispecies teams (researchers and researchers' pets) presented in the previous section. Although an attempt was made to involve the dog as a knowledge co-creator, rather than merely a co-protagonist in the investigated experience, I recognized that the perspective of the study was quite anthropocentric. The second study concerned pet-friendly vacation experiences. For this study, I identified and made contact with a company selected as a relevant case, but the fieldwork did not proceed. I had planned to carry out the fieldwork with my dog. In contrast to the dog-walking study, the period of data collection would be relatively short (one week), and the planned activities differed from my dog's usual routines. After some reflection, however, I realized that the dog would have become stressed by the fieldwork activities. Thus, the fieldwork was canceled, and the study did not proceed.

Multispecies mixed method: Combine traditional methods with the use of technology to collect relevant animal and human data.

By focusing on the relational aspects of animal encounters, both humans' and animals' perspectives on specific experiences can be investigated. This might be possible with technological devices that record relevant data about the animals and humans involved. The latter could be combined with more traditional methods, such as observations, interviews and surveys. The use of technological solutions might require following specific ethical research practices and rules. In addition, the use of technological devices on animals should be considered in light of the research's philosophical position (Guideline 1) as some practices that apply such devices can be invasive.

I have no experience with this type of multispecies mixed methods using technology. To my knowledge, no study in the tourism, hospitality and leisure literature has applied such an approach, which in some respects recalls the futuristic scenario imagined by Äijälä et al. (2021) and the videography study by Haanpää et al. (2019). Based on such studies, I propose that it might be possible to investigate animal-based experiences, such as dog-sledding tours, by collecting data from the animals (mainly through video and wearable technological devices) and tourists (through video, wearable technological devices and interviews). Such an approach would require multidisciplinary collaboration, including tourists and individuals who have knowledge of and experience working with the specific animals and technologies.

Research practical implications and impact on animals: Reflect on the possible effects of your research on the animals and how to make the research valuable for the animals themselves.

As researchers, we are usually asked to reflect on the practical implications and impact of our studies. We should reflect on what our research, the way we have conducted it, its results and their dissemination practically implies for the animals involved in the study as well as animals in general. It is my belief that we should strive to make our research valuable to animals, aiming to improve, or contribute to improving, their lives at the species and individual levels. This objective aligns with the main tenets of ecofeminism and the ethical considerations for research presented in the introduction. When entering the animal world to investigate it, principles and values derived from the view of animals as subjects should be respected with the aim not only of advancing human knowledge but also of protecting the animals and their environments and improving their well-being.

In my experience, while conducted with the best intentions, some studies about animal-based leisure and tourism activities may be used (for example, by the industry) to present in a better light practices that are not necessarily beneficial or harmless to the animals. This risk could be reduced by committing ourselves to making animals' voices more explicit in our studies. Through their engagement, and perhaps by adopting some of the methodologies presented in this chapter, scholars expressing animals' perspectives can develop, communicate and promote best practices. Eventually, such researchers may contribute to important improvements in animal conditions in tourism, hospitality and leisure. Two examples might be the transportation of pets via air travel and hotel policies regarding how rooms and common areas are designed. Improvements in animal welfare for captive wildlife, such as in zoos and aquaria, and wildlife encounters in nature, such as whale watching, might also be achievable in the not-too-distant future. More challenging are improvements in those contexts where animals are killed or abused (fishing and hunting, animal-based food experiences and certain events and festivals). Realistically, considering the animals' perspectives in these contexts and what they might want us to do could only lead to the abolition of such activities. We should ask whether we, as researchers (but not only as researchers), are willing to listen to animals' voices in situations that conflict with some of our most deeply rooted traditions and habits.

Conclusions and Recommendations

Based on the numerous and varied roles that animals play in our lives, and on growing scholarly interest in exploring animal issues in tourism, hospitality and leisure, this chapter has reflected on the methodological implications, challenges, and possibilities of research. The focus has been on studies aiming to represent the animals' perspectives on the activities in which they are involved. Based on a literature review and my personal experiences, this chapter has developed some guidelines for a methodology intended to underpin research about and with animals. More precisely, these guidelines concern reflexivity, philosophical and practical clarifications about the research, the researchers' knowledge of animals and the possible impact of the research on the animals. The guidelines include three main research approaches: fictional, multispecies ethnography and multi-species technology-based.

The chapter demonstrates that few scholars to date have adopted methodo-logical approaches in line with the growing recognition of animals, of at least some species, as sentient beings with an intrinsic value. Therefore, this chapter closes with an invitation to scholars who share such a recognition to act consis-tently in their research practices. The set of guidelines presented here may be a good point of departure for such engagement, which might bring us closer to understanding the animal world as well as our own. From an ecofeminist perspective, the final recommendation of this chapter is not to fear the cognitive and emotional engagement that might emerge from a compassionate inclusion of animals in our studies. Such inclusion will neither obscure our thinking nor limit our possibilities to research and influence human practices involving animals, as this chapter has strived to show.

References

Adams, C., & Gruen, L. (2014). *Ecofeminism: Feminist intersections with other animals and the earth*. New York, NY: Bloomsbury.

Äijälä, M., Jylkäs, T., Rajab, V., & Vuorikari, T. (2021). Designing future wildlife tourism experience: On agency in human-sled dog encounters. In G. Bertella (Ed.), *Wildlife tourism futures: Encounters with wild, captive and artificial animals* (pp. 126–139). Blue Ridge Summit, PA: Channel View Publications.

Banks, A., & Banks, S. P. (1998). *Fiction and social research: By ice or fire*. Walnut Creek, CA: Alta Mira Press.

Bertella, G. (2018). An eco-feminist perspective on the co-existence of different views of seals in leisure activities. *Annals of Leisure Research*, 21(3), 284–301. doi:10.1080/11745398.2017.1415152

Bertella, G. (2020). Animal-based experiences and animal experiences: Farm animals' perspective on human leisure in rural settings. *Annals of Leisure Research*, 24(5), 635–645. doi:10.1080/11745398.2020.1740603

Bertella, G. (2021). Interspecies communication and encounters with orcas. In G. Bertella (Ed.), *Wildlife tourism futures: Encounters with wild, captive and artificial animals* (pp. 98–110). Blue Ridge Summit, PA: Channel View Publications.

Bertella, G., Fumagalli, M., & Williams-Grey, V. (2019). Wildlife tourism through the co-creation lens. *Tourism Recreation Research*, *44*(3), 300–310. doi:10.1080/02508281.2019.1606977

Birkeland, J. (1993). Eco-feminism: Linking theory and practice. In G. Gaard (Ed.), *Ecofeminism: Women, animals, nature* (pp. 13–59). Philadelphia, PA: Temple University Press.

Burns, G. L. (2015). Animals as tourism objects: Ethically refocusing relationships between tourists and wildlife. In K. Markwell (Ed.), *Animals and tourism: Understanding diverse relationships* (pp. 44–59). Blue Ridge Summit, PA: Channel View Publications.

Campos, A. C., Mendes, J., do Valle, P. O., & Scott, N. (2016). Co-creation experiences: Attention and memorability. *Journal of Travel & Tourism Marketing*, *33*(9), 1309–1336. doi:10.1080/10548408.2015.1118424

Carr, N. (2009). Animals in the tourism and leisure experience. *Current Issues in Tourism*, *12*(5–6), 409–411. doi:10.1080/13683500903132575

Carr, N. (2014). *Dogs in the leisure experience*. Wallingford: CABI.

Carr, N., & Cohen, S. (2009). Holidaying with the family pet: No dogs allowed! *Tourism and Hospitality Research*, *9*(4), 290–304. doi:10.1057/thr.2009.10

Curtin, S. (2006). Swimming with dolphins: A phenomenological exploration of tourist recollections. *International Journal of Tourism Research*, *8*(4), 301–315. doi:10.1002/jtr.577

Danby, P., Dashper, K., & Finkel, R. (2019). Multispecies leisure: Human-animal interactions in leisure landscapes. *Leisure Studies*, *38*(3), 291–302. doi:10.1080/02614367.2019.1628802

Dashper, K., & Brymer, E. (2019). An ecological-phenomenological perspective on multispecies leisure and the horse-human relationship in events. *Leisure Studies*, *38*(3), 394–407. doi:10.1080/02614367.2019.1586981

DeMello, M. (2013). *Speaking for animals: Animal autobiographical writing*. New York, NY: Routledge.

Denzin, N. K., & Lincoln, Y. S. (2011). *The Sage handbook of qualitative research*. Los Angeles, CA: Sage.

Dhont, K., & Hodson, G. (2019). *Why we love and exploit animals: Bridging insights from academia and advocacy*. London: Routledge.

Donovan, J., & Adams, C. J. (2007). *The feminist care tradition in animal ethics*. New York, NY: Columbia University Press.

Fennell, D. (2011). *Tourism and animal ethics*. New York, NY: Routledge.

Gaard, G. (Ed.). (1993). *Ecofeminism: Women, animals, nature*. Philadelphia, PA: Temple University Press.

Gruen, L. (2011). *Ethics and animals: An introduction*. Cambridge: Cambridge University Press.

Gruen, L. (2015). *Entangled empathy: An alternative ethic for our relationships with animals*. New York, NY: Lantern Books.

Haanpää, M., Salmela, T., García-Rosell, J.-C., & Äijälä, M. (2019). The disruptive 'other'? Exploring human-animal relations in tourism through videography. *Tourism Geographies*, *23*(1–2), 97–117. doi:10.1080/14616688.2019.1666158

Hamilton, L., & Taylor, N. (2017). *Ethnography after humanism: Power, politics and method in multi-species research*. London: Palgrave Macmillan.

Harmon, J. (2019). Tuesdays with Worry: Appreciating nature with a dog at the end of life. *Leisure Studies, 38*(3), 317–328. doi:10.1080/02614367.2018.1534135

Herzog, H. (2010). *Some we love, some we hate, some we eat.* New York, NY: Harper Perennial.

Höckert, E., & Grimwood, B. (2019). Toward hospitable methodologies in tourism. *Critical Tourism Studies Proceedings, 2019*(1), art. 56. https://digitalcommons. library.tru.ca/cts-proceedings/vol2019/iss1/56

Hollinshead, K. (2013). The under-conceptualisations of tourism studies: The case for postdisciplinary knowing. In I. Ateljevic, A. Pritchard, & N. Morgan (Eds.), *The critical turn in tourism studies* (pp. 97–114). Routledge.

Israel, M., & Hay, I. (2006). *Research ethics for social scientists.* London: Sage.

Joy, M. (2011). *Why we love dogs, eat pigs, and wear cows: An introduction to carnism.* San Francisco, CA: Conari Press.

Kirksey, E., & Helmreich, S. (2010). The emergence of multispecies ethnography. *Cultural Anthropology, 25*(4), 545–576. doi:10.1111/j.1548-1360.2010.01069.x

Kline, C. (2018). *Tourism experiences and animal consumption: Contested values, morality and ethics.* New York, NY: Routledge.

Markwell, K. (2015). *Animals and tourism: Understanding diverse relationships.* Blue Ridge Summit, PA: Channel View Publications.

Nottle, C., & Young, J. (2019). Individuals, instinct and moralities: Exploring multi-species leisure using the serious leisure perspective. *Leisure Studies, 38*(3), 303–316. doi:10.1080/02614367.2019.1572777

Parry, D. C., & Johnson, C. W. (2007). Contextualizing leisure research to encompass complexity in lived leisure experience: The need for creative analytic practice. *Leisure Sciences, 29*(2), 119–130. doi:10.1080/01490400601160721

Parsons, E. C. M. (2012). The negative impacts of whale-watching. *Journal of Marine Biology.* Article e807294 doi:10.1155/2012/807294

Reinhold, E. (2018). How to become animal through writing: The case of the bear. *Culture and Organization, 24*(4), 318–329. doi:10.1080/14759551.2018.1488849

Richardson, L., & St Pierre, E. A. (2005). Writing: A method of inquiry. In N. K. Denzin & Y. S. Lincoln (Eds.), *The Sage handbook of qualitative inquiry* (pp. 959–978). Thousand Oaks, CA: Sage.

Serpell, J. (1996). *In the company of animals: A study of human-animal relationships.* Cambridge: Cambridge University Press.

Taillon, J., MacLaurin, T., & Yun, D. (2015). Hotel pet policies: An assessment of willingness to pay for travelling with a pet. *Anatolia, 26*(1), 89–91. doi:10.1080/13032917.2014.942327

Wilkinson, S. (2018). Being Camilla: The everyday leisure life of a captive chameleon. In N. Carr & J. Young (Eds.), *Wild animals and leisure: Rights and welfare.* New York, NY: Routledge.

Yeoman, I., & Postma, A. (2014). Developing an ontological framework for tourism futures. *Tourism Recreation Research, 39*(3), 299–304. doi:10.1080/02508281.2014.11087002

Yudina, O., & Grimwood, B. S. (2016). Situating the wildlife spectacle: Ecofeminism, representation, and polar bear tourism. *Journal of Sustainable Tourism, 24*(5), 715–734. doi:10.1080/09669582.2015.1083996

Chapter 12

Conclusion

Shiva Jahani, Fevzi Okumus and S. Mostafa Rasoolimanesh

In this chapter, the editors provide the reader with a summary of this edited book: *Advanced Research Methods in Hospitality and Tourism*. Within each paragraph, the reader will find a summary of objectives and content of each chapter. The editors aim to assist the reader in summative recall of what has been covered. Recent studies (e.g., Ali et al., 2018; Assaf & Li, 2021; Azer & Alexander, 2020a, 2020b; Boz & Koc, 2021; Rasoolimanesh, Ringle, Sarstedt, & Olya, 2021; Usakli & Kucukergin, 2018; Yang, Park, & Hu, 2018) have highlighted the importance of providing advanced research methods for hospitality and tourism scholars. To address these needs, this book covered updated and proven research methods with application in such topics as (1) mixed-method research, (2) scale development and evaluation, 3) psychophysiological tools of research, (4) text mining, (5) using archival material in research, and (6) analysis of social media, among others. While Chapter 1 explains the main purposes for publishing this book, each subsequent chapter focused on a specific research topic and provided recommendations and guidelines. Chapter 1 of this edited book is written by the editors. They explained the main purposes for publishing this book.

In Chapter 2, Jaylan Azer, Babak Taheri, and Martin Gannon provided a critical view of mixed methods research (MMR). The authors review how MMR within social science research has broader application including for the hospitality and tourism industries. The authors provided insight into the characteristics of MMR, demonstrating how it differs from a multi-method approach. The authors communicate that MMR can be challenging – the approach is time and resource intensive – and that researchers must have a range of skills. Following the discussions of MMR design as different methodological approaches in the field of hospitality and tourism.

The focus of Chapter 3 by Elizabeth Agyeiwaah was to examine the application of exploratory sequential mixed methods designs to the investigation of sustainability among small tourism enterprises. The author indicated that mixed methods research overcomes the weaknesses of single approaches to yield superior outcomes based on research questions. This author highlighted the value of mixed methods, especially to emerging tourism researchers.

Advanced Research Methods in Hospitality and Tourism, 213–217
Copyright © 2023 Shiva Jahani, Fevzi Okumus and S. Mostafa Rasoolimanesh
Published under exclusive licence by Emerald Publishing Limited
doi:10.1108/978-1-80117-550-020221012

Ali Bavik, Kuo Chen-Feng, and John Ap systematically evaluated the scale development procedures and psychometric properties of tourism and hospitality scales in Chapter 4. The challenges and some of the main limitations were identified, examined, and discussed. Noticeable methodological weaknesses in the scale development steps (i.e., number of interviews, pre-test, social desirability response bias check, and psychometric properties) were identified. This chapter concluded that there is a need for better reporting of the scale development procedures. Furthermore, this chapter may help future researchers to identify their limitations and direct their considerations in choosing and adopting scale development procedures in the tourism and.

In Chapter 5, Hakan Boz and Erdogan Koc proposed a framework on the most frequently used psychophysiological tools of research for researchers and practitioners interested in using methods other than the traditional methods. These authors presented neuromarketing applications in tourism and hospitality. The specific examples showed the outcomes produced by the neuromarketing and how they can be interpreted. Despite their advantages, the neuromarketing tools have several disadvantages as well such as (1) their cost, (2) level of expertise required to use these tools, and (3) limited number of study subjects with which the applications could be used.

In Chapter 6, Parisa Saadat Abadi Nasab, Neil Carr, and Trudie Walters discussed conducting archival research with photographs. Each photo has a story to tell for each photo recorded a moment of time loaded with meaning, giving the researcher an opportunity to extract insights about that particular moment, its social construction and the individuals both in the picture and behind the camera. In particular, family snapshots are records of human life and events, through which researchers can explore how individual and family behavior constantly changes. Yet it is not only photographs that are a rich potential source of archival material. The authors highlighted that archival material comes in a vast array of types and can encompass a long period of time, beginning today and heading backwards.

Continuing the discussion of examining existing data, Juan Pedro Mellinas and Eva Martin-Fuentes discussed in Chapter 7 the methodologies of examining Big Data in hospitality and tourism. For example, using the massive collection of data from websites, such as TripAdvisor, can be very useful in the investigation of different aspects of the field of tourism. The authors caution that the use of an appropriate methodology must involve quantifying aspects as relevant as sample size in relation to the universe of individuals under study. It is true that the TripAdvisor platform provides researchers with millions of reviews with which to perform their analyses more easily, quickly and economically, but it should still be considered that most people either do not review their experiences or use other review platforms. Having accurate data on the number of guests in hotels in each period would provide very accurate data on TripAdvisor review participation rates. Other websites also collect scores and reviews, such as Yelp, Holiday Check, Facebook, or Google Places. Empirical replications using other platforms to determine whether there are behavioral differences according to nationality may provide further insight to this discussion.

In Chapter 8, Gozde Ozturk and Abdullah Tanrisevdi discussed text mining approach with an example from cruise tourism. Online customer comments contain meaningful information for companies related to service problems, customer satisfaction or dissatisfaction, and more. Analyzing these comments undoubtedly provides a unique opportunity for the business to understand its shortcomings. In this chapter, two different rating prediction methods were proposed for determining important and unimportant aspects for cruise travelers about their cruise experience and the effects of their positive or negative feelings on the evaluation process from the customer feedback and comments. In the proposed system, the overall rating value is calculated according to sentiment and aspect probabilities of a given comment. In this way, it is possible to determine how much the aspects of comments influence the overall rating. By examining customer comments using text mining approach, it will also be possible for the company to determine its priority needs and perform budgeting according to said needs.

In Chapter 9, Ismail Shaheer, Neil Carr and Andrea Insch highlighted different steps for collecting and analyzing historical data from social media, in particular Twitter. Social media will continue to be employed by researchers given the numerous advantages and opportunities it offers as a source of information. The use of social media in research is particularly applicable to the tourism discipline as tourism providers increasingly utilize social media in the marketing and the delivery of services they provide. In addition, a large percentage of people around the world have adopted social media as a part of their lives, providing researchers with a window into their behavior, views, and desires. Although many new social media platforms continue to be introduced, Twitter remains a highly popular platform among researchers. Often researchers have a need to collect historical social media data in relation to a past event or ongoing events. It is possible to obtain sufficient longitudinal data from Twitter without having to rely on highly technical methods or incurring a significant financial cost. The data collection method outlined in this chapter is particularly suitable and applicable for qualitative analysis of Twitter data. This chapter highlighted the importance of studying social media through a qualitative approach due to the many benefits and opportunities it can offer for a more insightful understanding of the phenomenon studied. At the same time caution is urged. Social media-based research is valid and important but done correctly it is no easier than any other data collection process. Furthermore, while useful, social media data cannot answer all our research questions. In short, social media data should not be used as a short cut to undertake rigorous research.

In Chapter 10, Paulin P.L. Wong and Balvinder Kaur Kler provided guidelines for qualitative researchers. The authors combined focus group interviews, visitor-employed photography (VEP) and Q-method with photo elicitation. Tourism researchers who focus on uncovering the voice of the voiceless in understudied areas or communities should attempt the use of these methods. Participants feel respected when the research design incorporates activities and clarifies their contributions. Using this combination of methods and involving the participants through the process of data collection, the strangers-constructed focus group participants forged a sense of camaraderie due to the various data collection stages and the segments which needed their participation. This study showed that using this innovative data collection method, all participants enjoyed the VEP segment as well as the photo-elicitation with Q-sort. This chapter showed that, this combination of methods was systematic and illuminative using the example of deriving host community place meanings to a marine park.

Finally in Chapter 11, Giovanna Bertella focused on ethical issues and considerations when researchers are exploring animals and their roles in tourism and hospitality research. Based on the numerous and varied roles that animals play in our lives, and on the growing scholarly interest in exploring animal issues in tourism, hospitality, and leisure, this chapter has reflected on the methodological implications, challenges, and possibilities of research. The focus has been on those studies aiming to represent the animals' perspectives on the activities they are involved in. Based on a literature review and the personal experiences of the author, the authors developed some guidelines for a methodology to underpin research about and with animals. More precisely, these guidelines concern reflexivity, and philosophical and practical clarifications of research, the researchers' knowledge of animals, and the possible impact of the research on the animals. The guidelines include three main research approaches: a fictional approach, multispecies ethnography, and a multispecies technology-based approach. The set of guidelines presented here may be a good point of departure for such engagement, which might bring us closer to understanding the animal world as well as our own.

We, the editors of this book, thank all our readers for their interest our work. We hope that collection of the chapters included in this book would help students, faculty member and industry practitioners in their research projects. We also hope that our book will stimulate further research studies in the hospitality and tourism field.

References

Ali, F., Rasoolimanesh, S. M., Sarstedt, M., Ringle, C. M., & Ryu, K. (2018). An assessment of the use of partial least squares structural equation modeling (PLS-SEM) in hospitality research. *Journal of Contemporary Hospitality Management*, *30*(1), 514–538. doi:10.1108/IJCHM-02-2021-0272

Assaf, A. G., & Li, G. (2021). Introduction to the special issue: Economic analysis in tourism and hospitality—New methods and perspectives. *Journal of Hospitality & Tourism Research*, *45*(1), 3–5.

Azer, J., & Alexander, M. (2020a). Negative customer engagement behaviour: The interplay of intensity and valence in online networks. *Journal of Marketing Management*, *36*(3–4), 361–383.

Azer, J., & Alexander, M. (2020b). Direct and indirect negatively valenced engagement behavior. *Journal of Services Marketing*, *34*(7), 967–981.

Boz, H., & Koc, E. (2021). Service quality, emotion recognition, emotional intelligence and Dunning Kruger syndrome. *Total Quality Management & Business Excellence*, *32*(11–12), 1201–1214.

Rasoolimanesh, S. M., Ringle, C. M., Sarstedt, M., & Olya, H. (2021). The combined use of symmetric and asymmetric approaches: Partial least squares-structural equation modeling and fuzzy-set qualitative comparative analysis. *International Journal of Contemporary Hospitality Management, 33*(5), 1571–1592. doi:10.1108/IJCHM-10-2020-1164

Usakli, A., & Kucukergin, K. G. (2018). Using partial least squares structural equation modeling in hospitality and tourism: Do researchers follow practical guidelines?. *International Journal of Contemporary Hospitality Management, 30*(11), 3462–3512. doi:10.1108/IJCHM-11-2017-0753

Yang, Y., Park, S., & Hu, X. (2018). Electronic word of mouth and hotel performance: A meta-analysis. *Tourism Management, 67,* 248–260.

Index